SUCCESS

— *without* —

COLLEGE

ALSO BY LINDA LEE

One by One
(novel, 1977)

The Hand Book
(with James Charlton, 1980)

Out of Wedlock: A Love Story
(1982)

Working: My Life as a Prostitute
(with Dolores French, 1988)

Tom Hanks
(1999)

SUCCESS

— *without* —

COLLEGE

Why Your Child May Not Have to Go to College
Right Now—and May Not Have to Go at All

Linda Lee

BROADWAY BOOKS
New York

BROADWAY

A hardcover edition of this book was originally published in 2000 by Doubleday, division of Random House, Inc.

Broadway Books titles may be purchased for business or promotional use or for special sales. For information, please write to: Special Markets Department, Random House, Inc., 1540 Broadway, New York, New York 10036.

BROADWAY BOOKS and its logo, a letter B bisected on the diagonal, are trademarks of Broadway Books, a division of Random House, Inc.

Visit our website at www.broadwaybooks.com

First Broadway Books trade paperback edition published 2001.

The Library of Congress has cataloged the hardcover as:

Lee, Linda, 1947
Success without college; why your child may not have to go to college right now—and may not have to go at all./
Linda Lee. —1st ed.
p. cm.
"This book provides a road map for success and proves there is success without college."
1. High school graduates—United States—Case studies.
2. College dropouts—United States—Case studies. 3. High school graduates—Employment—United States—Case studies.
4. Education, Higher—Parent participation—United States—Case studies. I. Title.

LB2350.L45 2000
373.12'912—dc21   99-059364

ISBN 0-7679-0571-7

01 02 03 04 05 10 9 8 7 6 5 4 3 2 1

Contents

Acknowledgments

This book would not have been possible without the enormous support and encouragement (and time off) offered by my superiors at the *New York Times:* Barbara Graustark, editor of *House and Home,* and John Montorio, head of the style department. Thanks as well to the *New York Times Education Life Supplement,* which published the first version of this book in an article in August 1998 called "What's the Rush? Why College Can Wait."

For the Minnesota chapter, I relied on a young University of Minnesota journalism graduate, Jeannie Koranda, who trekked to White Bear Lake and helped me track down 1993 graduates. I'd also like to thank the others in White Bear who helped me and who are not mentioned in the book: Kevin Mackin, the principal of the high school; Susan Brott, the director of communications for the school and Stan Abbott, the managing editor at the White Bear Press. Jon Mikrut, a 1993 graduate who is mentioned in the book, put me in touch with dozens of other students. Similarly, Heather Zehm, who was working as a waitress in the town, handed the survey to her customers. Harry Mares, the former mayor, spoke to me. Neal Karlen helped me narrow my search. And my high school friend, Char Brooker, helped me understand the Minnesota education system.

Thanks as well to all of the press officers in the Army, Navy and Air Force who provided research materials and contacts. Aurora D'Amico at the National Center for Education Statistics in Washington, D.C., was invaluable in pointing me to the studies I needed. My agent, Mary Evans, and her assistant, Tanya McKinnon, were early advocates of the book. My editor, Jennifer Griffin, offered encouragement and support for an orphaned project on a rigorous schedule and kept the money flowing.

Chris Gaither, a journalism student at Berkeley, in California, helped me reach Scott Wainner, the web millionaire, and directed me to other computer gurus in Silicon Valley.

Marianne Rohrlich, a colleague at the *Times,* steered me to Tanner Zucker, the computer maven in New York. Rob Middleton, a Princeton dropout now living in Florida, gave me expert advice on notable dropouts and checked the list of those who never completed college. Rob has an amusing website called the College Dropouts Alumni Association that offered a number of leads.

The "year-off" counselors who are mentioned extensively in the book were instrumental in helping me formulate my ideas. So were the college administrators to whom I spoke. In talking to them I realized how much officials *do* care about young people. David Stein, head of communications at the North Carolina School of Science and Mathematics in Durham, directed me to a number of former students.

Then there are the researchers who helped me gather materials for the book: Robert, Vivienne, Alex, Annika, Evan and Gretchen. I am grateful as well to friends who read early versions of the manuscript, pitched in at the phone desk calling White Bear graduates and brought me hot meals when I was on deadline: Susan Senk, Gini Kopecky, Marc Wallace, Chris Filner and Lena Blau. Vieri Tucci had sharp eyes for mistakes and laughed in all the right places. Ansi Vallens, a friend who works with the United Federation of Teachers, insisted I speak to three people who became central to the book: Norm Fraley, Paul F. Cole and Thomas H. Haines. Douglas Feinstein, creative supervisor at the advertising agency Wunderman Cato Johnson, came up with the book's title during a walk with our dogs in Riverside Park.

Writing this book would not have been possible without the Internet, both for research and communication. And I am grateful to my companion, Beau, for his patience throughout. Lastly, my deep appreciation to Nan Mooney, who came into the project near the end as a researcher and fact checker and who made finishing the book, and getting it right, possible.

Introduction

You don't have to go to college.

That's very easy to say, and very hard to believe. Which is why you're holding a book in your hands instead of a postcard.

I said it to my own son, one of those bright kids who nonetheless didn't belong in college at age eighteen.

He didn't believe me, either.

My son ranked in the top 5 percent of people in the country in terms of IQ. He attended the Bronx High School of Science, where it is assumed that everyone goes to college. But still, he should not have gone to college at eighteen. He wasn't ready intellectually or emotionally. Put simply, he wasn't mature enough.

But try convincing a middle-class child of that. College, you see, is a class issue, and where my son grew up, in Manhattan, all kids went to college. They felt entitled to college. End of discussion.

I, like every other middle-class parent, had calculated his graduation date from college (the year 2000) at the time of his birth. How cool, I thought. The Class of Naught-Naught.

And here's what happened when my son actually went to college. During his first year, he broke his foot in two places jumping down the cement stairs in the dorm; went to the hospital and got his foot set, then prematurely took the cast off himself, because he got impatient for it to heal; got a D in a physics course, convinced me he should take it over to improve his mark and then got an F, the grade that is now on his record.

My son got two tattoos, the symbolism of which I cannot divine; refused to get an on-campus job because they all "sucked"; took out credit cards without telling me and then ran up $1,000 in new jeans, stereo equipment and computer games. He finished his first year with a 2.06 average, but that included a winter quarter (the quarter of the broken foot) in which he got a 0.71 average with the following grades: F, W, W, W, D and C. (I love how they put that 0 in front of the decimal point, just so you don't for a moment suspect your child really got a 7.1 average.)

I told his psychiatrist (because we live in New York and every middle-class kid who is underperforming has a psychiatrist) that I thought we should hold off on a second year of college.

She scowled. "You need to give him support," she snapped. "Kids like him need to know that their parents are behind them." And so I got behind him and took out another $15,000 in loans.

This is what he did in his second year: used the money I sent him for rent (because now he was going to live off campus, so he wouldn't be "distracted" in the dorms) to buy more video games and CDs, leaving an unpaid balance of $800 for the apartment. "I think it was for the damage," he told me when he moved out.

When I had visited the place, the damage must have been hidden behind the well-placed Day-Glo posters and the signs offering formulas for mixed drinks.

Did I mention that he equipped the apartment with black lights? There's one thing I can tell you, parent-to-parent. Black lights mean the same thing today that they meant thirty years ago: Someone's smoking pot and missing the 8 A.M. Methods of Evaluation class.

But hey. I'm a baby boom parent. How can I complain about pot, especially when politicians are cropping up left and right, elbowing each other out of the way to admit that they, too, smoked pot in college a long, long time ago.

His second-year adventures didn't stop there. His roommate with the 4.0 average moved out and his girlfriend moved in. They fell in love. In the winter quarter of his second year he achieved a 1.0 average, by keeping only one course, Packing Materials I, for a four-credit D.

Here are some other grades I learned about: S (satisfactory) does not count toward a GPA, nor does I (incomplete) or Z (audit).

Did I mention his driving record? He had to have a car, because . . . oh, I forget why, but he needed a car. (Certainly it was not to get to work.) And so I offered up $550 so he could have a very ancient Mazda RX7, a cross between a roller skate and a sports car, the perfect thing for winter driving in Rochester, New York.

You may ask how a body shop can charge $1,200 for repair work on a car that cost only $550, but then you wouldn't be following the logic my son uses: It was *worth* it to repair the car after the accident because he just loved the car so much. That was two weeks before he sold it.

The accident, you ask? Yes, there were seven (don't tell my insurance company), one of which was while he was driving his girlfriend's parents' car (oops, don't tell them, either).

It was at this point that I had a revelation. I was an enabler. I was guilty of what should count as an original sin: loving my son so much I completely separated his performance from my approval.

That was before I brightened up. Going to college is the reward for years of hard, test-taking, backbreaking work. A kid who doesn't do the work, or who sloughs off, who sneers at the Herbs at the Bronx High School of Science (the ones who can't keep up with the Nautica, Tommy, Guess cycle of cool clothing), the kid who plays nothing but rap music at home, songs whose only word seems to be "bitch"—this kid does not deserve to be sent to college.

No, I have become an advocate of Arrival of the Fittest. Mediocre students do not belong in college. Nor do kids (like mine) who wantonly throw their parents' money around. Do they know how much money plumbers can make? Are they aware that one hair colorist in New York City makes $500,000 a year? And she is no Harvard grad.

Kids like mine don't need a college education; they need an application to a good trade school. Buh-bye!

Sure, my son may one day go to college. But right now he's working. I've told him he can reapply to the First Bank of Mom when he pays off his credit-card debts, grows up and displays the drive and determination to do well in college. But I want you to know, I said it in a loving and supportive way.

And that is why I have written this book. My son's experience with college is more than just a cautionary tale. Think of it as a car accident, and of me as a crazed mom trying to find out why the brakes failed.

What I discovered is that my son is not unique. There are thousands and thousands of kids like him starting college every year. Some of them are slackers. Some are overachievers who burn out. Some can't handle the freedom. Some have chosen another path.

But what I've also found is that there is something terribly wrong with a college system that takes in so many (about 66 percent of high school graduates) and graduates so few (about 25 percent of those who enroll, after six years). And this is a system that can cost more than $100,000 for a bachelor's degree at a private school.

I could have spared my son two years of struggle if I had just convinced him to wait, perhaps a year, maybe longer, before starting college. While I was at it, I should have sat down with him and asked him a simple question, in a calm way.

"Why college?" I should have asked.

If his answer was "Because everyone else is going," or "It looks like fun," or "I don't know what else to do," I should have stopped those applications and tuition payments right there.

Let me put it another way. Try this: "Let's get married!"

"Why?"

"What else is there to do?"

You get the idea. And you can divorce a spouse. You can't divorce a bad record at college ("unless you go 'offshore,'" one helpful advisor told me, meaning a year in Dublin or Australia).

People shouldn't go to college just because they are suffering from a failure of the imagination. But in fact that's what my son and I had. We didn't know any better. This book is the result.

What I didn't know when I sent my son to college is that a lot of kids (some of them brilliant students) take time off. William R. Fitzsimmons, the admissions director at Harvard, says that Harvard encourages its students to take time off. "We urge them to get off this very fast train most of them have been on," he says. "In our admission letter, we talk about the idea of taking a year off, that it's a good thing to do."

For some kids, it's not only a good thing, it's an essential thing to do.

Cornelius Bull, the founder of the Center for Interim Programs in Cambridge, Massachusetts, is the grandfather of the movement that encourages kids to take time off. "If you don't know where you're going, any road will take you there," Neil says. In other words, if you're not ready at eighteen to commit to a field of study, you might as well go to Montana to build fences, or work in an orphanage in India. I wish I'd talked to Neil before my son headed off to Rochester, New York, to attend the rigorous Rochester Institute of Technology.

You will hear about Neil in this book. He's a charismatic guy, speaks in aphorisms and pretty much invented the business of counseling teens who aren't ready for college.

"I feel nobody for any reason should go to college at age eighteen," Neil says. "I say take your midlife crisis now."

Before World War II, only around 15 percent of the population went off to college, a place to study the classics or prepare to become a teacher. In 1941, only 10,000 people in the whole country took the SAT. Then along came two successive waves of change: first the G.I. Bill and second the baby boom. Today the United States is second among all countries in the percentage of population holding a college degree.

OK. What percentage is that?

I have posed that question to people all over this country. They will usually stop for a moment and consider. Then they will say something like "All my friends went to college, but it's a big country, so I'll say 50 percent."

Wrong, I tell them.

Twenty-five percent of all adults twenty-five years of age and older, according to the 1998 Statistical Abstract of the United States.

There's another way to look at it. How does the United States stack up against the rest of the world?

A 1996 study released as part of the Digest of Educational Statistics had 27.4 percent of Americans "of the theoretical age of graduation" in 1992 possessing a bachelor's degree, second to only one other country.

So if the United States is Number Two, who is Number One?

Answers usually go like this:

England, because of places like Oxford and Cambridge and those plummy accents and that interest in Shakespeare. (No. The United Kingdom had only 20.4 percent of its citizens twenty-five and over as college grads.)

France, because they seem so worldly and sophisticated. (No. France had around 16 percent.)

Germany, because of all those German engineers. (Nope. Germany had around 13 percent.)

Japan, where there's such an emphasis on learning? (No. Japan was high, at 23.4 percent, but still lower than the United States.)

Then one of those Scandinavian countries? (No. Sweden had

around 11 percent, Norway had 19.4 percent and Denmark had 22.1 percent.)

The answer is Canada, with 32.2 percent. (And right below the United States was Australia, with 26.3 percent.) Canada is a young country, it favors immigrants with high academic achievement and, besides, what else are you going to do there in January if not study?

And it's not that people in the United States go to college because they are so brilliant. If you look at the Third International Math and Science Study (TIMSS) in 1995, a study of one million students in twenty-six countries, students in the United States started in the middle of the pack in fourth grade (ranking right between those in Australia and Canada, but bested by those in countries like Singapore, Japan, the Netherlands and the Czech Republic), by eighth grade had sunk a little lower in the rankings, on a par with students in Scotland and Latvia, and by the final year of secondary school were ranked better than students in only two other countries, Cyprus and South Africa.

Does this sound like the United States is a country that deserves to send 66 percent of its high school graduates to college? No. We go to college because we *can* go to college. And we believe that skipping college will turn our kids into truck-driving louts, gum-chewing manicurists, butt-scratching carpenters, belching gas station attendants, or, said more politely, less well-rounded, less cultured, less interesting people.

But this is assuming that college actually educates people and turns them into cultured people, and that carpenters, gas station attendants and manicurists cannot be cultured people.

Anyone who says that has not been on a college campus lately. These days a college degree means, for a majority of students, a way to get a job, not to learn about the world.

In fact, one of my researchers on this book, Robert Costanos, a senior at SUNY Binghamton, in New York, thought I should call this book *Four Years, for What?* Robert claims he hasn't learned a thing in three years of college, but will finish his degree because "that's what I need in order to get a good job"—in his case, as a foreign correspondent or a travel writer.

So will his college degree, from a good school like SUNY Binghamton, translate into a good job? Thousands and thousands of students graduate with undergraduate degrees every year, each one of them expecting to turn that diploma into a glamorous, challenging job in which they will have a great deal of autonomy, perhaps travel to foreign countries and ideally become vested in an employee stock program. But even at the millennium, with the American economy on boil and unemployment at a thirty-year low, an awful lot of kids with bachelor's degrees are delivering pizzas.

And those are the ones who graduate. America has an extraordinarily high rate of enrollment in college, and an extraordinarily high number of college dropouts. According to government statistics, nearly a third of students who start college one year will not return to that college the following year. The graduation rates published in college catalogs are in fact for six years, not four. "That's pretty much the standard," one college admissions officer told me.

It took an average of 6.3 years to finish a bachelor's degree in 1993. In fact, only 26 percent of the students in one national study in 1994 had gotten a college degree within five years of starting a traditional four-year college. The numbers for students who started at community colleges were much lower.

I certainly didn't know that when I packed my son off to college. Nor did I know that only a third of the students get bachelor's degrees by the time they are twenty-nine years old.

In the two years since I started this book, I have been lucky to talk to advisors who believe in the resourcefulness of teenagers and their ability to succeed on their own. I have encountered pragmatic employers who chuckle at the difficulty of placing someone with a bachelor's degree in biology. ("They all want to be Jacques Cousteau," a man with Kelly Scientific, a temporary agency in Detroit, Michigan, told me. "But they don't know how to *do* anything.")

I have interviewed people from other countries who are astounded by Americans' obsession with college. ("In Europe," one told me, "no one would ever ask you at a party what you do or where you went to college. That would be vulgar. Your friends are the people you grew up with, no matter what they do for a living.") I have tracked down scores of people who did not get a college degree and who prospered anyhow.

I have met some delightful young men and young women who have chosen another course besides college. Some of them were bored with school, dreamers, druggies, academic washouts. Others were tired of the pressure, eager to get away from home, not ready to plug into another four years of school. Still others were the creative, artistic types who needed to get on with their lives. Or they were Internet entrepreneurs who were already making $80,000 a year and didn't see the point of getting a college degree . . . right now. One of them became a web multi-millionaire at the age of twenty-one, after dropping out of college because he had trouble with calculus.

What I have learned is that for the most part, kids come out fine. The smart and the restless. The young and exasperated. The drifting and directionless. The bored and the borderline. The bright and the ambitious. They make it, with or without college.

And this is what else I found: It is so easy to imagine a child who sails through school, gets top grades, plays tennis, goes to the prom, goes to a top-ranked college. That is the child we tend to see when we peer into the crib, into those bright button eyes.

It is another thing altogether to go down the road less taken, where the risks and rewards are not as well known, and certainly are a lot harder to explain to a coworker in the elevator. When someone asks, "What's your daughter doing?" they expect to hear, "She's in her third year at Northwestern," not "She's doing an internship in Bangladesh, then she's spending a Rocky Mountain semester with National Outdoor Leadership School."

Paulette Meyers-Rich, a mother of two sons from Minnesota, wrote me to say that both of her boys dropped out of the University of Minnesota without earning a degree. One reason her boys dropped out, she said, was "the revelation that after six years of all this (few graduate in four years these days), a degree in cultural studies or even journalism is not going to get one a lifetime's worth of work in a job that one wants to go to each and every day for the next forty years." One son switched to a technical program in graphic design; the other is supporting himself working in a restaurant while pursuing an interest in music. Meanwhile, she says, "they have seen their friends go deep, deep into debt and remain stuck in living situations they despise (with four roommates, or living at home), having to take whatever unrelated job anyway just to begin paying back the college loans, and so on."

While it is important to have an educated citizenry, she said, "The main thing young people are wanting from college these days is to get a job. A good-paying job that will buy them all the luxuries they believe they are entitled to and the hell with higher learning. This is not going to do us much good in the long run."

She, the daughter of a man who worked in a factory, knows that manual labor does not preclude an appreciation of art and culture. Her father, she said, would unwind by listening to classical music. He was a reader who went to museums and enjoyed theater and concerts. And he spent time involved with the community as a volunteer. Moreover, he was a man of great moral bearing. "These things are not reserved for the college-educated," she said. "There needs to be more respect paid to all types of learning. There has been such a class/status war going on in this country for so long, it's no wonder that even working-class kids don't want to take up a trade."

Taking up a trade, I should mention, is not the end of the line, either. An expert plumber in Connecticut—making far more money than I was—quit his job to teach fly-fishing in Montana.

And then there's the man I interviewed, in Austin, Texas, who had dropped out of junior college in his first semester and was running a toilet-paper-making machine before he happened upon the Internet and became a web-page designer. These days, Kevin Krall is raising $1.3 million from venture capitalists to fund a new web community.

So here's what you do if you envisioned your daughter being a lawyer and she tells you she wants to be a pastry chef, instead, if you think your son could make it as a doctor and he tells you he would rather be a tree surgeon—you accept it, that's what you do. Some kids, even some bright kids, do not belong in college. A few of them will have the self-awareness to tell you that outright. The others will give you a hint with a report card showing a string of W's and a couple of I's.

Take it from a mother who has been down that other, less traveled road: You do not love your child one bit less because he or she is a park ranger instead of a stockbroker. Remember when you told your children, "Whatever makes you happy"? Now is the time to find out if you really meant it.

Parents, life does not always turn out as we had planned. So let's begin: "You don't have to go to college."

Part One

COLLEGE ASSUMPTIONS

Chapter One

THE CASE AGAINST COLLEGE

All great truths begin as blasphemies.
—GEORGE BERNARD SHAW

Here is who belongs in college: the high-achieving student who is interested in learning for learning's sake, those who intend to become schoolteachers and those young people who seem certain to go on to advanced degrees in law, medicine, architecture and the like.

Here is who actually goes to college: everyone. That everyone includes the learning disabled and the fairly dumb, those who have trouble reading and writing and doing math, slackers who see college as an opportunity to major in Beers of the World, burned-out book jockeys and the just plain average student with not much interest in anything.

Think about your high school class. Now think about the 76 percent of those students (80 to 90 percent in middle-class suburbs) who *say* they expect to go to two-year or four-year colleges. You begin to see the problem?

Pamela Gerhardt, who has been teaching advanced writing and editing at the University of Maryland for six years, says she has seen a decline in her students' interest in the world of ideas. In an article in the *Washington Post* on August 22, 1999, she noted: "Last semester, many of my students drifted in late, slumped into chairs, made excuses to leave early and surrounded my desk when papers were due, clearly distraught over the looming deadline. 'I can't think of any problems,' one told me. 'Nothing interests me.'"

Her students, she said, rejected the idea of writing about things like homelessness or AIDS. Five male students, she said, wanted to write about the "problem" of the instant replay in televised football games.

Ever since the Garden of Eden, people have been complaining that things used to be better, once upon a time, back when. I suppose it is possible that, thirty years ago, students were just as shallow and impatient with education as they are today. But I don't think so. It could be that a college education is wasted on the young, but it is more likely that a college education is especially being wasted on today's youth.

Of course, there was a period twenty-five years ago when Cassandras argued that college was a waste of time and money. Around the time that *The Overeducated American* was published, in 1975, Caroline Bird wrote a book called *The Case Against College*. Her book has been out of print for decades. But there are arguments that seem very familiar to me: that Madison Avenue sells college like soap flakes, that going to college had become a choice requiring no forethought; that students weren't really there to learn and that college was no longer an effective way to train workers.

But primarily Ms. Bird argued that "there is no real evidence that the higher income of college graduates is due to college at all." She cited as her proof Christopher Jencks's report "Inequality: A Reassessment of the Effect of Family and Schooling in America," which pointed out that people from high-status families tended to earn more than people from low-status families, even if they had the same amount of education.

College, Bird pointed out twenty-five years ago, "fails to work its income-raising magic for almost a third of those who go." Moreover, she said, "college doesn't make people intelligent, ambitious, happy, liberal or quick to learn new things. It's the other way around. Intelligent, ambitious, happy, liberal, quick-to-learn people are attracted to college in the first place."

Or, as Zachary Karabell asked in the 1999 book *What's College For?: The Struggle to Define American Higher Education,* "on a more pragmatic level, does college truly lead to better jobs?"

He answered his own question with "Not necessarily. The more people go to college, the less a college degree is worth." He goes on to point out that the Bureau of Labor Statistics includes in its list of jobs that require a college degree "insurance adjuster" and "manager of a Blockbuster video store." Is that what you were foreseeing for Joey when you wrote that $25,000 tuition check?

Caroline Bird was outraged over the expense of college in 1975. A Princeton education, she said, would cost $22,256 for tuition, books, travel, room, board and pocket money—for four years.

Twenty-five years later, the price for that Princeton degree has grown to $140,000, including room and board and books, but not travel money and pocket change. It's even more than that, if you factor in the student's lost wages. Because of the low unemployment rates at the end of the nineties, anyone with the IQ to go to Princeton could make at least $15,000 a year with only a high school diploma, and perhaps more. So tack on at least $60,000 (if the student knows computers, make that $120,000) in lost wages while Jared or Jessica was busy at Princeton studying Shakespeare. That puts the price of a college degree from a fine Ivy League school at more than $200,000.

Is it worth it today? Perhaps even less so than in Caroline Bird's day, primarily because students no longer seem interested in ideas, and because it is so much easier to make money just by hopping onto the Internet.

"I agree that from the perspective of society as a whole, it would be better if fewer people went to college," Robert Frank told me. He's the popular Cornell economist, and the author of *Luxury Fever* and other books. "Economists often challenge this notion by citing studies that show significantly higher wages for college graduates," he said. "But all these studies say is that the people who attend college are better, on the average, than those who don't. They don't tell us how much value is added to them by attending college. From the individual's point of view, it still often pays to attend college, since employers so often use education as an initial screening device. Everyone wants the best-paying and most interesting jobs, after all, which assures that there will always be a surfeit of applicants for them. So employers who offer such jobs have every incentive to confine their attention to college graduates. But that doesn't mean that we'd be poorer as a nation if fewer people went to college."

An article in *Newsweek* (November 1, 1999) by Robert J. Samuelson said: "Going to Harvard or Duke won't automatically produce a better job and higher pay. Graduates of these schools generally do well. But they do well because they are talented." The article was titled "The Worthless Ivy League?"

Brigid McMenamin wrote a blistering piece in *Forbes* magazine (December 28, 1998) called "The Tyranny of the Diploma." Beyond listing the usual suspects in the computer field who did not complete college—Bill Gates, Michael Dell—she pointed to the young digerati who are making $50,000 to $80,000 a year and more at age sixteen. At a time when most kids in college say they are there "to get a job," these kids may well skip college in order to jump in on the booming Internet business.

Moreover, as Ms. McMenamin recounts, almost 15 percent, or 58 members, of the Forbes 400 (a yearly listing of the most successful business leaders), had either, as she put it, ditched college or avoided it altogether. In terms of wages, she said, brick masons and machinists had it all over biology and liberal arts majors. As a capper, she stated: "A hefty 21 percent of all degree-holders who work earn less than the average for high school grads." She didn't even bring up plumbers, electricians and car mechanics.

HIGH SCHOOL DROPOUTS

Almost half a million teenagers drop out of high school every year, according to the United States Department of Education. In New York City, half of the entering freshmen don't graduate from high school. There is every reason to be alarmed about high school dropouts.

Yet there is nothing stopping a high school dropout from becoming a plumber, or a computer programmer, and earning a great deal more than most holders of a degree in European history. One sixteen-year-old New Yorker, Cooper Small, dropped out of Stuyvesant High School in Manhattan in his junior year—over a bad grade in English, even though his GPA of 97.4 ranked him, he said, third in his class.

By that point he had begun working as a computer programmer, making $175 an hour. He then enrolled in Simon's Rock in Great Barrington, Massachusetts, as a freshman in college—without a high school diploma.

That's the millennial example: a seventeen-year-old who is off to college without a high school diploma, making more than his professors and doing it through building web pages.

OK, so those are the computer geniuses, the ones who may not even need a college education. But what about the kids who want to become doctors, lawyers, engineers, teachers? Fine, they should go to college, though I'll tell you, in the course of this book, about a medical school in the United States that takes students straight out of high school. Meanwhile, parents should be aware that in 1990, 75,000 people with college degrees were working as street vendors or door-to-door salesmen, 83,000 college graduates were working as maids, housemen, janitors or cleaners and 166,000 college grads were working as motor vehicle operators, according to the July 1992 issue of the *Monthly Labor Review.*

Jennifer might get that expensive degree in marine biology, but she also might just as easily end up a waitress/ski bum in Aspen who picks grapes in the south of France during the summer to pay for her room and board.

THE MIDDLE-CLASS BURDEN

Future doctors and lawyers constitute only a small portion of the students going to college. Going to college is epidemic, especially among middle-class families, whose students have nothing more in mind than just . . . going to college. These are students who have a sense of entitlement about the enterprise. They may enroll in business classes because that seems to be the way to get rich, or they may major in communications with some vague idea of getting into broadcasting.

They may buy term papers on the web (hey, dude, check out www.cheater.com, where term papers can be downloaded for free), argue with their teachers when too much reading is assigned in an English course and argue with their teachers again when they get a grade lower than a B-minus. These are the students who see their college degree as getting their ticket punched, so they can go out in the world and get a good job and become the consumers they have been raised to be.

Listen to Sarah Williams, who recently left a high position in marketing at Unilever to take a flier on an Internet start-up. "I found high school in Greenwich, Connecticut, pretty boring," she said. She enrolled in the University of Colorado and then dropped out. "I would never use 60 percent of what I needed in order to graduate," she said. "Jobs want people who are specialists," she concluded. "Not people who are well-rounded."

Or, as Mr. Karabell says in *What's College For?*, "Today's students represent a generation of pragmatists who want knowledge that they can apply to their lives." Mr. Karabell, who has taught at Harvard and Dartmouth, wrote that today's college students are looking for usable skills. And if they think that way at top schools, imagine the attitudes prevalent at the local community college.

Despite the fact that half of all college students matriculate at community colleges, which essentially offer training and remedial education, Mr. Karabell said, "The public still retains romantic notions of college and still sees a college degree as a special achievement."

Those romantic notions of success through college mean that parents treat all education up until college as mere prelude. Many middle-class parents buy homes in school districts where they are assured that 85 to 90 percent of graduates go to college—and where no guidance counselor would dare suggest otherwise.

At New York City's selective public high schools like Bronx Science, Stuyvesant and (in the humanities) Townsend Harris, the number of students heading off to college is close to 100 percent. And then there are the private prep schools, either day schools or boarding schools, for which parents pay up to $20,000 a year to guarantee that their children get into good colleges.

But here's a thought. College professors tell me that three-quarters of their freshmen have no business sitting in a college classroom. The professors were not talking about open enrollment, or remedial classes; they were primarily talking about spoiled, immature and lazy middle-class kids, the kind who are filling even some of the best college classrooms and who have no interest in studying what is being taught.

Saying that "everyone" needs to go to college (that is to say, everyone in the middle class) at age eighteen is just as arbitrary as saying that everyone at eighteen should become a race car driver or a concert pianist. Many kids just aren't ready. Some may never have the aptitude to do college-level work. And a surefire way to make sure that your reluctant son or daughter will never graduate from college (or experience the pleasure of learning for learning's sake) is to insist that he or she go to college "just to see what it's like." What they will see is that, for them, it's like *hell*.

ALLERGIC TO SCHOOL

The truth is there are students who are simply allergic to school. They have to be monitored in high school to do their homework. They skip school, arrive late, leave early. Cooper Small, the student who dropped out of Stuyvesant, says he skipped forty days of school his junior year, despite his stellar grade point average. Kids in Boston skip an average of twenty-eight days a year apiece.

And high school students have all the usual problems. They get pregnant. They get depressed. They do drugs. They get broken hearts. They get bored. One student at the Bronx High School of Science in New York dropped out a few months before graduation, even though he had a 1500 on his college boards and a full scholarship from Northwestern. The student said he was "tired of school," and took his GED. Good-bye, scholarship.

If this happened only rarely, you would have to say there was something wrong with the student. The fact is that it happens often enough to suggest there might be something wrong with the system.

Leon Botstein, the president of Bard College in the Hudson River Valley, believes that students should be turned loose at age sixteen from formal education and allowed to roam around a bit. In his 1997 book, *Jefferson's Children: Education and the Promise of American Culture,* Mr. Botstein, in a chapter called "Replacing the

American High School," proposes ditching high school as we know it. Too many hormones, he says, too little learning. His proposal: tenth grade, and then adios. The ones ready for college would go there; the rest would get work or vocational training.

High school, according to his theory, is the place that rewards the jocks and the cheerleaders, the best looking, not the academically gifted. (Or, if I might turn a movie industry witticism on its head, it's Hollywood, without the money.)

Staying in school, he says, damages the weakest students. "They stay in school, but they are bored," he told *The Christian Science Monitor* in May of 1999, after the shootings at the high school in Littleton, Colorado. "They can't concentrate. They gaze out of the window, dreaming about doing something else. They can't sit still. And they cannot divert the enormous energy they possess into something that makes them feel better about themselves."

BABY BOOMERS AS PARENTS

Thirty years ago, baby boomers (and I am one) fought to remove *in loco parentis* rules at colleges, to get rid of core curriculums, throw out the starchy old ideas about education and focus instead on getting back to nature, introducing pop culture and doing good deeds. While we were at it: down with materialism.

"In the sixties, students studied sociology so they could change the world; in the seventies they studied psychology so they could change themselves; in the eighties they will study business administration so they can survive," Landon Y. Jones wrote in his 1980 book, *Great Expectations: America and the Baby Boom Generation.* And what do you know? Business administration is the number-one undergraduate degree being offered today.

If anyone wants to know why today's eighteen-year-olds often seem to be at loose ends, lacking in values and uninterested in a liberal education, they need look no further than a study mentioned in Jones's book, "American Family Report, 1976–77," which defined middle-class and upper-class baby boomers as the "New Breed." "New Breed parents tend to be better educated and more affluent," the report said. "They represent the 'Haves' versus the 'Have Nots.' New Breed parents have rejected many of the traditional values by which they were raised: marriage as an institution, the importance of religion, saving and thrift, patriotism and hard work for its own sake. And they have adopted a new set of attitudes toward being parents and the relationships of parents to children."

As Jones pointed out, the World War II generation always put family first, themselves last. For the baby boomers, the first priority was themselves. As adults, Jones wrote, "the baby boomers have become the first generation of parents to be widely unavailable to their children," because mothers worked and married couples divorced.

Giving your children an expensive pair of sneakers is not the same thing as spending an evening focused on their social studies homework. As has become all too apparent to anyone who has tried to juggle work and home, money is not time.

I am not the only parent to wonder if I was too generous with my child, too eager to rush in and pay for solutions to his problems instead of waiting for him to solve them for himself. And part of the reason I rushed in with a checkbook and paid for a year at boarding school was that the entire process of educating children seems so relentless, there is no time to stop and wait for an organic solution. There seemed to be no way for me to just suspend him for a year or two and keep him out of the system until he was mature enough to plunge in.

Because almost everything we've done seems in retrospect to have been wrong, most baby boomers are becoming increasingly conservative with their children. The old adage that someone "would be without a heart not to be a liberal when they were young, and without a brain not to be a conservative when they were older" should be amended to say, "parents would be without a brain not to be conservative with their children."

When two schoolboys opened fire on their classmates in Littleton, Colorado, many middle-class parents immediately called for cracking down on teenagers. Suddenly there were suggestions that kids wear school uniforms, that curfews be established, that the drinking age be raised and violence eliminated in movies and on television. In other words, today's baby boom parents seemed to want to turn into parents circa 1958.

("Turn off that TV, Johnny, I don't know what that Elvis-pelvis guy is doing, but it shouldn't be shown in our living room!")

Yes, we have become our parents. But here is the difference. The World War II generation did not, for the most part, go to college. When baby boomers went off to those stern-looking, barrackslike dorms with long hallways and one phone at the end, they were setting out for a whole new world, one their parents did not comprehend.

When those baby boom parents send their own children off to college, they think it is an institution they understand. After all, they've *been* there. But college has changed.

Through market pressures and the inevitable sea changes that happen with any institution, college has become less rigorous. Moreover, the people going to college, our children, have completely different expectations from those we had. We wanted to change ourselves; they just want to make money.

It is the hallmark of every conservative to think that things were always better before. I thought that college would turn my son into an intellectual, someone like myself. For me, the newly hatched social conservative, college was about ideas, and about replicating myself. For my son, it was about getting away from home, being free, doing whatever it was his friends were doing and eventually getting a piece of paper that would entitle him to a job.

THE PAMPERED STUDENT

Because I wanted college to change my child, I coddled him into thinking that college was his right and punished him by assuming that college was essential. It wasn't easy to accept that a child *not* go to college, when a college degree is now required for (but not essential to) being a secretary or a police officer.

So parents wheedle and coax, demand and seduce their children into going to college. We complain that our children have a sense of entitlement, but meanwhile we have turned college into a *fun* place, and sold it to students as surely as television has sold Pokémon cards.

Students are not acolytes who arrive on campus to partake in a sacred ritual of education. They are savvy shoppers who have chosen a college based on skin-deep factors like the splendor of apartment suites (most students, raised with their own rooms, object to sharing a dorm room), the size of the swimming pool, the sophistication of the Internet connections and what's on the menu in the dining hall.

"It's a much more consumer-oriented generation of students and parents," said Connie Nicholson, an educational consultant in Osterville, Massachusetts. Note: The consumer-oriented students and their parents seem far easier to seduce with spangly, ephemeral things like a new gymnasium than by smaller freshman survey classes.

No one is saying that college students should live in squalor or not have a nice running track. But one father wrote me in amusement to tell me that his son had turned down a school in Boston because, get this, its football team played on artificial turf.

Colleen L. Casey, assistant transfer coordinator at Southern Illinois University–Edwardsville, said her colleagues have had some amazing requests from entering students. Among them she lists "Can I bring my water bed?" and "Can boyfriends and girlfriends share a room?" ("The student asking was serious, and this was a major factor in his decision," she said.)

Students arrive with televisions, VCRs, refrigerators, computers, cell phones, beepers and Bang & Olufsen stereo systems. They drive sports cars. Many of them do not understand the concept of doing without, or of students being as poor as church mice.

When colleges and universities found that nearly a third of the students who started as freshmen did not return the following year—despite the salad bars and Nautilus machines, the classes like The Biology of ER and the college restoration programs (for students whose grades put them in danger of being expelled)—administrations came up with another solution. Forget about the notion that college was the place where dissimilar people would learn about each other. Colleges now allow freshmen with similar interests to room together on the same floor or in the same dorm.

So if Jason is a practicing Buddhist, against smoking, drinking and eating meat, there is a floor waiting for him at a U near You. If Janelle listens to country-western music and wants a quiet study zone, there is a place where she will find like-minded people. Good-bye, diversity. Hello, People Like Me.

Meanwhile, undergraduate classes taught by part-time faculty and teaching assistants have risen to 47 percent in 1995 from 22 percent in the mid-1970s. Why? To save money.

It has become so important that kids go to college, so inconceivable that they do anything else, we have become almost comic in our eagerness to appease them. In the Education Life section of the *New York Times* (summer, 1999), this advice was offered: "If your son announces he did not take chemistry because the lab was scheduled during *The Jerry Springer Show,* don't risk alienating affections or parenticide by asking 'Do you know how much money I'm paying to send you to that school?' Offer to buy him a VCR to tape the show."

Aha. I see. A parent is not supposed to assume that the child is in college to, say, study chemistry and take the lab. A parent is supposed to understand that a student might want to watch day-time television instead.

In twenty years of working with teenagers and their parents, Neil Bull, the founder of Interim Programs in Cambridge, Massachusetts, has become flummoxed by parents who think they owe their children a college education. "I had a kid from Exeter," Neil said, referring to one of the top prep schools in the country. "This was a wimpy, feckless child, who got 1100 on his boards."

The kid had confessed to his father, a doctor, that he wanted to go to college to have a good time. "That father would be masochistically insane to send that kid to college," Neil said. "Most college freshmen are just falling-down binge drinkers."

OK, he's exaggerating. Less than half of college freshmen say they binge-drink once a week. But still, would any sane parent spend up to $30,000 a year on a kid who said, straight out, that he just wanted to have a good time?

IS IT EDUCATION, OR IS IT TRAINING?

Bottom line, why are kids going to college? They are going not to get an education, gain enlightenment, broaden their horizons, become better people. They are going to get those high-paying jobs. (And parents who have paid those tuition bills are certainly encouraging them to think about things like the size of their signing bonus on graduation.)

Perhaps it is because education has become so expensive that students have become so practical. As Ethan Bronner wrote in the *New York Times* in 1998, "The annual nationwide poll by researchers at the University of California at Los Angeles shows that two suggested goals of education—'to be very well off financially' and 'to develop a meaningful philosophy of life'—

have switched places in the past three decades. In the survey taken at the start of the fall semester, 74.9 percent of freshmen chose being well off as an essential goal and 40.8 percent chose developing a philosophy. In 1968, the numbers were reversed, with 40.8 percent selecting financial security and 82.5 percent citing the importance of developing a philosophy."

Now, it can be argued that "developing a meaningful philosophy of life" is a very sixties-ish thing to admire, but to me it seems to come much closer to what education and learning are about than "being well off."

Many colleges these days have become virtual trade schools, offering degrees in golf course design, massage therapy, business, business, business and computer programming. (I have no complaint with the disciplines, only with the notion that we have to bless them with a college degree.)

Placement offices have become the hotbeds that literary magazines used to be. In the American culture of big homes, four-wheel-drive trucks, conspicuous consumption and big-screen TVs, college has become a place to prepare students for a hot job market, not a hot discussion of Spinoza.

But in doing this, where colleges have sabotaged themselves. Training is much better done on the job or in narrowly defined, brief courses intended to do nothing more than teach NT networking administration. If colleges abandon the high ground of teaching the liberal arts, the notions of philosophy, the broad range of history, if they instead become diploma mills churning out baby business majors and computer science majors, there will soon be no reason to go to a liberal arts college at all.

So if personal growth is not the issue, better to just get the business experience yourself, or take a short-term course in the specific skill you need. Companies now offer certification courses for things that employers are actually demanding. Those range from "e-certification" in things like Windows 95 Power User for $25 on Tekmetrics.com on the web to several thousand dollars for the Microsoft Certified Systems Engineer program that leads to the coveted MCSE certificate. Cisco Systems, a networking company, offers a range of certificates from CCNA (Cisco Certified Network Associate) to CCIE (Cisco Certified Internetwork Expert), sometimes in high school. So while Jenny is working on her four-year B.S. degree in computer science, a high school dropout might zip by her with a CCIE, earned in a matter of months.

Colleges have a choice: They can either retreat to the high-minded school-on-the-hill notion of education and sacrifice 60 to 70 percent of their students. Or they can capitulate and become training institutions. Right now they are pretending to do one, while actually doing the other. Already the Culinary Institute of America in Hyde Park, New York, offers a bachelor's degree of professional studies, a B.P.S., in baking or culinary arts, a bachelor's degree recognized by the State Board of Regents. What's next, a bachelor's degree in pet handling, B.P.H., or a bachelor's degree in woodworking, a B.W.W.? Why do we have to justify a degree in cooking with a bachelor's degree? Because we still romanticize what a college degree means.

"Not everyone needs college, but everyone surely needs post-secondary education or training of some high quality, if they want a high-skill, high-wage job," Paul F. Cole, the secretary-treasurer of the New York State AFL-CIO, told me. He described a visit to Pueblo Community College in Colorado, where Cisco Systems, the computer networking company, has a certification program. A couple of dozen students were near getting their associate's degrees in computer programming, and "Cisco grabbed them for like $60,000 or $70,000 a person, hired them right there," Cole said, "people with a two-year technical college degree.

"Increasingly, because of the changing nature of work, and the increasing role of technology and understanding technology and other things you need to know in the workplace," he said, "those occupational and technical skills are becoming more important." The difference between the current level of training needed and the old vocational skills is that vocational training simply offered a narrow occupational expertise. To succeed today, Cole said, kids will need to learn occupational skills, but also need to read better, reason better and do higher levels of math.

Many community colleges, which are highly responsive to local job demands, are getting students who have already completed a bachelor's degree in the liberal arts, and who now need to pick up a skill in order to get a job.

But why take the bachelor's degree first? There are so many ways a kid can go out and earn money doing something he or she enjoys. Jill can get a certificate in horseshoeing (from the

Pacific Coast Horseshoeing School in Sacramento, California, 10 weeks, $3,350), an apprenticeship in herbal medicine at the Dry Creek Herbal Farm and Learning Center, in Auburn, California (nine months, $1,395), or learn feng shui consulting for a year at the Metropolitan Institute of Interior Design, in Plainview, New York, for $3,400. There is even a course that promises to teach students everything they need to know about book publishing in four weeks at the University of Denver Publishing Institute, for $2,750, as well as the better-known Radcliffe Publishing Course in Cambridge, Massachusetts, six weeks for $3,645, plus room and board.

IS ANYONE TO BLAME?

A baby boomlet will arrive on college campuses in the fall of 2000, a boomlet that will not peak until near the end of the decade. Soon we will have a million additional students graduating from high school each year and throwing themselves at the portals of higher education. That will lead only to more competition and more stress on students.

Already Harvard rejects half of its applicants who received perfect SAT scores (on the easier, recentered scale). How much more stress can kids take?

College will remain the benchmark as long as it is assumed to be the keystone to a middle-class life. In her provocative 1989 book *Fear of Falling: The Inner Life of the Middle Class,* Barbara Ehrenreich wrote, "Through professionization, the middle class gained purchase in an increasingly uncertain world. Henceforth it would be shielded, at least slightly, from the upheavals of the market economy. Its 'capital' would be knowledge, or, more precisely, expertise. Its security would lie in the monopolization of that expertise through the device of professionalization. Its hallmark would be higher education and, with it, the exclusive license to practice, consult or teach, in exchange for that more mundane form of capital, money."

But it is possible to see a college degree these days as a one-way ticket to . . . the middle, not the top. People like Peter Jennings, Tom Hanks, Woody Allen, Steve Jobs and Anna Wintour succeeded without that sheepskin, as did James Truman, the editorial director of Condé Nast.

"Don't talk to me about college," said Gary Levinsohn, one of the producers of *Saving Private Ryan*. Mr. Levinsohn, who grew up in South Africa, is a multimillionaire producer and movie executive. He does not have a college degree. "I have kids with college degrees who do my faxing for me," he said, laughing.

The creative types, the entrepreneurs, people who invent things, run things and dominate our culture (hello, Barry Diller) have often neglected to pick up a college diploma.

Meanwhile, perfectly good jobs—what my son called "butt crack jobs," like plumber, electrician and carpenter, plus truck driver, surveyor, air traffic controller, furniture restorer, cable puller, shop owner—are available for people who don't go to college. An entire generation thinks there's something sexy about sitting in front of a computer screen writing code, but something boring about repairing a car. And as for being a businessman, here's one acid test: If it's boring to own one garbage truck, why is it compelling to own 100? The answer, of course, is the difference between being a trash hauler and a trash mogul. But is the conversation at the end of the day that much different?

I am saying that most college students have not actually thought about what they are going to do with that college degree they are so avidly pursuing. They picture themselves being corporate executives, when in fact they are more likely to end up as low-level managers in charge of linens at Wal-Mart, or paper shufflers in the back office of a large and faceless insurance company. They might even end up in a more glamorous business—publishing, advertising, film—but shuffling papers all the same.

In fact, most students don't even know what jobs are available. Yes, there are those laughable aptitude tests (which predict with a kind of creepy certainty that everyone should become morticians). But most high school kids are goofy. They are dreamers. They still think they have a chance to become a champion soccer player or a famous actress.

Moreover, most of them could not accurately tell you what their parents do during the day. (I am an editor at a newspaper; my son would say I answer the phone, talk to people and look things up in a dictionary, not what my employer thinks it is paying me for.)

It used to be that parents ran small businesses, shoeing horses in the barn or repairing clocks, or worked as farmers or even on a production line in a factory. Children saw their parents work; they often helped their parents at work. Now kids visit their parents at the office, and come home without a clue as to what they do.

There are an awful lot of people sitting numbly in college classrooms who are in fact better suited to working with their hands, to being out on their own, setting their own workday, solving problems, actually helping people rather than reading textbooks and writing papers. But a lot of those jobs are, in fact, blue-collar jobs, and therefore beyond the pale for most children of the middle class. As Barbara Ehrenreich said of attitudes fostered in the 1970s: "The working class became, for many middle-class liberals, a psychic dumping ground for such unstylish sentiments as racism, male chauvinism and crude materialism: a rearguard population that loved white bread and hated black people." That's why Johnny's liberal middle-class mom is horrified if he suggests enlisting in the Army. In her mind, the Army is filled with all those people she has spent her life making sure he was better than.

And no wonder my son was initially dumbfounded when I suggested he look into becoming a car mechanic. "I want to do something that I'm not ashamed to say," he told me.

No wonder college professors look out at a sea of faces and despair. No wonder students lament that college is like high school with beer and dorms. Or that employers complain that college graduates have no knowledge, no depth and an interest only in getting a decent salary.

A RACE THAT IS NOT WORTH WINNING

We have taken the notion of competition over school enrollment to its logical and most absurd extreme. In 1998, one pregnant woman in West Palm Beach, Florida, Pam Knorr, got her doctor to induce labor six days early, so that her baby would be born before the September 1 cutoff date for admission to Florida's kindergarten. Forget whether this child will be ready for kindergarten in the fall of 2003; the mother was going to make sure that he was eligible. That's the kind of planning (and pressure) I'm talking about.

Not every child walks at the same age, one mother of five told me. Why should every child go to college at the same age? Why should every child go to college? Do we finally live in a society where every American child is "above average" and where only immigrants become plumbers?

It is also time that parents who have learning-disabled kids, or children with attention deficit, begin to accept that college may be a race their children cannot win. At least not when they are eighteen and still growing up and learning about themselves.

Robert Gilpin, a college counselor in Milton, Massachusetts, believes that far too many kids start college before they are ready. "Parents," he said, "you've got to listen to this. If you don't, you'll spend a lot of money, and miss an opportunity that your kids could benefit from."

It is a grave mistake to think that a child who struggled in high school will suddenly find himself in college. It happens, but far less often than parents would hope, and at a very high financial cost.

And if a high school senior—even a very good one—believes that college doesn't sound exciting, then that student should not go to college, at least not right out of high school.

Parents, are you listening? It's that simple.

Chapter Two

BART, BOBBY, OR BRENDA: DEALING WITH THE SLACKER TEEN

The condition of perfection is idleness;
the aim of perfection is youth.
OSCAR WILDE

Perhaps because this is such a hardworking country, we tend to idolize the slacker, and make fun of those who toil. Take a look (please!) at the devilishly clever 1999 film *Election,* which portrays a girl (played by Reese Witherspoon) so intent on becoming president of student government in high school that her mouth is permanently flattened into a grimly determined line.

Tracy Flick, as she is called, raises her hand so high in civics class that she seems to be picking coconuts. She knows more about student bylaws than the faculty advisor. She makes her own campaign buttons and bakes cupcakes for prospective voters. She even has the presence of mind to arrange to have the school paper photograph her casting her ballot in the election.

As much as I laughed at the striving, friendless Tracy, I saw a lot of myself in her, the overachieving girl in high school.

One of my son's best friends, Aaron, seemed destined for greatness from birth. The first time I heard of Aaron was when my son told me that this boy told him, on his first day of school, that he was forgetting his lunch. There you have it: My son was leaving his lunch behind in first grade and Aaron was there to remind him.

Aaron was not only brilliant at math, good at English and hardworking, but he was also on a citywide newspaper, started taking the SAT in seventh grade, went to elite summer programs limited to only really smart kids and competed nationally on the junior fencing team. There was no doubt, even in first grade, that Aaron was Ivy material. And so he is. He graduates from Princeton with a degree in computer science in 2000, completing his degree in the requisite four years.

If your child is like the fictional Tracy, or the real Aaron, read no farther in this chapter. If your child is hinting that he does not want to go to college, there are plenty of other chapters in this book for you. Your Jordan may not want to go straight to college. He may want to travel to Brussels (to intern at the Human Rights Watch) or work in a homeless shelter (to further his political career), or start his own Internet company. Your Jamikwa may feel she has a chance to become a pilot in the Air Force, or want to go to Choate-Rosemary Hall for a thirteenth year of school. They are going somewhere, even if it's not straight to college.

Then there are the rest of our children. Some of them have not yet had a chance to ripen. Some dawdled their way through school. Many have no particular goal in school. Some got into trouble. Some feel entitled to a college education even though they've done nothing to earn it. Some are bright but have learning disabilities. Some may not even be that bright. Many of them are lazy. Some are nearly criminal.

There are lots of ways to classify these kids. Robert Schleser, professor of psychology at the Institute of Psychology at the Illinois Institute of Technology in Chicago, has his own way of classifying students. "In my own work, we have the Bored, the Bothered and the Bewildered. The bored kid has attention deficit hyperactivity disorder. You sit down with a college textbook and you'll *become* ADHD," he said, laughing.

"We have a school system based on the bell curve," he explained. "The kids who are at either end don't do so well. On one end you have the bewildered kid with learning disabilities, who needs support on concepts. At the other end you have the bored kids who get the concept but can't stand the work. Then you have the ones in the middle, who are bothered by the other two."

"In my own case," he said, "I had A's until fourth grade and didn't see another one until after the military and Vietnam and doing blue-collar construction. Then I got straight A's for two and a half years. When I got to college it was a good fit for me."

Precisely.

One understanding mother of five, Kathleen Siegle, of Durham, North Carolina, just feels it is all a matter of maturation. "It's those readiness signs," she said. "If a child is eighteen months and not walking the same way as the others, we accept it. A person who's eighteen is still giving a lot of signals. Not everyone walks at twelve months. And not everyone who graduates from high school is ready for college."

PHYLUM, GENUS, SPECIES

Granted, some may just not be ready. I have my own categories for those kids; I divide them into Barts, Bobbys and Brendas.

Bart Simpson (on *The Simpsons*) is your classic slacker. "Underachiever, and proud of it" is his motto. In a 1990 episode of the television series called "Bart Gets an F," he patiently explains to a friend, "Only geeks sit in the front seat." The episode ends with Bart recalling a fact from history class and having his grade triumphantly changed from an F to a D-minus.

Bart is rebellious, hates doing chores, is strong-willed, plays a lot of pranks. When he thinks of the future, he imagines himself operating a wrecking ball. He gets frustrated with schoolwork and spends a great deal of time fantasizing. He tends to watch a lot of television (the ultraviolent *Itchy and Scratchy Show*, with episodes like "The Last Traction Hero"). He also fakes illness to avoid school.

Bart does not have a great moral compass, either. But what would you expect? His parents met in detention hall.

On the other hand, Bart's mom, Marge, may be dim, but at least she is good-hearted. It is Marge who said, in a 1991 episode: "Look, I know Bart can be a handful, but I also know what he's like inside. He's got a spark. It's not a bad thing. Of course, it makes him *do* bad things."

What to do with a child whose philosophy can be summed up with the words "Eat my shorts" and whose response to almost any question is "I didn't do it"? Well, after he was diagnosed with ADD, his parents tried a drug called Focusin. The drug turned Bart into such a monster, it came as a relief when the doctor put him on plain old Ritalin.

The reason we love Bart is that we all know Bart. I believe the Kevin Spacey character in the movie *American Beauty* is actually a grown-up Bart Simpson. Bart is merely an out-of-control kid. He wants what he wants, and he wants it now. If he weren't fairly dumb, he would be a master criminal. "Think how much more damage Bart could do if he were smarter," Norm Fraley of Kelly Scientific told me. "If he could think a little farther ahead, he wouldn't get caught."

So we've got our Barts, the kids who get called to the principal's office, who have notes sent home, who get suspended from school, caught smoking cigarettes, drinking beer. These are the ones who give their parents headaches, but they are no more deeply troubled than the Bobbys.

Bobby Hill, of *King of the Hill,* is quite simply, as his father puts it, "not right." Bobby is overweight, not doing that well in school. He's a space cadet who plays video games and eats junk food all day. His father sees him as a "Mama's boy," and perhaps his father is right. Bobby has always failed to meet his dad's expectations. (His father expects him to "be a man," play football and eventually grow up to go into the propane business.)

Instead, Bobby loafs around the house. His heart is in the right place. He's not the sort of boy who would blow up the girls' bathroom, except by accident.

Like all slackers, he is an underachiever. But some slackers have a little brio, a little flair. Not Bobby, despite his mother's hopes for him. Bobby is one big ball of disappointment—to himself and to others. "Something's just not right about that boy," his father, Hank Hill, says—repeatedly—on *King of the Hill.*

Bobby, too, was diagnosed with attention deficit disorder, definitely without hyperactivity. His parents put him on medication, but they weren't comfortable with the "new" Bobby, the talkative one who was full of energy and focused. And so they went back to the Bobby they knew: a little shy, a little whiny, and just, you know, not right.

And then we have our Brendas. On *Beverly Hills 90210,* the character played by Shannen Doherty is rich, popular and feels entitled to whatever it is she wants. Her Brenda was only with the show for two years but in that time Brenda developed a loyal television audience of people who were fascinated (and appalled) by her.

Another Brenda is the Brenda Patimkin made famous in Philip Roth's novel *Goodbye, Columbus.* That Brenda, played by Ali McGraw in the movie, was a strong tennis player who broke men's hearts. She, too, was a dyed-in-the-wool princess.

Brendas make the list primarily because of their sense of entitlement. If they got into a decent state school, they would complain that it was not "competitive" enough. One mother I know told me that her daughter (clearly a Brenda) refused to go to a $35,000 a year therapeutic boarding school because she didn't like the accommodations. This was a young woman facing a court date and who had just gotten out of rehab. "Look," her mother told her, "we're not sending you to Golden Door," a spa for the pampered. Nonetheless, this Brenda rejected the school. And won.

Brendas are obsessed with status symbols. They would pick a college on the basis of name alone. And, please, the college must allow them to bring their new car on campus as a freshman, otherwise they're Not Going, Mother.

In her farewell episode of *Beverly Hills 90210,* while the rest of the kids were going off to California State, Brenda was headed to Paris. (Granted, it was an attempt to get Shannen Doherty out of the show, but Paris is where the Brendas of the world *should* end up.)

One common complaint I hear about contemporary kids is that they, like Brenda, expect to have only the best. "Even young people I hire to work for me, there's this sense of not having to pay your dues," said Lisa Antell, director of admissions at Bridgton Academy in Maine, which consists entirely of kids in their thirteenth year of school. "The feeling is: You come out, you get perks."

And there you have it: Bart (the protocriminal), Bobby (the layabout) and Brenda (the arrogant one). One is not performing at all, one is performing beneath expectations and one expects more reward than her performance deserves. Needless to say, the types are not gender specific. Jobert can be a Brenda, just as Jillian can be a Bobby.

And not every kid is a pure type. My well-intentioned son was a bit of a Bobby with Brenda rising (Nautica, Tommy Hilfiger, Polo, Abercrombie & Fitch). He only had a flash of Bart when he was at boarding school.

SO SHOULD THEY GO TO COLLEGE?

Let me say first, this is not just a question of the expense. Even if parents have money to pay for private college, there is a very good reason not to send a child who is not ready: That child may hit a wall, flunk out or slink away in disgrace, and end up with damaged self-esteem. (By the way, in these politically correct times, no kid "drops out" of college; today kids "stop out.")

I asked Geoffrey Gould, director of admissions at SUNY Binghamton, an elite public university in New York State, to tell me some warning signs for kids who were not ready for college. He listed the following:

- Kids whose SAT or ACT scores were significantly higher than their grades. ("The exception is the student who feels freed upon leaving high school and home, and who then may be very emotionally ready and able to use his/her ability," he said.)

- Students whose academic performance is on a downward track. "Whoever they are, students with downtrends are less ready for college, both academically and emotionally, than those ending high school on a stable or 'up' note," Mr. Gould said. Similarly worrisome are kids who pick courses that are less selective during their senior year.

- Grade inflation that has tricked the student into thinking they are stronger academically than they really are. (A competitive college may come as a rude shock.)

- Students who seem especially interested in attending college close to home. "It may be for a very good reason, such as maintaining a strong family bond or economic necessity, or it may reflect uneasiness about making the break from home," he said.

- And finally, students who have been accepted only by a college far down on their list. "The students may be unhappy enough that they do poorly the first year," he said. "A youngster who feels like a failure as they begin college, because they are not at choice number one, will find adjustment more difficult."

"When one looks at freshman-to-sophomore return rates and four- or five-year graduation rates nationwide," he said, "it is clear that some of the items above as well as others are contributing to far less success than we'd all wish for."

The answer may be taking time off, he said, but "most high school seniors seem to find the notion of time off before college very hard to handle. They need to be reassured such a strategy may make things even better later, but it's a hard sell."

Another college admissions officer cautioned kids not to head to college if there is a sudden change in family fortunes, a death or illness, a divorce. The point: It's best for a child to head off to college with a clean slate instead of worries about what is happening back home.

And then there are the persistent fears every parent has of substance abuse. Even parents who smoked pot in the sixties may miss the signs of a child who is toking up before fifth-period biology. And as for drinking, how many parents don't check to see what is happening in the liquor cabinet, or take their child's word that it is her best friend who got into the single malt Scotch.

If you think a year off will loom like a giant void, ready to suck your child down into the nether regions of drink, drugs or lassitude, exactly what do you think that same child will do when she is five hundred miles from home and on a campus that stopped practicing *in loco parentis* about the same time that young ladies stopped ratting their hair and wearing crinolines?

If you look at recent statistics about deaths from alcohol poisoning on campus, you will quickly realize that a vulnerable child is far from safe at college. A study from the Harvard School of Public Health showed that 50 percent of males and 39 percent of females in college had been binge drinking in the last two weeks. (For him, five or more drinks in a row; for her, four.) Kids in fraternities and sororities were four times more likely to drink.

That daughter of yours would be better off working in an orphanage in a strict Muslim country.

HOW IS A PARENT TO KNOW?

Say you have a Bart, a Bobby or a Brenda in *your* house. This child expects to go to college because that's what everyone does. And you may have been going along with the idea and preparing to take out thousands of dollars in loans.

"You could take that money and have them travel around the world several times for what you spend on tuition," said Holly Bull, of the Princeton Center for Interim Programs, which arranges internships and travel for kids who are delaying starting college.

Your child may already have been accepted to college (of his choice or not). He or she may already be choosing what part of the dorm to live in: the vegetarian floor or the country-western music floor or intensive study floor (ha!) or the no-smoking wing. But until that child sets foot on campus, it is not too late to reconsider.

Of all the people I have talked to in writing this book, no one ever told me "I wish I'd gone to college sooner." A child who waits a year may gain a great deal; she certainly will lose nothing. Most colleges will let a student defer matriculation; many recommend it. And those who counsel kids who are searching for colleges tell me that a lot of those kids are going for the wrong reason.

"I and most of my colleagues deal with young people who go to college to get away from home," said David Denman, an independent college advisor in Sausalito, California "They're not going to read, write papers and explore careers. They're going to get away from their parents' rules. Those who spin out do so primarily because they can't handle the freedom.

"It's not that they can't handle their academic work," he said. "The college admitted them on the basis of the data that says they can do the work, but no one has given them a maturity test. They've had the SATs but not the test for maturity."

Well, folks, here's the test for maturity.

A 1400 on the SAT is not going to help your daughter at Princeton if she has bad work habits and no focus. The following questions are meant to help you rate your child's drive and discipline, both aspects of maturity. Those qualities will help make up for a weak SAT or ACT score. Contrarily, a smart kid who has never developed drive and discipline is going to get into trouble, quickly, at a competitive school.

Admissions officers are paid to keep just such kids (high potential, low achievement) out of the top-tier schools. Parents, on the other hand, will try everything from bribes to pressure to get that child in.

In a word: Don't.

You should look at the following checklist if your child is raring to go to college, but you're not sure he or she is ready. You might also take the quiz if your daughter herself says she's worried that she won't be able to handle the work and the freedom. You should do the test especially if your child has a learning disability that will make college that much harder.

Check off any of the following statements that describe your child. Note that there are both positive and negative attributes; points are added or taken away accordingly. And after the quiz take a look at what some experts on teens and college have to say about those questions.

☐ 1. If asked to do a household task, the teenager will invariably say, "Why should I?"

☐ 2. The teenager finishes things he or she starts, whether it is a school assignment, a household chore or a hobby.

☐ 3. Your child has defaced, gouged, torn or otherwise tortured an assigned textbook or library book.

☐ 4. Your child has often forgotten to bring home forms for you to sign for events like trips, appointments or special events at school.

☐ 5. Your son or daughter has developed a technique for studying for a test, like reviewing material, making flash cards, writing outlines or rereading chapter summaries.

☐ 6. Your son or daughter is analytical about what he or she did wrong; he knows which questions he got wrong before he gets the test back; she takes blame for her mistakes. ("I messed up," rather than "The question was stupid.")

☐ 7. When assigned a research paper, your child starts by going to the library or searching the Internet long before the paper is due.

☐ 8. If given a choice between watching a favorite television program and getting an important paper finished, your child would opt to watch television first.

☐ 9. Your child has expressed an ambition to be the best in a field, whether it is music, sports, flower arranging, academics, modeling, whatever.

☐ 10. Your teenager may not be good in everything he or she does. But in his or her area of interest, he or she will work through the night on something. (Note: talking on the phone and playing computer games do not count; repairing the computer does.)

☐ 11. Your child has a hard time breaking a task down into component parts, and is often overwhelmed and confused by assignments or requests.

☐ 12. Your child tends to hang out with (and identify with) the children who have no solid plans for the future.

☐ 13. When your child gets a bad grade, he or she will bring up kids in class who got a *worse* grade.

☐ 14. You can remember at least one time when your child overcame great obstacles to get a school assignment or activity done.

☐ 15. After getting college catalogs, your teenager sat down and eagerly paged through them, identifying courses and programs to pursue.

☐ 16. Your child often says things like, "The course is too hard," "My teacher hates me," "I don't understand the assignment" or "This class is stupid."

☐ 17. Even if the assignment is too elementary for your child, he or she will work on it thoroughly and carefully.

☐ 18. Your son or daughter gets frustrated easily and gives up on things, even things that are almost finished.

☐ 19. Your teenager always seems to be short of cash and borrowing money; for him or her, immediate gratification doesn't seem soon enough.

☐ 20. Given a choice between being a big fish in a little pond and a little fish in a big pond, your child would rather be in a big pond.

SO WHAT NOW?

College is a very expensive way for your child to find himself, and a bad experience may mean that he never goes back. So add up the following scores and then think about reconsidering the type of school your child will attend or whether he is ready to go at all. (At least talk to your child about your concerns.)

I call this the "Functional SAT Score." If the Functional Score is significantly lower than the child's actual SAT score (or ACT score), you have three choices: ignore it, suggest a school farther down the food chain (a two-year college instead of a four-year college, public school instead of private school) or ask your child to take some time off before entering college.

It's okay for a parent to say, "We think you should wait." In fact, it is right to *insist* your child take some time off. It's your money. You are the adult.

Remember, the point is not getting into the college, it is getting out. The smart kid who is lazy and unmotivated is probably not going to make it. A kid who waits and grows up, who learns a little bit more about the way the world works, just might.

You will notice that the quiz is divided into questions about discipline (getting the work done) and drive (an internal will to succeed). Discipline can be taught (it's what boarding schools excel at). Drive is more difficult to instill. A child with discipline but no drive may end up a file clerk; one with drive but no discipline may end up a thief.

Below is the scoring, along with some thoughts about the questions from employers, educators, counselors, psychiatrists and parents.

1. If asked to do a household task, the teenager will invariably say, "Why should I?" (30 points come off the SAT score for lack of drive; ½ point comes off the ACT.)

EXPLANATION: I'll take the first one. Your son or daughter is not being cooperative on the little things, and college is a big thing. It is a collaborative endeavor: You put up the money; he or she puts in the effort.

Children who aren't grateful to their parents will not think twice about wasting their parents' money. You know the cartoon image of a person's conscience, the little elf that sends the student to the library instead of to the lounge to microwave a pizza and watch what's on the WB? A kid who says, "Why should I?" has a serious conscience deficit.

You could say, "It's immaturity," and point out that it's fairly common. No matter. A teenager who says, "Why should I?" when asked to help around the house is being surly and shouldn't be rewarded.

2. The teenager finishes things he or she starts, whether it is a school assignment, a household chore or a hobby. (Plus 50 points on the SAT for drive; plus 1 point on the ACT.)

EXPLANATION: Tom Hassan, dean of admissions at Phillips Exeter Academy, a prep school:

"High school students face many challenges that they could easily brush aside, and many sometimes do. They might put off tackling challenging calculus problems or daunting college admission essays in order to watch television or socialize with friends. Procrastination seems to be an inevitable part of adolescence.

"Teenagers, though, who stick with the task, even if that comes close to a deadline, impress admissions officers. These students are the ones who will succeed in their studies and in life beyond college.

"But how do admissions evaluators identify the students who finish what they set out to do? Clearly, standardized test scores don't reveal much of this trait, other than being able to show up on time one Saturday morning to color in the bubbles with a No. 2 pencil.

"Careful readers of admissions files pay particular attention to the language used by recommenders. They like to read about students who come to class stimulated by what they have read, students who are able to talk about it in class. They also like to see students who have pursued a hobby with passion and persistence. Large numbers of tardy references and unexplained absences understandably put them off.

"Admissions evaluators are looking for students who take full advantage of what is available to them and do so with vigor and sustained commitment. These students will in turn be the reliable contributors at their schools."

3. Your child has defaced, gouged, torn or otherwise tortured an assigned textbook or library book. (Minus 30 points on the SAT for discipline; minus ½ point on the ACT.)

EXPLANATION: Sure it's easy to write in the textbook, to circle the questions to be answered or underline the parts that will be on the test. And what's the difference if a book is thrown into a corner at the end of a school day, or used for first base in a pick-up game of softball? Here's the difference. My son valued his comic book collection and his car magazines. They were carefully stacked by date and treated with reverence.

Not so his textbooks. He thought nothing of drawing super-heroes on the front cover or writing "This sucks" inside. The spines on several of his books were completely gone by the time the course was over. Was he trying to tell me something of his feelings about American history? I didn't think so at the time. I do think so now.

And note here: I am not talking about the student who is so passionately involved with what she is reading that she cannot help but write in the margin, "This is *so true!*" That's another matter.

4. Your child has often forgotten to bring home forms for you to sign. (Minus 40 points on the SAT for discipline; minus 1 point on the ACT.)

EXPLANATION: Carole S. Fungaroli, Ph.D., professor of English at Georgetown University and author of *Traditional Degrees for Nontraditional Students* (www.traditionaldegrees.com). "'Forgetting' documents, even those for fun activities, means your child is mentally elsewhere. Picture a telephone that is off the hook, or a computer line that has dropped the connection. Your child is so unattached to school that she or he has no idea what those pieces of paper mean, or why they should matter.

"I understand distraction because I *was* this child, back when I struggled in high school, and eventually in my first failed college effort. Today, as a Georgetown professor, I see this disconnectedness often, but only in my most at-risk students.

"You can't fix this, but a boss probably can. A demanding job will convince any daydreamer that—whoa dude—the devil *is* in the details! Paperwork matters, especially when it connects to your paycheck, or to your continued employment.

"Work will be especially effective if your child does not have the family finances to fall back on in case of quitting or (gasp) firing. Most of these young adults go to college later in life with a commitment to do exceptionally well."

5. Your son or daughter has developed a technique for studying for a test, like reviewing material, making flash cards, writing outlines or rereading chapter summaries. (Plus 40 points on the SAT for discipline; plus 1 point on the ACT.)

EXPLANATION: Gail Reardon, an independent counselor in Newton, Massachusetts, who helps students structure time off:

"I see a lot of these kids. They have been organized, on track and have gotten into the schools they want. They've been on a fast track since the age of three. They've met with great success, but to do this they have had to lead their lives in a certain way.

"While they will probably do very well at college, this kind of child would also benefit from a year that allows them to explore other parts of themselves and other perspectives. Sometimes all that's missing is a different tempo of life, and kids can get that almost anywhere outside the United States.

"Which is not to say that I urge them to be disorganized or irresponsible. Instead it's good to give them an experience for which there is no right answer. It's a chance for them to get in touch with their instincts."

6. Your son or daughter is analytical about what he or she did wrong; he knows which questions he got wrong before he gets the test back; she takes blame for her mistakes. ("I messed up," rather than "The question was stupid.") (Plus 50 points on the SAT for drive; plus 1 point on the ACT.)

EXPLANATION: Bob Schleser, professor of psychology, Illinois Institute of Technology:

"There are two components here. One is the recognition of their error, the other is accepting responsibility. Attribution theory says that we make causal statements about our success and behaviors. It can either be a very narrow attribution, or global: 'I messed up on my test' versus 'The question is stupid.'

"The narrowest, nonadaptive, view can become: 'I messed up, I always mess up.' Or, it can go the other way: 'I didn't mess up, I never mess up.'

"A good student will say, 'It wasn't a lack of ability, it was a lack of effort on my part.' Someone who accepts responsibility and sees a mistake as something that can be corrected is the one who will succeed. Students have to be able to do that, to say, 'I didn't make the effort but I can; I don't have the ability now, but I can develop it.' You need both in college. How we answer this question answers how we're likely to do and to respond to obstacles."

7. When assigned a research paper, your child starts by going to the library or searching the Internet long before the paper is due. (Plus 30 points on the SAT for discipline; plus ½ point on the ACT.)

EXPLANATION: Al Newell, Dean of Enrollment, Washington and Jefferson College, Washington, Pennsylvania:

"If your child is exhibiting this type of behavior, as a parent you should count your blessings. One of the factors that distinguishes those students who excel in college, as opposed to merely surviving, is the ability to manage time. If a student is accustomed to planning, organizing and staying ahead of academic tasks, he or she will have an advantage in the transition to the greater freedom of college life. Chances are this sense of organization and drive will manifest itself in the application process, eliminating some of the stress and perhaps even improving the student's chances for admission."

8. If given a choice between watching a favorite television program and getting an important paper finished, your child would opt to watch television first. (Sorry, this is pretty common, but minus 30 points on the SAT for discipline; minus ½ point on the ACT.)

EXPLANATION: Note the words "important paper." And consider this—when this teenager is in college, there will be many more temptations than a favorite television show, including partying in the dorm, beer, drugs and sex. A child who will watch a television show before tackling that paper is a child who does not know how to defer gratification. The question is: Does a parent forbid a child to watch TV until the paper is done, or leave it to the child to figure out?

Geoffrey Gould, director of admissions at Binghamton University, believes that parents should leave it to the child: "When children learn to make decisions that work for them, confidence is instilled. Parental support is essential as children learn to weigh alternatives and understand the benefits and consequences of choices. The child given options to consider is more likely to work with parents to find strategies that leave everyone feeling okay. It's no surprise that anyone would choose recreation before work, or television before a term paper. A brief stint of relaxing TV followed by getting down to work makes sense, as the rewarded, refreshed student should then be content to study. On the other hand, the reward of TV *after* study can work for some, but that won't work for all. Only when a student seems unable to compromise or make balanced choices should parental mandates be used. It's not easy at first for children to see the benefits of hard work, but praise for it helps. In time, self-regulation will rule, and long-term benefits will accrue.

9. Your child has expressed an ambition to be the best in a field, whether it is music, sports, flower arranging, academics, modeling, whatever. (Add 50 points for drive on the SAT; add 1 point on the ACT, even if the ambition is to be the best rapper or cartoonist; even if the ambition is to be the best bank robber. Ambition is ambition.)

EXPLANATION: Norm Fraley, manager of distance learning for Kelly Scientific, a temporary employment agency:

"Ambition to be the best, even if it is only for a few minutes, reveals the existence of seeds of greatness. Any desire to be the best at anything is great leaps beyond having no focus at all; it is a decision to do something. Ambition cannot exist without a goal or at least a vision.

"However, execution of the desire is another matter. Part of the way into the activity, your child may find that he or she really does not want to be the best or even continue doing it at all.

"This is also a good thing. As parents we should encourage the practical decision of cutting losses and refocusing efforts on those things that are more important. This helps build a healthy self-esteem by empowering the child to act upon their decisions."

10. Your teenager may not be good in everything he or she does. But in his or her area of interest, he or she will work through the night on something. (Note: Talking on the phone and playing computer games do not count; repairing the computer does.) (Add 50 points to the SAT for drive; add 1 point to the ACT.)

EXPLANATION: David Rynick, executive director of Dynamy, an internship program in Worcester, Massachusetts:

"We often praise young people who can do everything well. But students who have a passion for an area of life or study will often outperform the well-rounded student in the long run. Their interests may change over time, but their experience of working hard and achieving results is one of the most transferable skills they can have.

"One word of caution: If your child's area of interest is narrow, make sure they are headed for a school that will allow them to spend a lot of time in that area. A student with a passion for mechanical drawing should not have to sit through two years of liberal arts classes to get to do what he or she really cares about."

11. Your child has a hard time breaking a task down into component parts, and is often overwhelmed and confused by assignments or requests. (Take away 50 points from the SAT for discipline; take away 1 point from the ACT.)

EXPLANATION: Perri Klass, associate professor of pediatrics at Boston University School of Medicine and Boston Medical Center, pediatrician at Dorchester House in Boston:

"These are kids who can't do things that are plainly within their intellectual grasp—they can't deconstruct a problem, a task or a project into its manageable, attackable steps and therefore, often after a lot of time and effort, they become discouraged and disgusted and quit without finishing. This sometimes gets misinterpreted as an attention problem, or a motivation problem, when in fact it's an efficiency problem—these kids are so inefficient in the way they tackle projects that they use up their attention and their motivation. They see only the whole, only the glorious and unattainable goal, and they just can't break it down. In a sense, they miss the trees because they see only the forest.

"Of course that larger vision, in the right setting, can be an advantage. Your child may one day be the person who always sees 'the big picture,' may be the idea lady or the visionary. But in the meantime, complex algebra problems and essays on *Catcher in the Rye* and scale replicas of the solar system can be sheer hell."

12. Your child tends to hang out (and identify with) the children who have no solid plans for the future. (Take away 50 points from the SAT for drive; take away 1 point from the ACT.)

EXPLANATION: Holly Bull, Center for Interim Programs, Princeton, New Jersey:

"Instead of viewing this scenario with distress, and judging your child to be aimless and lacking in drive, stop for a moment and consider the dearth of choices your child is facing. The operative phrase here is 'solid plans for the future,' because it usually translates into going to college.

"It is not inconceivable that your child is thoroughly weary of the classroom after what might be seventeen years of schooling and is, in a sense, exhibiting plenty of drive *away* from this one socially preferable choice.

"Do not panic. It is a mistake to assume that this is a permanent attitude or position; your child may simply require a temporary break from what often feels like an academic grind. Why not look for alternatives and offer your child more choices? Aside from working at a job, there are plenty of interesting programs and internships that provide young people with the chance to explore different areas of interest in an engaging, hands-on way. If and when they head to college, and most usually do, they will be more focused and mature, as well as reinvigorated, and can take full advantage of what college has to offer.

"If your child is hanging out with kids who, in addition to having no plans for the future, are actively getting in trouble in the present, it may come down to an issue of your own child's self-esteem. Even here, offering another choice and a fresh start may be the answer."

13. When your child gets a bad grade, he or she will bring up kids in class who got a *worse* grade. (Take away 30 points from the SAT for drive; take away ½ point from the ACT.)

EXPLANATION: Mel Levine, professor of pediatrics at the University of North Carolina, Chapel Hill, and cochairman of the board of All Kinds of Minds, a nonprofit institute for the Understanding of Differences in Learning:

"Personal accountability plays a significant role in academic success. There are many students who are said to have 'an external locus of control,' which is to say they have great difficulty perceiving their own roles in day-to-day performance. When they have difficulty, instead of wondering what they could have been doing differently, they look around for some external force (often a human force) to blame for their seeming inadequacies.

"They may invoke, alternatively, bad luck, a teacher who discriminates against them or some form of unfairness in testing. Regardless, the student seldom is able to feel personally accountable for his or her performance, especially when the outcome is not particularly positive. However, there are some students who feel so out of control of their performance that when they actually succeed, the laudable results are attributed to luck. In college, personal accountability is a key to success. College students need to accept responsibility for their day-to-day performance. Those who are in the habit of sidestepping accountability may rationalize their way into failure and 'learned helplessness' during the college years."

14. You can remember at least one time when your child overcame great obstacles to get a school assignment or activity done. (Add 50 points to the SAT for discipline, add 1 point to the ACT.)

EXPLANATION: Here's how life works: One person is dutiful and does his job reliably and on time; the other is the one who jumps in only when there is a crisis and saves the day. Which one is the hero? The one who comes through in a pinch. Why? Because we love stories of people who overcome the odds. In thinking about your child, remember that courage matters. The kid who finished the cross-country race with a pulled tendon, or the kid who finished his science fair project even when he had the flu, is the one who can reach inside and find those extra reserves that make for a triumphant finish. This counts even for the young person who goes out on stage in *Our Town* with a raging case of acne. Being able to buckle down and come through when everything is going against you is a great predictor of success. Never bet against the dark horse with courage and spirit and heart.

15. After getting college catalogs, your teenager sat down and eagerly paged through them, identifying courses and programs to pursue. (Add 50 points to the SAT for discipline; add 1 point to the ACT.)

EXPLANATION: Several of my consultants did not believe there was such a student, but I was that student. College for me represented an enormous opportunity, and I was hungry for it. So hungry I began college in the summer, right after high school graduation, with a course on logic.

But perhaps today, with sophisticated course offerings at the high school level, the grand buffet of a college course catalog is not that exciting. At least that's what Cornelius Bull, the founder of the Center for Interim Programs in Cambridge, Massachusetts, felt when he saw this question. Prepare yourself, because Neil is highly skeptical of the notion that eighteen-year-olds are ready for college.

Cornelius Bull: "I don't think that college catalogs eagerly paged are going to provide much of anything in the way of revelation about a college other than geography and boilerplate. And I don't think that identifying college courses is what one should be doing in the senior year of high school. But then I don't think that *any* high school senior should go directly to college. They don't have enough wisdom, perspective or experience to take advantage of this very expensive four-year sabbatical that kindly parents are providing.

"Can they do the work? Of course. Any idiot can do college. What they should be doing is visiting college campuses with a competent counselor. At each college names should be procured of recent grads who should then be called for advice; catalogs tell one absolutely nothing of value. There is no hurry for kids to romp through college. If they have spent twelve years being schooled, and often not educated, it's time for a break. Remember that George Bernard Shaw said that the only time his education was interrupted was when he was in school. Wise words."

16. Your child often says things like "The course is too hard," "My teacher hates me," "I don't understand the assignment" or "This class is stupid." (Take away 50 points for drive from the SAT; take away 1 point from the ACT.)

EXPLANATION: Dr. Edward Hallowell, author of *Connect* and co-author of *Driven to Distraction:*

"Signs of emotional distress or significant learning problems often go ignored for a long time, not being addressed until a lot of unnecessary damage has been done. Early signs of such problems are comments like, 'I hate school,' 'The work is too hard' or 'School is stupid.' Instead of lecturing such a child, or punishing him, or wringing your hands or rolling your eyes, the first step should be to get a solid handle on what is going on.

"Look underneath the negative remark, and you might find a treatable cause, like a learning disability, depression, an anxiety disorder or just massive misunderstanding between the child and his teacher. Once you have a handle on the problem—a diagnosis, to use the medical term—you can make a rational plan that actually might lead to constructive change, instead of simply leading to more struggle and no progress.

"As a psychiatrist, I have seen time and again, indeed every day in my office, the transformative power of a proper diagnosis and treatment. It all starts with knowledge. Sometimes you need to consult with an expert. But whatever you do, make sure you look underneath the negative statements your child might make, instead of just taking them as annoying expressions of negativity or irresponsibility."

17. Even if the assignment is too elementary for your child, he or she will work on it thoroughly and carefully. (Add 50 points to the SAT for discipline; add 1 point to the ACT. A personal note: An awful lot of routine work on the job is too easy. I do work every day at the office that is too easy. That should not be a standard for deciding if a project is worthy of your attention.)

EXPLANATION: Kenneth Hoyt, distinguished professor in the Department of Counseling, Education and Psychology, Kansas State University:

"The concept of excellence is applicable at all levels and kinds of education. A commitment to completing all assignments in the best possible way is a valuable ingredient in successful career development. The concept of 'good enough' should never be adopted. Whether the assignment is 'hard' or 'easy' has nothing to do with the concept of excellence. This kind of commitment is sure to be helpful at many times both in the quality of the work each of us does and in our personal satisfaction with our accomplishments."

18. Your son or daughter gets frustrated easily and gives up on things, even things that are almost finished. (Take away 50 points from the SAT for drive; take away 1 point from the ACT.)

EXPLANATION: David Rynick, executive director of Dynamy in Worcester, Massachusetts:

"The challenges of college come in all different forms—from sharing a room with a roommate to new expectations for performance and behavior in the classroom. Your son or daughter's attitude when the going gets tough is a good indicator of how they will respond to those challenges. Learning a whole new set of social and academic skills means being willing to keep going even when you are sometimes confused and unsure of the final result.

"The ability to follow through, especially on things that don't appeal to you, is a necessary skill in college (and in life). An assignment that is 90 percent complete but not turned in gets the same grade as one that was never started."

19. Your teenager always seems to be short of cash and borrowing money; for him or her, immediate gratification doesn't seem soon enough. (Take away 30 points from the SAT for discipline; take away ½ point from the ACT.)

EXPLANATION: Money equals time, something that will become clear to your child when he or she starts working for an hourly wage. All teenagers occasionally squander their money and end up short. But if your child makes a habit of it, it could spell big trouble down the road. If he squanders money now, he will squander his time when he's at college. And if she doesn't know how to handle cash when she's under your supervision, what is going to happen to her when she gets on a college campus, where credit cards are given away like popcorn?

20. Given a choice between being a big fish in a little pond and a little fish in a big pond, your child

would rather be in a big pond. (Add 50 points to
the SAT for drive; add 1 point to the ACT.)

EXPLANATION: There are people who can make perfectly satisfy-
ing lives for themselves by opting to live and work in a smaller
community. Still, it's the child who is ready to jump into the big
pond (who is ambitious and ready for a challenge) who is more
likely to succeed at college. Deke Smith, an independent college
counselor in Cambridge, Massachusetts, and Portland, Oregon,
would like to differ with me:

"Many students begin the college search process with the idea
that 'big is better.' It's my observation that, while this may be true
for the very bright, focused and aggressive student, many students
will be better served where the faculty greets them by name on
campus; they can more easily participate in class discussion and
can more likely be chosen for leadership roles in undergraduate
organizations or play on intercollegiate athletic teams. In their
adult lives, this early experience with leadership and participation will very likely prove beneficial in virtually any career.

"An appropriate match between the student and the college
will in the long run be the primary determining factor for success—far more so than the reputation of the college at the time
of application."

A WORD OF DISSENT

When I sent the questions out for review, Norm Fraley, who
works at Kelly Scientific, took the quiz himself. "I lost three hundred points," he said, "and I sailed through college."

What made the difference, I asked?

"I loved chemistry," he said, "and I always knew that was what
I wanted to do."

He believes that inspiration and dedication will trump things
like discipline every time. "Discipline is not the way I do it," he
said. And he's not fooling. At one point in his career, he went
from working in aerospace to working with hot dogs. Now he is
a strategic thinker for Kelly Scientific.

So all of the above should be amended with this one idea. If
Jocasta is in love with music or dance or physics, if she lives and

breathes it, then yes, she should go on to college (or some kind of school) to study it.

She may struggle with her English classes, if she is disorganized. She may have difficulty fulfilling her math requirement. In fact, if she is singularly focused, she may eventually have difficulty fulfilling the distribution requirements in American colleges and may not graduate.

If she is, like Norm, in love with one thing, and if she has an entrepreneurial bent, she may also become the next Bill Gates, someone who did not need a college degree to succeed. She is, in fact, more of a Tracy Flick than a Bart, Bobby or Brenda (none of whom has any intellectual focus).

So if you have a child like Norm . . . never mind.

Chapter Three

IT'S A MIRACLE THEY
SURVIVED HIGH SCHOOL

> Alice: "Would you tell me, please, which
> way to go from here?"
> Cheshire Cat: "That depends a good deal on
> where you want to get to."
> —LEWIS CARROLL,
> ALICE'S ADVENTURES IN WONDERLAND

It would be very easy to create the perfect high school. All we would have to do is figure out in advance which children would end up at Harvard studying American history, which ones were best suited to leaving school at sixteen to become web millionaires, which ones needed extra hours for rehearsal as dancers or musicians. If we had a way of separating the brain surgeons from the tree surgeons, the plumbers from the poets, we could make a perfect high school.

In the last chapter I talked about what's wrong with kids. This chapter is about what's wrong with education. As a parent, it's a lot easier to blame the system than your own child. And if anyone is looking for something to blame, high school, that cauldron of unrealized ambition and fully realized hormones, is a great place to start.

Eighty years ago, America opted for "comprehensive education," which could loosely be defined as "one size fits none." The schools simultaneously prepared students to be everything from tailors to ministers, from housekeepers to boatbuilders. Comprehensive education is the reason that I went to a school in Minnesota where Future Farmers of America shared homerooms with Future Teachers of America.

Our model of education is something like this: Fill those little minds with a wide variety of facts for twelve, thirteen, fourteen years; then assume that little bits of knowledge will seep out for the rest of a person's life, no matter what he or she ends up doing. It's a kind of water tank/drip irrigation system of instruction. Twelve years of filling the water tank, a lifetime of information dripping out. None of it very dynamic or interactive.

Meanwhile, parents of children who are destined for Harvard (what one educator mischievously calls "gifted parents") will do almost anything to get young Jared out of the comprehensive school and into gifted and talented programs, magnet schools or, failing that, private schools. "Who among us is not ready to intervene in our child's school whenever we are concerned that his or her ability to learn may be in jeopardy," Robert L. Fried wrote in the December 1998 issue of the *Phi Delta Kappan*. Mr. Fried outlines in his piece, titled "Parent Anxiety and School Reform: When Interests Collide, Whose Needs Come First?," a "fairly lurid image of status-conscious parents demanding that the school district perform a kind of educational triage to separate out and lavish attention on their own academically promising children, leaving others to suffer."

That applies just as well to status-conscious parents whose Barts, Bobbys and Brendas are not academically promising; such parents can be even more desperate to find the teacher who can unlock their child's inner scholar. In terms of educational politics, most parents flunk the test of altruism.

Then there is the rank hostility to education that, in this country, is based primarily on school taxes. This comes up most often when someone proposes building a new high school. And with one million *more* American children born in 1991 than in 1975, there are going to be lots of proposals to build new high schools. From a low of 11,338,000 kids in 1990, high school enrollment will hit 14,579,000 in 2005. In 2007, Nevada will see 70 percent to 90 percent more kids graduate from their high schools than in 1997. Nevada might be an extreme case, but the country as a whole will have 16 percent more high schoolers graduating in 2009 than in 1999.

Taxpayers (particularly retirees) see high schools as desirable only because they keep teenagers off the streets. It is not by accident that most new high schools are built far from Main Street, in some cornfield at the edge of town. Town planners say it's because schools these days need space around them for soccer fields and swimming pools. But deep down most planners will admit that the last thing citizens and store owners want to see is a thousand teenagers in baggy clothes, pierced tongues and orange hair swarming out of a school building, getting into cars and peeling out, or yelling and joshing with each other as they walk down the street.

Better to put them on buses and safely disperse them back to wherever they came from. Truth be told, we don't like teenagers, at least not in large groups and certainly not those who belong to someone else. We're afraid of them.

There may be good reason for that. Crime statistics show that in 1996, kids age ten to seventeen committed 40,000 robberies and 58,000 aggravated assaults in the United States. "[E]ven as the attention adults pay to individual teenagers has apparently declined, the degree to which adults fear them as a group has unquestionably increased," Thomas Hine said in his 1999 book, *The Rise and Fall of the American Teenager.* The growing number of teens down the road will inevitably mean a growing number of crimes.

Taxpayers will therefore build high schools, somewhere out at the back end of beyond, and will insist that students stay there until sixteen, seventeen, even eighteen—if only to guarantee that the kids are under some kind of control and kept out of trouble. "There are only two places where people feel like they're doing time," noted David Denman, an educational consultant in Sausalito, California. That's why teenagers often feel that school *is* jail.

Morton Egol is the managing director of Arthur Andersen's Schools of the Future project, which contributes advice and equipment to the Alameda Public Schools in Alameda, California. "Students compete for grades, taking examinations graded on a curve, and are ranked by A's and F's, which guarantees a significant failure rate," Mr. Egol said in a speech in June of 1999 at a conference on Learning for the Twenty-first Century. "The prospect of average or failing performance, and pressure to perform, crushes out natural love of learning. . . . For most students, school has become an onerous place."

With the "standards-based" curriculum advocated by reformers these days, even more students will fail to measure up. So students rebel openly, or covertly, by failing to show up for class. According to a study by the American Council on Education, 34.5 percent of college freshmen in 1998 said they had overslept and missed class in high school, compared with 18.8 percent in 1968.

Cornelius Bull, the founder of the Center for Interim Programs in Cambridge, Massachusetts, says many children can't tolerate high school. "Kids all the time say, 'Why should I be there? It's a waste of time,'" he told me. "There is rank boredom in the schools. They don't *want* to learn French." He points out that most teenagers would pick up French in a matter of months if they simply went to *live* in France.

High schools, Neil says, are eager to provide answers, but unwilling to listen to questions. "The system is very user unfriendly," he says. "It treats everybody the same. It assumes boys learn the same as girls. And it doesn't seem very relevant. Talk to most kids about what they're getting out of it, and it's real thin."

His organization finds more and more middle-class kids who want to quit school at sixteen or seventeen. "I am working with two high school sophomores now," he says. "They said to their parents, 'This is pointless.' They came in, and in each case we're getting them out, one to Australia, one to Alaska. Maybe they'll get a GED," he added blithely. "Whatever works for them."

Robert Gilpin, the founder of Time Out Associates in Milton, Massachusetts, notes, "There are other ways to get through high school than high school." He often sends students off to work with their hands. "I found twenty-three programs that build boats," he said.

Although parents feel their child will be marked for life by not completing high school—and that is how I felt when my son was thrown out of boarding school—there are alternatives. Rich parents have always resorted to a sort of backdoor system (study abroad, "postgraduate" years, a series of private schools) that will provide a wayward child a way to get into college or secure a good job.

The low-rent version of that is the GED, a substitute for a high school diploma. Just as there are rich dumb kids who find redemption through expensive alternative schools, there are smart poor kids who find redemption after taking a GED. Consider this story of a young woman born in Morristown, New Jersey.

Her parents ran a furniture store. This child loved to read but hated school. In an interview in 1994 in *Interview* magazine she said, "I have been out of school since I turned seventeen, and there has not been a single Sunday night since then that I haven't thought, 'Well, at least you don't have to go to school tomorrow morning.'"

She was expelled from high school in New Jersey (where she earned money working at the local Carvel ice cream store) and got her equivalency degree. It was only after getting a job reviewing B movies for Andy Warhol's *Interview* magazine that she found her acid and highly original voice.

Fran Lebowitz is one of the prime chroniclers of our age (*Metropolitan Life*) and writes charming and droll children's books. She should be the GED poster girl, an example of stunning achievement from the land of equivalency degrees. Below a certain income and intelligence level a GED can be a source of shame; above that level, it can become an eccentric accoutrement on the way to a successful life. Peter Jennings and John Cheever were both thrown out of prep schools and never received their high school diplomas.

Some college admissions officers are going to be happier to accept a piece of paper from the Wilds O' Maine Boat Building School (or a GED accompanied by an SEC filing on the kid's latest Internet venture) than a so-so recommendation from the guidance counselor at Aging Suburban High School. After an admissions officer goes through enough applications from children who are home-schooled, and children who have been in charter schools, and those who want college credit for their Rocky Mountain semester at the National Outdoor Leadership School, that boat-building school is not going to look that odd. And note: MIT does not require a high school diploma.

And yet dropping out of school remains a threat, especially for marginal students who do not have the option of $20,000-a-year "bridge" schools in Massachusetts or $3,000-a-month boat-building programs. The dropout rate in New York City is 50 percent. Florida's Education Commissioner, Tom Gallagher, shocked his local school boards by declaring the state's actual 1998 graduation rate to be only 48 percent, based on his revised calculations. His innovation? To count how many kids actually graduated from high school instead of including those who got a completion certificate (for the requisite seat time) and those who merely took their GEDs.

Ask a school what its dropout rate is, and you will often get a number that deserves scrutiny. I had assumed dropout rates were calculated as the number of children who graduate from high school compared to the number of children who had started twelve years before (adjusted for kids who transferred or were held back). Not so.

I noticed that Madison, Wisconsin, was arriving at its graduation rate by comparing the number of students who graduated to the number of students who entered twelfth grade (thus leaving out kids who had dropped out of school somewhat earlier).

Tim Potter, a research technician in the Madison school system, wrote back: "You are not the first person to question the validity of twelfth grade graduation/dropout rates. They don't make a lot of sense." He did add that the Wisconsin State Department of Instruction was going to change its definition for the 1999–2000 school year to calculate dropout rate as the number of students entering ninth grade versus those graduating. (Well, it's an improvement.) Meanwhile, he himself wondered how many of Madison's dropouts earned a GED. "The state was not willing to share this information," he said.

Goals 2000: Educate America Act (Public Law 103-227) stated that "by the year 2000, the high school graduation rate will increase to at least 90 percent." Ha.

This country is nowhere near making that happen. The education branch of the Organization for Economic Cooperation and Development (OECD), based in Paris, found that a decade ago, the United States ranked eighth among twenty-two OECD nations in graduation rates. In 1996 the United States dropped to twenty-third, ranking second from last, ahead of only Mexico. More than 93 percent of students in Belgium, Finland, Japan, New Zealand, Norway and Poland graduated from high school or its equivalent. In the United States, the rate was 72 percent (and that includes GEDs).

FORGOTTEN BY WHOM?

The kids who don't even get as far as a high school diploma are often referred to as the "forgotten half." If our high schools were better at offering courses that actually appealed to restless teenagers—in which, as one kid told me, "we actually get to *do* something"—then high school graduation rates might not be so low.

But here's the problem: Let the country come up with such a program, like one called Tech-Prep, and parents are wary because they believe that someone is trying to *keep* their kids out of college. Because we have a pluralistic society, and because prejudice reigned for much of two centuries here, parents of low-income and minority children will often stand in the way of their kids getting practical educations, because of their fear of tracking, or of shutting doors. For all of our respect for the differences between people, the one difference that is hardest for us to accept is that some people are smart and deserve to go to college and that others are better destined to vocations and trades. It becomes especially hard when a college-educated, middle-class parent discovers that Julie wants to go to work on the Alaskan pipeline or that Jed wants to study cake decorating.

Tech-Prep, authorized in 1990 under the Carl D. Perkins Vocational and Technical Education Act, will spend $111 million in federal money during the fiscal year 1999–2000 to encourage and organize free preparation at the high school level for high-paying jobs in technology. What Tech-Prep is attempting to do is revamp the old Vo-Tech programs that led to jobs in manufacturing for low-functioning students. The new Tech-Prep (aimed at the middle students who might benefit from training as technologists) is trying to teach computing skills and health care skills.

Nancy Smith Brooks, director of the Appalachian Regional Commission Liaison Office, an independent federal agency established in 1965, said that "the federal share, although small, has historically fed legislation that has pushed the states in certain directions: Tech-Prep, the integration of academic and vocational, gender equity."

Tech-Prep deals with high-tech, high-wage skills; the program is meant to begin in high school and continue in community college. Today the fields range from restaurant management and paralegal to advertising design, radiology, dental hygiene and veterinary technologist, construction, culinary arts and computer-aided design.

"Information technology is very popular," Ms. Brooks said. "You can start in ninth grade." The point of Tech-Prep, she said, was to offer "seamless education," where a student could work toward an associate's degree or a certificate from a community college while still in high school.

Some of the best Tech-Prep programs, she says, are in South Carolina, in Spartanburg and Greenville and at Tri-County Technical, a community college. "Those three really serve the community," she said. "Tri-County is one of the *best* tech prep programs in the country. One of the things they have done successfully is build a strong relationship with the state department of education. South Carolina does not start a vocational education program unless they know there is a need." In other words, Tech-Prep trains kids in a field where there is a demand for employees. Your tax dollars are actually at work here.

But recruiting for some Tech-Prep programs meets resistance from parents. A 1995 report on Tech-Prep by the Department of Education found that the program in Gainesville, Florida, "must overcome a common and long-standing prejudice: that vocational education is for youths who cannot make it in college and who can work effectively only with their hands. Preference for the university is also common among parents. A 1990 survey revealed that two-thirds wanted their children to go to college, and more than half preferred a four-year college." This despite the fact that parents recognized that two-year degrees could get their children high-paying jobs.

The report recognized "an almost universal demand among parents and students for high school programs that lead to college, as well as a distrust of traditional vocational programs that might not."

A Tech-Prep program in Springdale, Arkansas, found that one way around parents was to disguise the nature of the program. "Given the universal guidance process for all students and the intentional avoidance of a distinct Tech-Prep program identity," the report said, "the Springdale consortium does not specifically recruit students to a Tech-Prep program and does not identify a student as a 'Tech-Prep participant.'" That despite the fact that more than 40 percent of the students in Springdale High School do not plan to go to a four-year college and do take one or more vocational courses. Because of the overwhelming belief in this country that everyone must go to college, kids who might benefit from training as a health technologist, say, or a graphic artist, instead will labor through an academic program they are not suited for and that they do not like, just so they can go to college. This is insanity.

SO WHAT'S HIGH SCHOOL FOR?

Because Americans have difficulty recognizing a truly educated person without a piece of paper (it would seem far too classist and way too unscientific to say "I know one when I see one"), we have come up with nearly meaningless standards. We have page-one stories about the numbers of kids who graduate from an increasingly meaningless high school system and about the rising or falling SAT scores and also about school systems in New York helping their students cheat on achievement tests. We point at the numbers of kids getting Regent's diplomas, those passing national (or international) achievement tests in reading and math. We assume that because the American economy was so strong at the end of the century, we must be doing something right in terms of education.

But ask yourself how many recent American high school graduates could write a reasonably intelligent paper on any subject—excluding sports, hunting, movies, television and pop music. If anyone proposed that *half* of its high school's graduates could do that, I would rush to that school immediately to see the miracle for myself.

Wait, you say. That's not the only criterion for being educated. And you're right. Holding an intelligent conversation or writing a decent paper are just two skills. They are, however, skills that are required in college. Kids who can't do either probably should be heading in another direction. For those kids who cannot discourse on the French and Indian War, why not become expert carpenters, bricklayers or electricians?

"I'm not much of a book person," Chris Thomas told me. She graduated from White Bear Lake High School in Minnesota in 1993 and took a two-year degree as a medical secretary. Now, she says, at age twenty-four, she makes $12 an hour as a medical transcriptionist. "There are people who graduated from college and they work for eight, nine dollars an hour," she said. "I'm not one who says you have to go to school."

What high schools should be doing is coming up with alternative programs that actually interest unhappy students, that offer them an immediate application for what they learn and that teach them something they can use in the outside world. Just because it isn't college oriented doesn't mean it can't be good.

IF SCHOOL IS BORING, LEAVE

Many kids report that they are bored with school; they don't see the point of sitting in class and they know they can get away with cutting class.

In "An Ethnographic Study of Low-Achieving Students Within the Context of School Reform," in *Urban Education,* May 1999, Patrick W. Lee wrote about struggling students at Emerson High School in Oakland, California. "Cutting classes was a practice developed early on for many respondents during their freshman year and quickly developed into what several students referred to as an 'addiction.' Every student, when asked why they failed to attend classes, immediately responded that boredom kept them away."

Students at the school, he wrote, "often did not see the classroom as a site for exploration or reflection." Moreover, they understood that cutting classes would go largely unpunished. "[T]hey claimed that in classes taught by apathetic teachers, they could readily and frequently cut, receive no reprimands, and still pass their courses. Because they sensed a lack of immediate consequences to their cutting, most said they chose not to attend classes because they were 'able to get away with it so easily.'"

And it's not just struggling students in struggling schools. When my own son attended Bronx High School of Science, one of the few times I opened a letter from the guidance office and breathed a sigh of relief was when they had confused my son with another boy, one who had cut class 132 times in one semester.

Which is one reason Leon Botstein, the president of Bard College in Annandale-on-Hudson, New York, has suggested that high school end at sixteen. "The routine daily experience in high school is an object lesson" in boredom, he writes in *Jefferson's Children: Education and the Promise of American Culture.* "Young people learn how excruciatingly slowly time passes." In a country in which a significant number of students entering college have to take remedial courses, he laments that "a young person comes to college at age 18 without a serious love of reading, without a reasonable comfort level with mathematics and without a basic concept of science or history" as well as "sloppy habits in terms of concentration and memory." His conclusion: "The last two years of high school, particularly the senior year, are a waste of time."

Instead, he says, those who are ready to go to college should go at sixteen—to a place like Simon's Rock, which is run under the aegis of Bard. (People went to college even younger in the nineteenth century, he argues; they can do it now.) Or kids can go to a community college, where they will sit in classes with people in their twenties and thirties, people who are serious about getting an education, or at least a certificate in something practical.

Those Barts and Bobbys who "barely survived high school," as he puts it, can work or enter the military. Or they can get a practical education, under which he includes dance, art, music, designing, acting, as well as the areas usually dismissed as vocational education.

Neil Bull argues that a kid who is allergic to high school— and the kids he sees, it must be noted, are middle-class kids with affluent parents—needs to take an internship, become an apprentice, do good deeds or travel.

"You proceed by indirection," he says. "Our society thinks that's dalliance. But you have to have faith in the kids. How many times do you get the opportunity to sample things, even if they are irrelevant?" He is not saying that education is unnecessary. He is saying that some children may need to get their education outside of school.

Most adults are nostalgic about high school, the football games, the rallies, the homerooms, proms, lockers, even the macaroni and cheese in the cafeteria. But from a teenager's point of view, school is like a never-ending company evaluation, where every gesture is open to criticism and where movements throughout the day are monitored. At no other time in life will people feel so thoroughly, and unfairly, judged.

Ambitious students who are competing for admission to the top schools are also supposed to find time to volunteer at a nursing home, or run for student council president (like the toxically ambitious Tracy Flick in the movie *Election*), in between fencing and luge lessons. Meanwhile, everyone from parent to guidance counselor to peer is asking them if they've picked a college yet. And if it's MIT, they'd better start calculating just how their family is going to come up with $34,700 a year for tuition, room and board, books and supplies. That's pressure.

WHERE THE GIRLS ARE

These days, girls are becoming the majority of college graduates. And that starts in high school, where girls simply do better. "Where Are the Guys?" asked a paper in the Mortenson Research Seminar on Public Policy Analysis of Opportunity for Postsecondary Education (October 1998). (Don't worry: The report is a lot more fun than the organization's name.)

"Males are in serious trouble in higher education," the report said. "Males are disappearing." The paper noted that males received 85.3 percent of college degrees in 1870 and only 44.9 percent in 1996. It predicted that in 2007, nearly 60 percent of college graduates would be women. So much for Ophelia.

The report says that more women go to college, and that even more critically, more women *stay* in college. In fields like education that practice affirmative action in order to attract men, the report said, the result is that "almost any breathing male who walks in the door is enrolled while women are sometimes placed on a waiting list for admission.

"This raises the ugly specter of preferential admissions treatment for unmotivated, unprepared males at the expense of educational opportunities for motivated, prepared, ready-and-waiting females."

An administrator at a large East Coast university, who did not want to be quoted on this subject, told me, "There's no doubt that girls make better students. Boys are lazy. I think it goes back to a different level of focus. The easy way to say it is that we have a larger number of young women who receive merit scholarships."

But instead of it being *good* news that women are the ones on the college track, it may turn out that college will be seen as less desirable simply because more women go there. Think about it. Any field dominated by women is dismissed by the culture as less significant and, therefore, less worthy of high pay: nursing, secretarial work, teaching. Judith Sturnick, director of the American Council on Education's Office of Women in Higher Education, said, in the February 8, 1999, issue of *U.S. News & World Report,* that "when there begins to be a predominance of female members in any area, the value of that area goes down."

Meanwhile, there are those problem boys. Karyl Clemens, senior assistant to the president of Hartwick College, in Oneonta, New York, told me, "Parents wring their hands over sons, especially, just wondering when they are going to wake up and smell the coffee. The good news is that they do, eventually."

The bad news is that "eventually" turns out to be around age twenty-five to twenty-eight. For anxious parents, that can be a long, long wait.

The *U.S. News & World Report* article laid the blame for fellows not going to college squarely on the good jobs that boys could nab right out of high school. Males, it said, were "tempted by fast cash in a boom economy, preferring $30,000 starting salaries in such fields as air-conditioner maintenance and web design to four years of *Beowulf* and student loans."

That *U.S. News* story went on to say that some experts "foresee a time not too distant when degrees are not so prized, and skipping college might be a wiser career choice." With high schools becoming training schools for Microsoft and Cisco Systems, can the college-prep track even compete?

While girls may continue to stick with higher education, high school boys increasingly gravitate toward fields that tend to pay good wages, fields like computer programming, auto mechanics and truck driving. When I say it's a miracle "they" survived high school, I am talking disproportionately about boys.

Steve Bott, of St. Paul, Minnesota, graduated from a private high school in 1992 with a B- average. He was accepted at some good private universities, but decided to attend the University of Minnesota because of his parents' monetary situation. He dropped out before the end of the first semester.

"It quickly became apparent that I am not a 'sit in a classroom' kinda guy," he wrote me. Over the next four years he took the kinds of jobs you can get with just a high school degree: movie theater assistant manager ($5.50/hour), warehouse shipping clerk ($7.50/hour) and data-entry temp at a large bank ($8.50/hour).

In less than a year at the bank he was permanently hired as a mortgage document auditor at $9 an hour. Three years later he became a systems analyst and senior member of the management team, earning $37,500—more than he'd be making, say, after a similar time as a high school teacher.

Steve has taken some college courses over the years, and says he knows he will have to finish a degree if he wants to advance at the bank. At the same time, however, he says, "My high school friends who did finish college right away all have huge credit card and student loan debt, while I am debt-free. I paid off my new car loan in just twenty-one months and rent my own apartment, while planning to buy a home by the end of next year."

His biggest worry: that his younger brother, the straight-A student, will see dollar signs and skip college.

"I make it clear to him that my way hasn't been the easy way," Steve said. "Hopefully, he will make the right choice for himself."

BAD BEHAVIOR? NO WORRIES!

While there are high school girls who accidentally set fire to their bedrooms, drink too much and steal from their parents' friends, it is primarily boys who require creative embellishments on the recommendations written by college advisors. Boys predominate in special-ed classes, have more diagnosed learning disabilities, turn in sloppier papers, give lip to their teachers, get suspended more often, tend to drop out more and see less point in participating in band, the school newspaper and civic organizations.

No matter. High school guidance counselors have been instructed to find a college for each and every student who wants to go, even if the student is a known slacker, and especially if the school is solidly middle class. Everything depends on that college acceptance rate: local real estate prices, bragging rights and peace among the soccer moms. Parents have sued school districts over guidance counselors who were not enthusiastic enough in writing recommendations. It appears that even a student who spends four years slouching around the back of the classroom gets a letter attesting to his "potential," "curiosity" and "interest in public service."

"We have our ways," one high school guidance counselor who requested anonymity told me. "If a student just doesn't measure up, we have to pretend he's a good candidate. But we'll put at the bottom of the letter, 'If you have any questions, please call me.' That is a warning sign. If they call, I can tell them the truth."

Parents, you see, believe that their child deserves to go to college, and not just a state college but a name-brand school. How do I know? Because I took my son out of Bronx High School of Science when the guidance counselors there suggested that they would not steer him toward a four-year college. I sent my son instead to a $20,000-a-year boarding school that practically guaranteed he would get into a good college.

The reason I am writing this book is that I was wrong and Bronx High School of Science was right, though they certainly were not eloquent in explaining their stance. "We have a lot of *good* students here" is the way they put it.

THE ADMISSIONS GAME

"There are times when we know more about a student and the circumstance than will ever come through in a letter of recommendation or in written format," said Larry A. Griffith, director of admissions at the University of Delaware. He has, as he puts it, "worked both sides of the desk," trying to get kids into college as a guidance counselor at a boys' high school in Washington, D.C., and trying to assess candidates at Delaware and before that at Brown University.

When he was at the boys' school, he said: "I had a young man, extra good in sports, who was being tapped for his athletic prowess. He was an amazing athlete, but he had a lackluster academic record.

"When it came to applications, several colleges looked at him," he said. "Then they looked into the transcript and many said, 'Whoa. This kid is not ready to go.'"

He knew the kid was not ready. "He had not connected academically," Mr. Griffith said. "At a fundamental level he did not believe in himself as a student." But when Mr. Griffith tried to alert the parents to that reality, they rejected the idea. The boy insisted on going to college.

"He did not graduate, to my knowledge," Mr. Griffith said. "It was very unfortunate, and it has stuck with me to today. If he'd gone to a different place or taken a postgraduate year or gone to a community college . . ."

Geoffrey D. Gould is director of admissions for the State University of New York at Binghamton, where about 70 percent of freshmen graduate in four years, and 80 percent graduate in five years. When he and his staff look over applications for admission, they have the pick of the crop. More than half the students they accept will be in the top tenth of their high school classes. But even so, they are aware of the ways in which schools "sell" their students and try to make all their students appear above average.

"Grade inflation and other grading-system changes in high schools that seem to inflate school performance are insidious and misleading to families," he said. "The school that sends 65 percent of its students home with a 90 GPA or better gives parents and students the mistaken impression of excellent performance. Schools that have GPA's going up as high as 145 are distorting reality and undermining credibility. In a competitive society, I can understand the impulse or goal, as one school principal put it years ago, 'to get all our seniors into the upper half of their class.' However, it doesn't really contribute to good educational practice."

An amusing *Wall Street Journal* article in May 1999 not only explained how a student could earn a 5.0 on a 4-point scale (advanced-placement classes carry extra credit) but also that parents with children in private school feel their children deserve top rankings. "I do see a disturbing trend of consumerism," Al Newell, dean of enrollment at Washington and Jefferson College in Washington, D.C., told me. "It's 'I've paid this tuition, and I have a right to expect my son or daughter to get into this school.'"

Parents who pay top dollar do not expect their children to be ranked in the bottom half of their class. It's the American predicament: the inability to accept that anyone can be below average.

The *Wall Street Journal* article went on to point out how school administrators can make most of their students *above* average: If a bad student drops out, or moves to another school, the school can leave him on the class rolls, so that he pushes another student into the top half; if a good student transfers out, they remove her immediately, to make room for a student who remains. The article also points out that, rather than be sued over who actually deserves to be class valedictorian—the one who took all AP

courses or the one who didn't—some schools are dropping ranking altogether. (Bill Gates's high school class didn't rank students;
Bill Clinton was ranked fourth in his class in high school.)

Meanwhile, elite colleges, even public ones, are becoming more
demanding—both because of the increasing pool of candidates
and because politicians have noted that if you admit fewer people
to public colleges, you end up graduating more and spending less.

In April, when those thin and thick envelopes go out, kids
wait and worry. Twenty and thirty years later, people remember
how many schools they applied to and how many accepted
them. And some still talk of the shame of getting into only their
"safety" school. Or not even that.

It's no wonder that Neil Bull, who sees two hundred anguished
kids every year who want out of the system, says: "I think the kids
just need surcease. They are going to live forever. I say take your
midlife crisis now. Stop the choo-choo train you're on."

SO HOW DID WE GET HERE?

We could start with Socrates, but it's easier to look at Thomas
Jefferson. Five years after leaving office as President of the United
States, he wrote in a letter, "The mass of our citizens may be
divided into two classes—the laboring and the learned. The
laboring will need the first grade of education to qualify them
for their pursuits and duties; the learned will need it as a foundation for further acquirements."

Jefferson proposed three grades of education in a letter he
wrote in 1823: "1. Primary schools, in which are taught reading,
writing, and common arithmetic, to every infant of the State,
male and female. 2. Intermediate schools, in which an education
is given proper for artificers and the middle vocations of life; in
grammar, for example, general history, logarithms, arithmetic,
plane trigonometry, mensuration [measuring things], the use of
the globes, navigation, the mechanical principles, the elements of
natural philosophy, and, as a preparation for the University, the
Greek and Latin languages. 3. An University, in which these and
all other useful sciences shall be taught in their highest degree;
the expenses of these institutions are defrayed partly by the public, and partly by the individuals profiting of them."

Those three principles—the laboring and the learned studying together, free education and the pursuit of rigorous studies—would become the foundation for the American education system a hundred years later.

Which brings us to "tracking," a word that inspires anger and consternation among parents and educators. No matter if one class is called the "bunnies," the "A's," the "maple trees," the "laborers" or the "pumpkins," parents say again and again that they do not want their children tracked, unless (of course) their children are on the "gifted and talented" or accelerated track. There's a reason Americans are so against tracking, and it's ingrained in the formation of our current school system.

Education was made compulsory in all states between 1852 (Massachusetts) and 1918 (Mississippi). Because the American school system is made up of fifty separate systems, each state makes up its own rules for entry and exit. In 1996, the states' requirements broke down this way, according to the Education Commission of the States.

Ages at which children must be in school:	*Number of States:*
5 to 16	5
5 to 17	2
5 to 18	2
6 to 16	13
6 to 17	1
6 to 18	4
7 to 16	15
7 to 17	4
7 to 18	2
8 to 17	1
8 to 18	1

So children could legally enter school in one state as late as eight, then move to another state and leave as early as sixteen.

The kind of public school they go to, comprehensive schools, emerged from a debate at the beginning of the twentieth century about whether American schools were going to follow what was condemned as the "elitist" traditions of European schools (most particularly, German schools), or whether American schools were going to be "democratic," with everyone given the chance to learn Latin.

Comprehensive education means that everyone in a town or neighborhood would go to the same school whether they were going to work in a factory (laborers) or going off to Harvard (learners). And in those days, the preponderance of students *were* laborers; only 11 percent went to college.

Comprehensive education won out in a crucial document, the Commission on the Reorganization of Secondary Education's "Cardinal Principles of Secondary Education" in 1918, which presented a curriculum that offered only health, "fundamental processes," "worthy home membership," vocation, citizenship, "worthy use of leisure" and ethical character. Nonetheless, Andrew J. Coulson, in his comprehensive book *Market Education: The Unknown History,* notes that one educator at the time considered the curriculum "almost hopelessly academic."

One of the pillars of comprehensive education was that students would, at least once a day, gather in a homeroom that would seat farmer next to stenographer next to scholar, not a fact that was acknowledged on *Beverly Hills 90210,* or, for that matter, *The Wonder Years.* Even if the high school students had different course loads, they would be together for homeroom and band and graduations. It was a democratic ideal that was sidetracked as soon as the first "special" (in the old sense of the word) schools opened.

"Out of a strong commitment to serve individual needs, specialized courses and programs proliferated to the point that the existence of variegated course offerings alone has become the sole criteria for the now commonplace label 'comprehensive high school,'" the quarterly *E.A.Q.* argued in December 1998. "From a historical perspective, to date, the comprehensive high school model remains at best half implemented."

And so, in a city like New York, students begin to diverge in elementary school and junior high. An eleven-year-old in New York, headed into the sixth grade in public school, may have to decide if she wants to go to "science" school or an "academy" to learn Latin, two of the minischools that existed, for instance, inside my son's public middle school, I.S. 44 in Manhattan. Located on the Upper West Side of Manhattan, I.S. 44 was a comprehensive school, in the sense that the regular intermediate school children (primarily black and Hispanic) ran through the same hallways and up and down the same stairs. But except for a few instances of the "regular" students knocking down the smaller, younger, nerdier and much whiter science and academy students, there was nothing democratic or comprehensive about the experience. The students never so much as shared a homeroom.

And intermediate school in New York City is just practice for the ultimate in tracking, the New York City high school system that sends kids at age fourteen into a staggering array of special schools, from Transit Tech, to Automotive high school or Business or Culinary or Science or Music and Art or Dance Tech, the last a program run by Elliot Feld that teaches ballet and modern dance within a high school system. At the time my son was going through all this, I was appalled at the possibilities (especially at the thought he might end up at Transit Tech, learning to repair subway cars).

This, I said at the time, was worse than the German system, where kids were sent at fourteen to be apprentice watchmakers. Now I have switched sides. These days, I've decided, the only thing wrong with the New York City system is that businesses are not involved in each and every one of the schools and that the students for the most part don't do real work or get paid.

Paul F. Cole gained his position as secretary-treasurer of the New York State AFL–CIO through his work on various state and national teachers' groups. Paul is an interesting guy, with one foot in schools and one foot in industry. Because of that he is one of the engines behind the National Skills Standards Board, a government group that rewards people for what they know rather than how long they have been sitting in a classroom. In an interview in his office in Albany, Paul discussed some of his most passionate beliefs about American education.

"We almost demean work in some instances," he said. "It's a very different tradition in Europe; the Germans, the *Meisters* and so on, are very highly thought of. What you have in Europe and many Asian countries is a system where you move efficiently and smoothly from school to work." What he is talking about, of course, is the same system that a hundred years ago this country rejected as elitist, because it tracked people into either academic or nonacademic programs. In Germany, for instance, one track will have a young man or woman leave more formal schooling behind at fourteen to begin working as an apprentice (for pay), while taking some classes that apply to his or her work.

"In the United States we don't have any such system," he said.

PREPARING FOR CAREERS IN TECHNOLOGY

Parents need to understand that the new technology-based economy will require far more people with technical skills than people with general liberal arts diplomas. "With technology happening, there has been a shift downward," said Norm Fraley, Manager of Distance Learning at Kelly Scientific Resources in Detroit, Michigan. "What it took a full-tilt chemist to do has shifted downward to technicians. The machines are doing more, and the machines can be run by people who just run machines.

"Five years ago that was not the case," he says. "Now there's glorious new stuff, quarter-million-dollar systems. Right out of the box a chemist is not required." Instead, a trained technologist can do the job, he says. "It's 'Call the maintenance guy if this thing ever goes over *that*,'" he said. "The responsibility is being shifted to technicians."

This is not to say that every kid should become a lab technician. If a child loves science and wants to spend four years studying science, and if the parents have the money, that child should definitely go to college. But read what Norm has to say about college graduates first.

Highly educated himself—he once worked on the space shuttle—Norm says he dreams these days of finding college dropouts. "If they have the skills, we've got the knowledge," Norm told me. Through an online training program, he says, he can teach anyone who has the all-important "hand skills" how to perform technologists' jobs.

"I can't teach sculpting, goldsmithing over the web," he said. "But knowledge transfer, no problem."

What Kelly Scientific Resources has found is that it must train freshly minted college graduates, because so few of them have employable skills. "I hold universities responsible for kicking out these sad-state-of-affairs graduates," Norm said. "Johnny can't read and Joe Chemist can't do the math."

He's not joking. Things that chemists learn in their first year of college, he says, like the chemistry of a pH-buffer solution and doing titration, are gone by the time they graduate. Why? "Because there are three years of keg parties between when they learned it and when they apply it," Norm said. "I don't know if there's proof that the educated cells go first," he muttered, "but the new grads coming out don't know how to do basic math."

As a result, companies who hire these college grads have to pull senior scientists out of their labs to teach new hires to do the job. "Someone who is in the lab has to teach it to you," Norm said. "That is, if you are brave enough to let them know you don't know. Most people just screw up. It's painful for employers who train someone. But it's worse for a temporary agency like ours. We can't afford to do that."

His solution has been to create Internet-based remediation. "For twenty-five dollars I can say, 'Go take that course,'" he said. "If they pass, I know they've learned it. They are able to refresh themselves for the important stuff they learned in the first year."

He notes that he is offering vocational training as an adjunct to university learning. "I think we need to bust that learning-training stereotype," he said. "And get it out there that training is teaching how to do something functional." Some universities are now asking to use Norm's training courses for their first-year chemistry majors.

And don't get Norm started on the need for apprenticeships. "Apprenticeships were, for hundreds of years, proven to be the best way to create masters," he said. "With the creation of public education came the loss of apprenticeships. And someone called this progress."

Master craftsmen did not need college, he said. "Now our model of a master is someone who spent far too much time in school," he said. Businessmen, in his experience, merely patronize highly paid, freshly hired M.B.A.s. "They hope that in the next two years they'll catch on and learn something."

"In the scientists we see the same thing," Norm said. "The simplest degree is a biology degree. People come out of school to change the environment, but they can't do anything. They are depressed. They are upset. If we are lucky enough to get them a job washing glassware, that's it—because they can't do anything else. They say, 'I didn't get a four-year degree to wash dishes.' And we say, 'So why did you get a biology degree?' If they go to microbiology or biochemistry, *then* they can get a job. But general biology? No."

Colleges and universities continue producing graduates with fantasies of saving the whale he says, because "university departments need to justify their existence." Instead he would prefer to find college dropouts, he says—"people who said, 'I learned enough to go on to do what I need to do.'"

Meanwhile, he says, colleges continue to graduate students with useless degrees. "Hope you had fun at the keggers, because that's all the good college did you," he said.

So perhaps it's time to consider a certificate in C++ or Linux, an associate's degree in mammography, or a two-year certificate in homeopathy. The problem is that middle-class parents are far more likely to approve of the first than the last, because computers not only offer a clean work environment but also might pay off big time if the company goes public. Still, not everyone could (or should) go into computers.

The American high school system remains fragmented and mostly unresponsive to the real needs of students who are not book-smart or headed for college. So let's take a very anecdotal look at how three other countries—Britain, Germany and Japan—deal with high school.

THE BRITISH SYSTEM

Lucie Young, a writer in her thirties who now lives in New York, explained to me that English schools didn't have any general education programs till late in the last century. "It served the Victorians not to educate," she said. "They wanted kids to clean the chimneys. Their notion was to *use* the young, rather than educate the young."

Students in Great Britain, at around the age of sixteen, take their O levels in up to ten subjects. There are no multiple-choice questions. Students are expected to write essays for courses like history and English. Exams in foreign languages require translating from Latin to English and again from English to Latin. In a living language like French there would also be an oral exam. Many students leave school forever at sixteen, after completing the O levels, but they leave with a pretty thorough education.

And here is where the British system becomes interesting. Instead of requiring students to take a broad range of courses in both science and the liberal arts if they go on to further education, students are not allowed to take math, say, if they failed their math O levels. "If you required people at British universities to take math, half of the literary figures would have done without a university education," another product of the system told me.

Even in the O levels, the British schools rank their students first, second and third level. "Third stream they put you in for C.S.E., a Certificate of Secondary Education, i.e., not first class, which means you're headed for a technical college typing course," Lucie said. "You're the dunce of the class. It's not remedial. You'll probably leave school at sixteen and stack shelves."

For students who do well on the O levels, there are the A levels, usually prepared for in what the British call "sixth-form colleges." Already the system sounded a lot more fun than American high schools. "Our English teacher used to take us down to the pub after class," Lucie said. But the course work was also much more rigorous. At the A-level exams for English Literature, she said, students would be asked to write essays on tragedy in Shakespeare and recall huge chunks of text, along with the critical commentary about it.

Most students will take three A-level courses, but those who want to try for Oxford or Cambridge will do four. In Britain, people differentiate themselves academically, not through sports. "No one gives a toss if you're good at tennis," she said. "If you went to Sussex and said 'I have three A levels and was fabulous at track sports,' they'd roll their eyes and think you weren't serious."

Here's the part that astounded me. If a student is not trying for Oxford or Cambridge but for one of the other British universities, they go for an interview and, in a sort of weird bicker arrangement, angle for the lowest offer. If a university really wants you, she said, they will make you a "two-C" offer, meaning they will take you if you fail one of your A-level courses and get C's in the other two. Lucie said, "You aspire to get the lowest possible grading."

College in Britain lasts three years instead of four, and ranks you when you come out as well. "Firsts," she said, "are pretty rare and if you got a third class degree it meant you were a stoner."

She eventually took an additional year at the University of London studying journalism, or, as she put it, "hatches, matches and dispatches" (births, marriages and deaths) but says that the most important part of her training was the two-month internship, which landed her at a job at a health magazine, despite her considerable smoking habit. "No one cared about your degree," she said. "They just cared if you could write."

Frances Anderton, a British woman who lives in Los Angeles,

where she produces a radio show, went to The Bath High School/Girl's Public Day School Trust, a very formal place that was one of a number of such schools subsidized by the government. "They were founded at the end of the nineteenth century for young ladies who would end up as governesses, or marry someone who would go off to India," she said. "They encouraged sciences and a lot of sport. It was a Victorian tradition: You had to have a sound body if you were going to run the empire."

"At our schools you were on a conveyor belt to your A levels," she said. "I gave up on physics by the time I was fourteen. Maths, biology, French, English and history were required. Chemistry I dropped at thirteen. I was very under-equipped in the sciences when I left school."

Frances and her friends applied to the University College, London. "We'd heard that if they wanted you in the arts department, they'd give you a two-E offer. Even if you were doing three A levels."

Frances swears that they were all told they would be accepted if they failed one of their A-level exams and barely passed the other two. "I know I went off thinking I was home and dry. Two E's. We just relaxed and I don't think any of us did well on our A levels. I think I got a D in German. We were being kids and we wanted an easy life."

"We were brought up to think the American system was absurd, with an overemphasis on sports and an underemphasis on analysis. We were told Americans just reeled off the facts."

The minute they finished their A levels they decided to take a "gap year," the traditional British year off before starting university. And she informed me that college education, per se, was not considered a solid way to judge someone's intelligence, success or character. Perfectly nice girls went to cooking school, or art school. (Studio arts, acting, music and so on were not taught at universities but in polytechnics.)

She also laughed at the idea of going to university to learn how to write. "One attitude was that those absurdly earnest Americans thought you had to go to journalism school," she said. "In English journalism you just make things up about people— it's hopelessly irresponsible. The Fleet Street reporter in England is like a little terrier. And then there's the more relaxed men of letters, the Noel Cowards. You weren't supposed to work hard at it.

You'd just sit down and write something. You certainly didn't go to school and study it. That would be kind of vulgar.

"Americans believe in working hard. The English believe working hard is vulgar. You were supposed to do brilliantly, but with the greatest of ease."

An American who went to Oxford noted one further oddity about the English University system. When he was given his Oxford bachelor's degree, he was informed that "if I wasn't arrested in the next two years," the degree would magically turn into a master's degree.

"It's part of the snobbery of the Oxbridge system," Lucie said, when I asked her if this could possibly be true. "But I think you'd have to do something really vile that made all the papers in order to keep it from turning into a master's."

I was incredulous so I checked further. This is what Sarita Bhatia of the British Department of Education and Employment told me: "It is true that while at Oxford or Cambridge that after a certain amount of time a Bachelor's degree will automatically become a Master's degree. The graduate does not have to do anything except 'continue to live' for a certain amount of time. The college they attended will then apply for them to receive an M.A. It is important to point out that other universities such as Edinburgh, automatically give their graduates M.A.s, so it is not unusual to do this."

THE GERMAN SYSTEM

Axel Hertlein is thirty-three, and lives in Lichtenau, Germany. In his fluent and polished English, he explained that he had hated school, where he studied "basic math up to Pythagoras."

"At the modern secondary school, I was very bad," he said. "I failed eighth grade, and had to do it again. I had a chance to go to the ninth grade in the comprehensive school. Instead I went to the government employment office. I was asked what I was interested in, and they did a little test. They suggested car mechanic, and at fifteen years, at that age, it interests you."

He took training as a metal worker. "All the mechanical jobs, it doesn't matter if it's a car mechanic or blacksmith or machine mechanic. It's the same metal training." And even though he was only fifteen, the government began paying for his health insurance. He got $500 to $600 a month in salary, and the government was contributing to his retirement insurance. Like any worker, he also got vacations and holidays. In other words, he was being treated as if he were a grown man.

"I was a skilled worker, and with a little bit of training on the job I could do what I was asked to do." He notes that the German system, which seems so rigid, is in fact full of loopholes. There are second acts. "You can go back as I did for one, two or three years to a modern secondary school, like a high school, for more education: math, physics, chemistry. It's not a trade school or a special college. It's where you learn math and language.

"In the apprenticeship I found something I liked," Axel said. "And I became very successful. That was after I was one of the worst in the modern secondary school—really the worst of all."

Axel today is a master machine technician (the steps are apprentice, journeyman, master). His company sends him out with a team to fabricate and install assembly lines. He makes enough money to enjoy frequent trips abroad, which is where I encountered him, visiting his sister in upstate New York.

The other end of the spectrum in Germany is the gymnasium, the tough college prep school. When Laura (Hunter) Halvorson graduated from White Bear Lake High School, she decided to spend a year in a German gymnasium.

She stayed with a family in Düsseldorf whose son had lived with her family in White Bear Lake. While she had graduated from a rigorous academic course of study at White Bear, she knew she would not be ready for the last year of the gymnasium, the thirteenth year. Instead, she elected to go to the gymnasium's twelfth year. "It was challenging. Once I got over the language barrier, I found everything was focused on analysis and pulling things apart. On being able to discuss their opinion on almost anything."

She particularly remembers a two-hour German literature course with about twenty students. The teacher was very soft-spoken and would enter the room quietly. "He would start us out with one question and then sit back for two hours. I think, for the most part, it was a pretty orderly discussion. It never got ugly." But it was spirited and thorough, and led almost entirely by the students themselves, with the teacher jumping in only to offer another possibility.

"I took several of the tests," she said. "I think the only test I was truly given a grade on was my English class. They said I didn't merit a grade in the others.

"I found the math interesting. I had been in the advanced calculus class in White Bear. In Düsseldorf I took the required twelfth-grade General Math. Where we started out in Germany was exactly where my advanced calculus class in White Bear ended up. That really shocked me. And they had advanced math beyond that."

The German education system is stripped bare of anything other than academics and sports. There are no extracurricular activities. No band, chorus, debate club. School also runs six days a week and practically year-round, and the main courses are two hours long.

"I think there's a different school ethic," she said. "You're there to go to school and focus on your studies. Here you're going to be with your friends."

"To be able to get a diploma from the gymnasium, you have to take a final exam, the *Abitur,* and they take it very seriously," she said. "If you are hoping to go on to university your score determines where you can go and whether you can get a study spot."

It is worth mentioning one more thing about the German education system. All college is free and paid for by the government. But to get into desirable professions, a student has to have superb grades on the *Abitur.* Such positions are limited by a system called *numerus clausus,* which regulates the number of students allowed to enter.

"For many academic subjects a ceiling of first-year students is stipulated beyond which universities do not enroll students," Paul Windolf wrote in *Expansion and Structural Change: Higher Education in Germany, the United States and Japan, 1870–1990.* "Since the number of applicants for such subjects as medicine, biology, architecture, psychology, management science and chemistry is always higher than the number of university places, students are selected according to their grades at high school, but military service or service in a hospital (for medical students) may also be helpful."

The British system as described by Lucie Young and Frances Anderton was clubbish and elite, while accepting that some students might rather be studying art or cooking. The German system is highly organized, and yet flexible. No surprise, it does a remarkable job in training people for technical trades. The Japanese system, which has been entrenched for decades, is going through a period of upheaval. Many of the assumptions—that students must study incessantly to pass exams to get into high school and then college, that learning must be rote and without any creative element, that a good university degree is an automatic ticket for lifetime employment—are being challenged. A steep Japanese recession increased the level of criticism.

Note, when the economy of a country is strong, other countries begin copying its system of education. If the economy is weak, the thinking goes, it must be the fault of the schools. Japan's recession evoked the usual amount of breast-beating. Hikota Koguchi, dean of academic affairs at Waseda University in Tokyo, was quoted in a 1999 article in *The Christian Science Monitor:* "You can see it in the bureaucratic quality of Japan today. Society has lost its vitality, we don't have enough creative, original minds. Having a university full of people who can only study isn't all that good anymore. Unless we correct the overemphasis on egalitarianism, there's no future for Japan."

THE JAPANESE SYSTEM

The Japanese students I spoke to are in their twenties and studying in America. They agreed that the pressure on them to study was intense.

Kanako Ohara is now studying for her Ph.D. in sociolinguistics at Georgetown University. She remembers what it was like to study for the tests to enter high school, which is not mandatory in Japan.

"Entrance time to high school is in spring, so the winter break is the last possible cramming time, the most important vacation." She and the other fourteen-year-olds in her middle school almost all did the *juku,* the famed Japanese cram schools.

"That's when I, for example, went to *juku* for twelve hours a day for two weeks. We can devote all our time to prepare for the entrance examination. People glorify it. *Juku* teachers would tell us something like, 'There's this great student who lost all her hair from stress, that's how much she studied.' All of the legends.

"To have stress is glorified," she said. "You've got to study. If you're not cut out for it, you don't have to go," she said. "You can go to vocational school to be a mechanic." Kanako is from a fairly prominent family in Fukuoka. "I've never known anyone who never went to high school," she said.

"You do have to work hard at it until you go to a good

college," she said. For college admission, students apply to particular programs within particular colleges; each requires a different test. And since the tests are given only once a year for admission in the spring, if a student fails to get in, he or she has to wait another year and prepare all over again.

But once in college, things ease up remarkably for Japanese students. "Once you get to college, it's very difficult to drop out," she said. "People really protect you. A lot of people never go to class or open a book. Professors take attendance, and friends answer for you. You can just take the test and pass."

Since my image of Japan was of a country where people never kicked back and relaxed, I checked this out. And indeed, I was told that professors seemed to believe that students had worked so hard getting into college, they deserved a break before entering the world of the salaryman. *Business Week* from November 1998 noted: "Japan's grade schools are intense and focused on rote learning, but its universities are too lenient. Once students pass their entrance exams, they are expected to use their time to learn to get along with other potential leaders. There are few tests and little homework."

Kanako told me that in Japan, as elsewhere outside the United States, students go to medical school directly from high school. "So of course that's not easy. If you're in a special field like science and medicine, those are tough. But not humanities, literature and philosophy."

One expert on attention deficit told me, "You'll never see any ADD in Japan." So I asked Kanako: did she know of any children in Japan who simply did not like high school, or who had learning disabilities, who fidgeted in their seats and couldn't pay attention?

"If you don't work," she said, "they kick you out. Some kids suffer from ADD, but they're off the regular track. Unless they're exceptionally bright it's not likely they'll make it in the Japanese system. Not only do you have to be very well-rounded, but you have to be the same as everyone. You have to have the same kind of attention span."

"Any kind of disability," she said, "be it manic depression or depression, that's considered a shame. It's a shame culture."

Artists, designers, dancers take training after high school and most likely do not go to college. "After high school some people get training for furniture-making or textiles, house-builder, carver. In Japan there are a lot of craftsmen and they need a lot of training."

WHICH OF THESE SCHOOLS IS NOT LIKE THE OTHER?

If this kind of anecdotal evidence is compelling, it shows that students in Great Britain, Germany and Japan are far more likely to work hard in high school, primarily because there are drastic consequences. A student who did not go on to A levels in Britain could not go to Oxford. A German student had to make it on a particular track or was dropped down to a lower track, with fewer options.

In Britain, once past the O levels, a student did not have to take any more math. In Germany and Japan, math is considered an essential part of education and is rigorous. In Japan, the hardest part is getting into a university. In Britain, with its first-, second- and third-class degrees, the hardest part may be getting out with a respectable rank.

College is four years in some countries, three years in others. And although experts in America claim that 5 percent of the population (at a minimum) have ADD, two young women who grew up in Japan did not believe they had ever met anyone who had ADD. And despite the strenuous schooling in German gymnasiums, the overall eloquence of the British population, the diligent work ethic prevalent in Japan, the college statistics in all three countries may come as a surprise. In Germany in 1997 only 30 percent of students went on to college, in Japan it was 44.2 percent and in England 40 percent, while here in the United States a full 66 percent of high school graduates go on to college.

One of these schools systems would probably be the right place for almost any American student. The problem is that parents and children must deal with the school system they've got. Yes, there is the charter school movement, and some of the more successful academies have reverted to uniforms and *juku*like schedules of drilling and memorizing.

The problem for parents is finding a system that works for their child. And even the best suburban schools, like the one I looked at in White Bear Lake, Minnesota, fail some students, despite their substantial budgets, their learning theories and their best intentions.

Chapter Four

WHITE BEAR LAKE, MINNESOTA

Go Bears.
—*FARGO*, 1996

In the Coen brothers' mordant comedy *Fargo,* one of a pair of dimwitted prostitutes from this town mumbles, "Go Bears." As one movie guidebook said of the film, "just about everyone here is a borderline moron with an annoying accent."

"After that movie came out, at a teachers' convention, I had more people go by me and look at where I was from," said Ted Blaesing, Superintendent of Schools for the White Bear Lake area. " 'Go Bears.' That's all they'd say. I could have raised a ton a money selling 'Go Bears' T-shirts."

I knew what my son's experience of high school and college admission was like. I had read the numbers of college dropouts from the Centers for Education Statistics in Washington, D.C. But I was curious. What would happen if I looked at a high school class that graduated in 1993 to see how many of the kids had gotten their bachelor's degrees? And what had happened to the kids who did not?

The 1993 class was of particular interest to me, since there were fewer people born eighteen years earlier, in 1975, than at any time since the post-war baby boom. As a result, the teenagers graduating in 1993 had all the opportunities: Colleges were desperate for students; businesses were desperate for workers. Moreover, the class of 1993 graduated into the longest economic expansion since World War II.

I picked White Bear Lake somewhat at random as a typical and rather ordinary Midwest suburb. But White Bear Lake turned out to be far from provincial. In a display of multiculturalism, the school board meetings in White Bear frequently begin with a recital of the Masai warrior greeting *"Kasserian ingera,"* "And how are the children?" The traditional Masai response is "All the children are well." The Reverend Patrick T. O'Neill of Framingham, Massachusetts, once said, "I wonder how it might affect our consciousness of our own children's welfare if in our culture we took to greeting each other with this same daily question." And so the school board of White Bear Lake asks, "How are the children?"

As Ted Blaesing told me, "You can't say, every day, the kids are all right."

He proved it to me by sending me a book written ten years ago, *A Death in White Bear,* about the abuse and murder of a child in that town in 1965, the year I graduated from high school in a town about thirty miles north of there. The murder, by an adoptive mother, was not discovered until twenty years later.

But Ted needn't go so far back to find trouble. In the fall of 1999, the high school was shaken by the suicide of a sixteen-year-old student who hanged himself. The kids who graduated in 1993 also lost a classmate, a sixteen-year-old girl who died suddenly in tenth grade.

One 1993 class member, Eric Anderson, was paralyzed from the chest down in a diving accident in the lake in 1996. At least two class members have been to jail, one for stealing and the other for drugs.

And despite the recitation of the Masai greeting at school board meetings, racism has been a problem in the town. Students told me, "They got the *white* part of White Bear right." The class that graduated in 1993 had more than five hundred students. Four of them were black, nine were Asian, one had a father who was Native American. Even that diversity was deceptive. "In White Bear there are two or three colored kids and one was adopted by a white family," said Cindie Wisener, a member of the class of 1993. "Asians, too, are adopted by white families."

Jon Mikrut, a member of the same class, was born in Korea and adopted by a White Bear family at the age of four months. The night I met him he was hanging out at the unpretentious White Bear Bar with other young men who had graduated in 1993. Amid a lot of beer-drinking, and general ribbing and shouting, one of them referred to Jon in his presence as "slant eyes."

I asked Jon the next day how he felt about it. "It's all right," he said. "We rip on each other all the time."

Another classmate, Ryan Mims, said that he had encountered no overt racism. "I was one of the only black people at White Bear," he said, "but I was never made to feel out of place." After trying community college and technical college, Ryan said, "I have a decent job delivering furniture that allows me to get outside and enjoy the outdoors while meeting a whole lot of interesting people and making good money."

A 1996–97 state survey put the Minneapolis "minority" population at 66 percent and the St. Paul "minority" population at 57 percent. The survey put White Bear Lake's minority population at 4 percent. The suburb, population 26,000, lies only twenty minutes from downtown St. Paul. Beyond the village and the lake are suburban developments stretching in every direction around nearby Otter, Goose and Ham lakes.

Freshmen and sophomores attend class in a 1919 building that sits near the center of old White Bear. Juniors and seniors are crammed into a "new" school building, an ever-expanding one-story group of brick modules begun in the 1970s in a markedly suburban area south of the lake. The students walk across school lawns that in November are crunchy with dried cigar-shaped droppings from unwelcome flocks of Canada geese.

The comprehensive range of courses in White Bear Lake High School's 1999–2000 catalog include thirteen Advanced Placement courses, including microeconomics, four bridge courses (with college credit), studio art courses, advanced computer applications, biochemistry, Law 1 and 2, advertising, money management, multimedia computing, child development, working with "exceptional" (multiple-handicapped) children, consumer economics, interior design, kinesiology, auto technology, architecture, drafting, construction technology, advanced calculus, treble choir, jazz ensemble, European studies, philosophy, music theory, earth and space systems, and a course in Minnesota vertebrates. There are many more, including six semesters of Spanish, French or German. Cross country is a major sport in the town and the superintendent runs marathons. "I run by things," he said. "That's how I know what's going on."

Presumably there would be enough here to keep any student interested, but kids will always find a reason to complain. "You don't have to do anything in high school," Joe Madden, a member of the class of 1993, said. "You just sit there. You don't even have to do your homework. It was way too easy." Six years out of high school, he was pursuing a degree in business at Augsburg, a private college in Minneapolis, while supporting himself as a carpenter.

During the 1992–93 school year there were 1,105 students in the eleventh and twelfth grades but only three-and-a-half guidance counselors. "We try to look at each student individually," said Jan Femrite, one of the school's counselors. "But this is more like triage. Because it's all eleventh and twelfth graders, the whole focus is on graduation."

In 1993, 75 percent of the school's graduates planned to go to college, 58 percent of them to four-year schools, 17 percent to two-year colleges. Another 10 percent planned to attend technical schools. Just like the British school system that turned its polytechnics into universities, the State of Minnesota recently combined its technical colleges and its two-year colleges, a nod to the fact that there is demand for practical degrees. White Bear's local community college, Lakewood, and its local technical college, Northeast Metro Tech, thus became Century Community College.

The class of 1993 had mean SAT scores of 487 verbal and 562 math (before recentering). The mean SAT scores for the country in 1993 were 423 verbal and 479 math. So the White Bear students averaged more than 100 points above the norm on their combined scores. Sixty-six percent of the class took the ACT test and had an average composite score of 22.1, well above the national average that year, 20.7.

I got surveys from more than one hundred students, evenly divided between men and women. They were contacted through the Internet, by mail, phone, a newspaper ad in the local paper, newspaper stories, radio and in person. The surveys asked eight questions about what the students did after high school and how they felt about college.

According to the surveys, 62 percent of the students completed bachelor's degrees within six years. (Thirty-six of them were women, twenty-six of them men.) The percent graduating from college may be on the high side because of the nature of White Bear, or it may be on the high side because of sampling errors. Of the first ten students who responded to the survey via my website, all but one had graduated from college; of the five students I later found in a bar in White Bear, people who had been contacted repeatedly but had not responded to the survey, none had graduated from college. The students who responded to the mailed survey were presumably more likely to be those who had completed college.

Of the rest, 17 percent earned AA degrees or certificates and 21 percent had no further diplomas. Almost all of them told me they were expected to go to college—by their parents, their teachers, their classmates and themselves.

What surprised me about the kids who answered the survey was the hostility about education from many of those who got college degrees, and the extraordinary success of some kids who had no college at all. Much of that success was due to work in computers and technology. And this should be a comfort to parents: The kids, even those who had a rocky start, seemed to turn out pretty well.

THE WHITE BEAR PHILOSOPHY

Minnesota is a progressive state. In 1991, it and California were the first states to pass charter school laws. In addition, Minnesota has more than 7,000 bridge students, who begin taking college classes for free while they are still in high school. It is a state that cares deeply about its education system.

On the other hand, the state's governor, Jesse Ventura, is not a college graduate but a former professional wrestler and a populist maverick. Early in his first term he proposed letting college athletes play sports without having to take those pesky college classes.

A study by the Minnesota House of Representatives in December 1998 showed that the number of students who were going on to colleges (including two-year colleges) in the state had dropped from 48 percent in 1987 to 40 percent in 1996. (Figures were higher for predominantly white metropolitan areas like White Bear, much lower for the areas of the far north, like the Iron Range.)

The study blamed tougher admissions standards, as well as an improved job market that allowed teenagers to get employment straight out of high school. Moreover, the study pointed out that it was the "marginal" Minnesota students who appeared to be less likely these days to head to college. While the perception was that something should be done about the situation, to me it seemed evolutionary. Marginal students (perhaps students who did not belong in college) had decided to go elsewhere. Was it possible that by 1996 Minnesota's teenagers had decided that there were credible alternatives to college?

School officials in White Bear Lake, at least today, seem eager to accept alternatives to college. Rolf Parsons, who sits on the school board and had a daughter in the class of 1993, said: "I've tossed around the idea that everyone had to do something else for a year after high school. It would serve everybody better."

Mr. Blaesing, the superintendent of the schools, said: "I have long grappled with, how do we prepare the kids who don't go into college? Maybe they're going later, they may start in a local business. But they are the most entrepreneurial group. They have the ability to step out and do things on their own. They are the ones who start companies in the garage. It's kids who don't have the academic record to access college right away who start out washing cars and the next thing you know they are cleaning sky scrapers."

Mr. Blaesing comes by his admiration for blue-collar work partly by background—his father was a masonry contractor—and partly by exposure to the German apprenticeship system. The Fulbright Commission sent a group of educators, including Mr. Blaesing, to Germany for a week, and Mr. Blaesing returned a fan. "They feel you need to know every job to run the place," he said. "Start from the bottom. They value that as a society. We tend to think that is beneath us.

"What do we ask when you graduate from high school?" he

asked rhetorically. "Where are you going to college? That's what our values are, and that's unfortunate." But if that is the school's philosophy, the 1993 students did not hear it.

Mr. Blaesing came to White Bear just as the class of 1993 was getting ready to graduate. But he feels he knows 1993's graduates pretty well, since one of his daughters graduated from another high school that year.

"They are focused kids," he said. "They basically want a job. They have good work ethics and they seem to have their priorities right in life. They think things through. And they have good social consciousness."

Three of the students who responded to my survey went on church missions after high school. Two that I know of went into the Peace Corps after college. A number, including Sara Hargesheimer, have gone into special education. She now works in an inner-city school in St. Paul that is 30 percent Asian, 30 percent black and 30 percent white. Sara, who attended the University of Wisconsin, Stout, also revealed to me the reason so many kids from White Bear went to school in Wisconsin. Not only is there a reciprocal education agreement between the two states, but Wisconsin's tuition is about $1,000 cheaper, textbooks can be checked out of the library for the term and, this is a big plus, Wisconsin has a law that allows underage students to drink in a bar with their parents. "So on parents' weekend, you can go out together," she said.

Of the sixty-two White Bear students in the survey who graduated with bachelor's degrees, ten became teachers, twenty-one took liberal arts degrees in fields like languages, biology, history, English, physics, political science, economics and (the most common liberal arts degree) psychology. Seven became engineers. There were five business majors. Three specialized in kinesiology or athletics.

The other fifteen bachelor's degrees were in practical fields like hospitality and tourism, watershed management, occupational therapy, design communications, industrial design, applied management, marketing management, information systems management, community health. And there were four graduates in broadcast/media. (One is now on the air in Peoria, Illinois.)

Jill Dybdal, who was elected "most likely to succeed," has her bachelor's degree in psychology and computer science. David Kuczynski, the class president, got his bachelor's degree in journalism and advertising from the University of Wisconsin, Madison. One of the two official "class clowns," Christie Mastchke, earned a bachelor's degree in psychology from Grand Canyon University in Phoenix in five and a half years. Benjamin Butters got a B.A. in physical education from Dartmouth College and is now back at White Bear, teaching.

Some people who responded to the survey were passionate in their defense of a college education. Bridget Siebenaler, who got a degree in business and speech from the University of Wisconsin, River Falls, said, "You need college to discover who you are and learn more about cultures, values and society."

Bill Bennett, who earned a degree in industrial engineering from Purdue, argues that a college degree is essential. "What college really teaches you is how to learn, how to survive and how to interact with people," he wrote me. "The amount of technical information learned in college is insignificant, even in a technical profession such as my own. What a college education tells an employer is that the individual has gone through the process of learning how to learn, of maturing intellectually, being shown the drive and discipline to undertake a difficult task and conquer it." Bill now works as a manufacturing engineer for Active Power in Austin, Texas.

Similarly, Jeremy Nietz, who got a bachelor's degree in biology and a master's degree in physicial assistant studies (both from Marquette University in Milwaukee, Wisconsin), defended college education: "It isn't only the academic knowledge that you gain in college," he said. "You have the opportunity to learn how to interact with personalities from different backgrounds, culturally and socially, and make mistakes in a controlled environment."

People like these are, of course, the kinds of students everyone would agree should go to college. They went to school for the right reasons: to establish a career, build a body of knowledge, explore themselves. College would be a far more interesting place if the majority of the students were like them, or like Brian Wagner, who got his bachelor's degree in information systems management from Luther College in Decorah, Iowa. Brian said, "My personal experience in attending a liberal arts college was life-changing. I had the opportunity to explore my beliefs and values. I discovered my passion in life."

Christie Doxsee, with a biology degree from the University

of Wisconsin, Madison, proclaimed, "Having a college education decreases ignorance, increases self-esteem and challenges a person to seriously think about amazing things."

But it was just as common in the survey to hear from people who did not have an inspiring college experience and who questioned the value of the degrees they earned. Anne M. Johnson, who earned a master's degree in exercise physiology from the University of North Dakota said, "I'm done with school. The experience you gain is invaluable, but I think universities need to begin teaching more practical applications."

Carrie Anderson, who got her bachelor's degree in education from Winona State University in Minnesota, said, "I do not use my ever-powerful degree. I am a full-time flight attendant for Northwest Airlines, Mesaba Airlines. I didn't require a four-year degree to get my flight attendant position, that's for sure."

Susan Harper got a business degree from the University of Iowa, but found, like many kids, that she needed specific training to get a job. "I ended up majoring in marketing, which I have no use for in my current job," she said. "I wish I had gone into computers the first time around." She is now working as a software test analyst in St. Paul.

Bridget Gaffney, who got her degree in psychology from the University of Wisconsin, Eau Claire, complained: "I think college is overpriced. Personally, I'm glad I went, but I believe you can be just as successful without a degree. I'm not sure it was the best way to invest $20,000."

I also heard from a number of people who said that the best thing about going to college was partying. And those were people who graduated.

Then there were the White Bear students who dropped out of college. "To be honest, I was not ready," said Michael Millington, who attended Mankato State University in Minnesota. "I think a year of junior college or working after school would have better prepared me." He noted, however, "Had I known that I would be working in a profession that does not require a college education, I probably wouldn't have gone." He now works as an independent insurance agent.

Of the one hundred people who responded to the survey, seventeen (eleven male, six female) earned technical degrees, certificates or associate's degrees, including one electrician, a large-appliance repair person, an auto technician, a person who studied mechanical drafting, another who took a course in being a receptionist, a person who briefly became a prosthetic technician and a number who were trained in computers.

Tony Benshoof earned a two-year degree and is headed for a four-year degree in business and computer science despite a schedule that keeps him traveling throughout Europe for six months of the year as part of the U.S. luge team. Two of the respondents went for the Microsoft Certified Systems Engineer certificate, which qualifies them to earn a minimum of $50,000 a year, without college. Chad Jungers earned a certificate from Brown Institute in computers and now is making around $40,000. The average per capita income for people in the Minneapolis–St. Paul metropolitan area was $26,797 in 1997. So only six years out of high school, many of these kids are doing far better than their parents, and certainly better than their high school teachers, in terms of salary.

Robert McDermot earned a diploma in mechanical drafting. "I think that hands-on higher learning is the way to go," he said. "Those are the people that will get the opportunities just because of the experience."

Jill Marie (Chavie) Cessna, a shy young woman who came to meet me at Decoys, a local sports bar in the center of the town of White Bear Lake, studied for her receptionist's diploma at Pine City Technical College. But she instead took a job as a teller at U.S. Bank in St. Paul, a bank that promoted her and trained her at their own expense. She now processes commercial loans.

Jason Cairl's story is inspiring. Jason was one of twins born two months prematurely. His brother was fine, but Jason, who weighed only two pounds four ounces at birth, developed cerebral palsy. His mother helped push his wheelchair into Decoys for his meeting with me.

While Jason most wanted to go to school with his twin brother and with his sister, born a year later, for most of his life the White Bear schools were not equipped to deal with a student in a wheelchair. Finally, in tenth grade, when he was a year behind, he was able to join his brother and sister in school. He graduated from high school in 1993 but, because of transportation problems, it took him six years to earn his associate's degree in human services from Century Community College. Now he is working as a recreation program leader in an after-school program for elementary school children.

"We give snacks, go on field trips, try to build self-esteem," he told me as he used his arms to push himself upright in his chair. "I've always accepted my disability. I don't think the world owes you anything."

Then there are the remainder, twenty-one people (twelve males, nine females) who did not get any kind of degree. A surprising number of them have become quite successful. Three of them went into the Army, one into the Navy. Many took brief courses in computers. As Shannon Omvig, who earned a bachelor's degree in English and communications, said, "I know many people who have high-paying jobs who never attended college."

Jason Woller went to the Benchmark computer training school and is now two tests away from earning his Microsoft Certified Systems Engineer certificate. He is working as a systems engineer for a computer consulting company in Minneapolis.

Although the preponderance of the kids who did extremely well without college did so in the areas of computers and technology, there were some who found solid employment in other fields. Eric Anderson worked at Minnesota Life insurance company before being paralyzed in that diving accident at the age of twenty-one. "Right before my accident," he said, "I went to a job interview with about twenty other people, most of whom had college degrees, and here they were doing the same thing I was." A lot of kids from his class, he says, went to technical school and are now earning $50,000 a year. "I never considered going to college," he said. "I know I would've just partied it all away."

These days, in addition to speaking in schools about the dangers of head injuries, Eric, a remarkably self-possessed young man who is in a wheelchair but has use of his arms, is teaching himself about computers.

Bryan Lagergren dropped out of community college and is now working at his stepfather's archery business. "College is a joke," he told me, standing in a back room at the White Bear Bar. "If anything you need hands-on training. I make good money selling archery products, targets, deer scent. You don't need to speak Spanish to do that."

Jason Blumenthal went to trade school and became a cement finisher. He now works full-time in construction and makes $26 an hour. "Not a book person," he said. "Even high school was mostly a waste of time."

A STUDENT WHO DIDN'T GO TO COLLEGE

Jon Mikrut, the Korean-born White Bear graduate, is an interesting study. He is tall, handsome, levelheaded and has an impressive bearing. The other young men who hang around the White Bear Bar defer to him. "He's the responsible one," one of them said.

He is also the one who encouraged Adam Hejny to be the class streaker at the homecoming game senior year, and the one who hatched the senior prank that nearly got the class president suspended.

"We were sitting in economics class and I said I had heard it was cool to grease piglets and turn them loose in the school," Jon told me. "But they went to an auction and bought one-hundred pound hogs." Not quite as amusing when turned loose in a school building. And damned hard to catch.

He may have made the suggestion, he said, but he had perfect deniability: "I didn't *do* anything," he said, thus displaying the kind of leadership potential that could mark Jon as a future business executive.

Like most of the other students I met at the bar, Jon carries a cell phone. His has more than thirty of his classmates' numbers in its memory bank. One photo in the yearbook shows a crew of boys partying at his house: Jon is bare-chested in the middle of the group, wearing pooka shells around his neck and looking like a potentate.

These days Jon works as a car salesman, making an average of $50,000 a year. He told me he plans to live in White Bear Lake the rest of his life.

Jon got A's in high school and was ranked eighty-second in his class, in the top 20 percent, "as bad as I was, hanging out, skipping class and partying." He was accepted at a four-year college in River Falls, Wisconsin ("far enough to have to leave home, but close enough to come back often," he said), but decided at the last minute that he didn't want to go. "I wasn't sure what I wanted to do," he said.

It is only now, he says, that he is thinking of getting more education. "People are always yelling at me to get an education," he said. "I've gone about as far as I can go in this field in terms of earnings." And so at twenty-four, Jon is thinking of beginning a second career. Maybe in computers, he said.

THE SCHOOLTEACHER AND THE COMPUTER GUY

Heather Zehm, a 1993 White Bear graduate, got her teaching degree from Texas A & M. After doing her practice teaching in Texas she decided to move back to White Bear. While she was waiting for her certification in elementary education, which would pay her about $26,000 a year to start, she was working as a waitress at Decoys and living with her family.

"To be a teacher you have to have your degree," she said. "But I'm in debt for $12,000 and it really wasn't worth it. If I did it over again, I'd pick a field that offered more financial opportunity, like a degree in business or marketing."

One way to judge a student's popularity and success in high school is by counting the number of photographs that appear in the high school yearbook. Heather's picture appears seven times. Frank Milhofer's picture does not appear at all. Instead he is listed as an "alternative/night student."

I arranged to meet Frank at Decoys. A good-looking young man with a firm handshake and a steady look, Frank had joined the Army as a tank driver after high school. When he got out, the Army paid him $800 a month for schooling. He tried community college but wasn't enthusiastic. Then he woke up one morning with a revelation.

"I always thought computer people were jerks," he said. "Then I started thinking about Bill Gates. He may be a nerd, but he can buy whatever he wants."

Frank immediately went to Century Community College and signed up for Introduction to Computers. "Once I started doing something I liked, I got only A's," he said. He figures he has completed about a year of classes at this point.

Through a temporary agency, he got a job as a tape operator on a mainframe computer for Fair Isaac, a company in the Twin Cities that does computer programming for clients like the U.S. Postal Service. Rather quickly he moved to the tape library. After five months he applied for an opening as a programmer. "I bought a book off Amazon on MVS JCL," he said. "I just learned it from a book, along with Q Basic."

Eventually Fair Isaac sent him to Washington for a week to learn assembler language. "The assembler class was $1,500 plus $1,300 for travel," he said. "All together it came to $3,500 for one week and they paid it all. I could have gone to college full-time for a semester for what they spent to send me to Washington for a week."

By now Frank knows three computer languages: assembler, Basic and JCL. He has signed up to learn Cobol. With the experience he has, he said, and Cobol, he could make $60,000 a year.

"Right now, I make about $40,000 a year, plus quarterly bonuses and a dollar for dollar match on my 401K for the first 3 percent of my salary," he said. "And I like the work. I put on my headphones, can wear anything I like. People wear jeans, have long hair." One of his White Bear classmates also works at Fair Isaac. Jamie Larkin graduated with a four-year degree from Augsburg. The two of them now do the same job, despite the difference in their education.

"So," Frank said, leaning in for the kill. "I have one question about my class."

And that is?

"I want to know, has anyone become a millionaire yet?"

It was about at this point that Heather, the teacher-waitress, came to our table. "I thought I recognized you," she said to Frank. They talked for a bit. When she momentarily left our table, Frank confided, "She'd be a great sales rep. She's got the personality." (Let it be noted that Heather is the kind of statuesque young woman who, if she became a teacher, would seriously impact the psyches of her boy students for years to come.)

When she came back, Heather, who stands five foot eleven, was soon bending down at our table and hanging on Frank's every word. "Let me give you my card," he said. "You should think of coming to work at our company."

Heather demurred, saying she didn't know anything about computers.

"An account representative makes $39,600 to start," he said. "My girlfriend does it, and she doesn't have any college at all. If you become an account manager, you make $64,000."

Heather took his card.

A MOTHER'S LAMENT

I stopped on a Sunday morning at the largest Protestant church in the area, St. Andrews Lutheran Church in nearby Mahtomedi, which draws a number of parishioners from White Bear. The bustling Sunday 10:10 A.M. service had drawn an overflow crowd. Three of the pastors were milling around in an attached reception hall along with several of the lay leaders and at least one high school French teacher from White Bear.

I met with the senior pastor, the executive pastor and John Straiton, the associate pastor. They all looked monklike, in their long white robes, and bore a striking resemblance to one another: balding, glasses, graying beards.

Pastor Straiton nodded sympathetically when I mentioned the number of White Bear graduates who felt they were not ready to go to college.

"We have a baccalaureate service for graduation," he said. "And often the students who aren't going on to college don't show up." He looked at me carefully. "It's because of the stigma, you know. The stigma of not going to college. And that's not right."

It's not right especially considering the number of White Bear students who did so well without college. But there is no organization that celebrates the kids who went the other way, who skipped college and got on with their lives.

Later that day, at the Keys Coffee Shop and Bakery, I met Kathy Schwartz, the mother of four. She had sent me a note about her son Eric, who graduated from White Bear in 1993. "I think high schools should take more time helping students explore their options and feel okay with saying college is not for me," she wrote. All the teachers ever preach, she said, is college, college, college.

Her oldest child, a daughter, sailed through college. That was not the case with her three sons. "Eric had in his mind that he *had* to go to college," she said. He started at the local community college, but it didn't work out. He felt like a failure. Then one day he came home and told his parents he was enlisting in the Navy. Now he was on an aircraft carrier in the Persian Gulf. It was the Sunday before Thanksgiving and Kathy and her husband would be celebrating the holiday without two of their sons. Another boy was in the Army in Kosovo.

Kathy sat talking with me over a piece of the Keys' pecan pie. "The teachers have one mind-set, but there has to be more than one direction," she said plaintively. "All the teachers have been to college so that's their mind-set."

"When you say you're not going to college," she said, "they tell you you won't amount to anything."

"The job Eric has in the Navy—he launches the planes—the captain says that it's the hardest job there is. The captain said, if you can do this, you can go out and do anything. I think that's the first time Eric has ever heard that," she said.

All of her kids are good kids, she said, though Eric was a wild one. He was intelligent but it was a kind of intelligence that did not translate into schoolwork. "That stigma," she said. "I don't know when it starts, but I think we do a real injustice to the kids who don't go to college. We need to slow down here, four years, six years, whoa. It takes some kids more time than that." Her son Stephen will get out of the Eighty-second Airborne in September 2000, but says he is *still* not sure if he's ready for college.

"I always knew my kids were special in their own way. I'm a woman of faith," she said. "I do pray a lot for my kids. I leave it in God's hands. I don't know what else a mother can do."

She was talking to me, she said, because she felt there was something wrong with the system that made kids like her sons feel bad about themselves. Our thinking about all this, she said, needed to change. As Sara, the special ed teacher, said when we met, "Why don't people build on their strengths? Aren't we all much happier in things where we can succeed?"

And there we have White Bear, a typical town in that its students predominantly opt for college—because, despite the town's enlightenment, they do not hear of any alternatives. The system worked for those kids who sailed through college and got good jobs in their fields. It worked considerably less well for those who plunged into the wrong majors, dropped out, stopped out and felt like failures in what they were told was the most important thing to do: Go to college.

Chapter Five

ARE THEY BROKEN, AND SHOULD WE FIX THEM?

The two most common elements in the universe
are hydrogen and stupidity.
—HARLAN ELLISON

A child may not be ready for college because she wants to go live in Bali. Or a child may want to skip college because he's a computer genius and is too busy starting his Internet business. A child may find himself on an aircraft carrier in the Persian Gulf. Children may put off college because they want to work for a while, or volunteer for a church mission. But probably the most common reason a child will not be ready for college is because of a learning disability or attention deficit disorder, the inability to sit still or concentrate or finish a task.

On this, I'm with Perri Klass. In her column in *Parenting* magazine in September 1998, she wrote: "I wonder from time to time whether there's anyone left anymore who is just no good at math. Or anyone who is just a slow reader. . . . Nowadays, my children's friends and my friends' children who don't do well in one subject all seem to end up officially diagnosed with learning problems."

Perri Klass, associate proffesor of pediatrics at Boston University School of Medicine and pediatrician at Dorchester House in Boston, often sees parents who are looking for a diagnosis of their child's problem. "For reasons I don't fully understand," she wrote, "many parents would rather have a child with a documented learning problem than one who's just a rotten speller."

When I was growing up in North Branch, Minnesota, we had the usual assortment of class clowns, mostly boys, who seemed to spend an inordinate amount of time goosing one another and making farting sounds with their armpits, blurting out animal noises and generally hee-hawing their way through the year. They constituted a separate tier of students. The class clowns were neither the smart, studious ones, nor the dull, out-of-it losers, nor the jocks and athletes nor the cool kids. Tom Hanks says he was a classic class clown, horsing around and offering up silly commentary to slide shows.

Back then, students actually hoped they would have a couple Tom Hankses/class clowns in the room with them, someone to break up the infernal tedium of sixth grade and the study of Minnesota state history (a subject that was, at least, blessedly short). In the fifties and sixties, fewer kids were expected to go to college. They took the SAT precisely once. That was during their senior year. No one practiced for it. They just took it and then they went to state college.

Back then, it was easier to follow your father into the archery business, or work at the farm equipment dealership, or join your mom's real estate business or take over the farm. You could make a good living at things like that; college was for smart kids who were going to be lawyers or doctors or teachers.

Psychiatrists were a far-off thing, and dealt strictly with problems like schizophrenia. No one was looking to haul North Branch's crop of class fidgets and clowns into a shrink's office for a diagnosis. Teachers and kids alike just understood that some kids were goofy and couldn't sit still. Today, working-class families may still have those attitudes.

If anyone wants an example of a typically restless kid, he is right there in *Huckleberry Finn*. When an old maid tries to give Huck a spelling lesson, he says, "She worked me middling hard for about an hour, and then the widow made her ease up. I couldn't stand it much longer. Then for an hour it was deadly dull, and I was fidgety. Miss Watson would say, 'Don't put your feet up there, Huckleberry'; and 'Don't scrunch up like that, Huckleberry—set up straight'; and pretty soon she would say, 'Don't gap and stretch like that, Huckleberry—why don't you try to behave?'"

Even Huck Finn came around to like schoolin', in his own fashion. "At first I hated the school, but by and by I got so I could stand it," he says. "Whenever I got uncommon tired I played hooky ... " For more than a hundred years, we've admired Huck's independent spirit, but such an attitude today would land a middle-class kid in a boarding school, for sure, or with a counselor.

Some of that is because our expectations for our children have become so overwhelming. Back in the fifties and sixties, when many of today's parents were growing up, families consisted of at least three children, sometimes more. With an heir and a spare and a few more than that, parents were able to see the differences in their brood. It was obvious that some were good at school. Then there were those who worked hard at their math tables, bless them, sitting at the kitchen table with wetted pencil in hand and a furrowed brow. It was clear they were never going to be scholars.

Some kids had good hands and could sit for hours doing crochet work. Where I grew up, every girl had to learn to sew and every boy made a gun rack in shop class. Some kids were musical or mechanical or boisterous or shy.

No one kid was supposed to be good at everything. It was not expected that we would all go on to school. And if one of us ended up living at home until the age of 30, hunkered down in an upstairs bedroom, and having an occasional drink, that was okay, too. It was nice to have someone to help with the storm windows and the yard work. People actually used the term "late bloomer," and smiled.

Now the shy kid is depressed, the boisterous one is hyperactive, the bad speller is learning disabled (dysgraphia), the class clown has attention deficit, the late bloomer has issues with separation and maturation and the kid who starts drinking is self-medicating.

FROM THE ADMISSIONS DESK

"It just seems to me I get more applicants every year who say, 'diagnosed ADD his junior year,'" said Lisa Antell, director of admissions at the Bridgton Academy in Maine, a school devoted solely to thirteenth-year education. "I understand that, but we don't make a lot of accommodations here for those kids. That's the philosophy of the school.

"I think sometimes my feeling is that these parents want to be able to say, 'He has a learning disability,' instead of, 'He doesn't have the intelligence, he doesn't have the horsepower.' It's easier to say. It's easier to say, but he shouldn't be thinking about college."

When she goes on the road to talk about Bridgton, she often encounters guidance counselors who tell her that every kid in their school *must* go to college. "I disagree with that," she said. "There's a reason more than half of them don't finish college. They don't belong there in the first place."

EVERY CULTURE MAKES ITS OWN CLASSIFICATIONS

Two thousand years ago, a system of yoga laid down nine obstacles that could prevent a person from reaching his or her goals: languor, illness, self-doubt, indifference, laziness, love of a good time, false illusions, difficulty in concentrating and the difficulty in continuing to concentrate. If that were a horoscope, I would say my son was born under that sign. But only when it involves schoolwork or demanding reading.

Put a mechanical problem in front of him (or a car magazine) and he will be up all night. He is like a young Tom Edison, a natural tinkerer, magic with his hands. My son could rewire a stereo faster than I could find the "on" button. He once redid our family lawyer's entertainment center while we were there for dinner. As long as my son was around, I was sure to have surround-sound from the television and a car wired up with every conceivable gizmo and a working radio. It goes without saying that he was also able to fix every component of my computer and intuitively understand software. "I don't know," he said, "kids just know these things."

What should a child's goal be? Doing the thing he loves? (For my son, working with cars or stereos or computers.) Or doing the thing we say he should do? (For him, go to college and take freshman composition and courses in history and philosophy.) To put it another way, would there be any diagnosis of ADD if we did not require our kids to sit in crowded, stuffy classrooms doing rote work and studying boring subjects so they could go on to college and do more of the same?

One favorite consolation for parents of kids with ADD is a list of famous people with ADD and learning disabilities. When my son was younger, I was constantly told by friends that "Albert Einstein flunked math." First of all, hello. My child was not Einstein. And second, what kind of expectation did that present?

Fine, you can struggle with your multiplication tables. But nothing important has been done since Heisenberg's Uncertainty Principle, so get busy on that one.

Sure enough, Albert Einstein turns up on lists of people who supposedly have ADD or other learning disabilities, along with Galileo, Alexander Graham Bell, Mozart, Stephen Hawking, the Wright Brothers, Beethoven, Winston Churchill, John Lennon, Leonardo da Vinci, Tom Edison and Cher. Does that make anyone feel better?

As romantic figures, the creative geniuses, the scalawags and misfits, rogues and cads are compelling. They are not quite as compelling when they are sitting in the upstairs bedroom, playing Quake instead of doing their term papers, or rewiring the basement when they are supposed to be reading *Moby Dick*.

And yet it is possible that some of those misfits will turn out to be ideally suited to our modern world. "We do a lot of diagnosing of normalcy," said Robert Schleser, a professor of psychology at the Institute of Psychology at the Illinois Institute of Technology in Chicago. "We give it a fancy label. We make it a mental illness. When our kids do what we did, we don't like it. We say 'oppositional disorder' and make them stop. We're hypocrites."

As for attention deficit disorder, "we've called it a mental disorder, a cognitive disorder, but I suspect these kids are important players in the new millennium," he said. "It takes a good deal of focus to read a book. Now the biggest complaint parents have is that their kids are on the computer. But these kids are not ADD at all on the computer."

That restless kind of energy that kids with attention deficit have is "perfect for surfing the Internet," he said. "They don't get bogged down with a topic."

Professor Schleser calls himself "wildly nonlinear."

"I cannot sit down and read a book," he says, "but I can read five books at a time. I'd shoot myself if I had to watch one movie at a time. The bottom line is if you find the right environment, you get the job done."

Professor Schleser, by the way, does not even believe in the diagnosis of ADHD. "I believe in the symptoms created by a rigid structure that says there's a certain way to get things done," he said. "It's you linear thinkers who are doing it. It's a linear thinking society, so call the priest, the policeman or the psychologist when someone doesn't fit in."

Kids who won't do boring, repetitive homework assignments are, he says, freethinkers. Why should someone do forty pages of workbook problems, he said, "if people like me got the concept the first time out?" (All right, settle down, you linear thinkers who say, "You do forty pages of workbook problems because that's the *assignment*.")

There's nothing wrong with getting an education outside of the schoolroom, he says. "There's something to be said for the education the world provides," he told me. "In my era, you were just as apt to get in the car and go to California. You learned something about the world.

"You've got to look at your kid. I'm going to invest my kid's time and energy and a fair amount of dollars—what's the best return on my investment? To truck him off to college where he doesn't want to be in classes he doesn't like? That sets up damage to the self-confidence because of a bad fit.

"I see a lot of guys, late teens, early twenties. They drive their parents crazy. I call them Buzzards. They're just hanging around. I tell parents, 'Leave them alone. They're just percolating.'"

SOMETIMES PARENTS KNOW TOO MUCH

Michael Lyles is the director of admissions for the Fenster School, a boarding school near Tucson, Arizona, for under-achieving students and kids with learning disabilities. He told me that parents sometimes deliver their children to the school with thorough dossiers. One mother arrived from England with her Ph.D. thesis, which she had written about her son's attention deficit hyperactivity disorder.

"She handed us his life story in her Ph.D., a case history from kindergarten up to his enrollment at Fenster," Mike told me. "That's what we see. A lot of kids being diagnosed with a lot of things, and sent to expensive therapeutic programs that cost $70,000 to $80,000 a year."

Fenster told this kid's mother to keep her notebooks and instead instituted their program of small class sizes, strict supervision of homework and immediate rewards or consequences. The Fenster School doesn't do anything draconian, he told me, but they do have a 150-acre campus, and "it's immaculate," he said.

This particular kid, who arrived from the underground scene on the streets of London with "no discernible GPA," Mike said, as if talking about a pulse, graduated from Fenster with a 3.2 average and entered the University of Arizona. "He was one of our leaders," Mike said. "We never knew what he was going to wear. Every day was Halloween. But he graduated, and he graduated with self-esteem intact."

AND OFTEN PARENTS PUSH TOO HARD

There is extraordinary pressure today for children to be everything for their parents, even material for a Ph.D. thesis, even material for a book. And if a parent has only one child, that child has an even greater burden. From Mozart in the womb, through the tension of kindergarten admission (yes, kindergarten), through the Sylvan Learning Center and batting coaches for eight-year-olds, and the prep classes for the PSATs and the enriched summer programs, right up through decimal-counting analyses of the child's final GPA, we treat our kids like some kind of Frankenstein lab experiment, a testament to our own hubris and an assertion of the idea that every child in America must be above average, and academically competitive.

And if a child does not measure up, there has to be a reason. Huck Finn could say, "I had been to school most all the time and could spell and read and write just a little, and could say the multiplication table up to six times seven is thirty-five, and I don't reckon I could ever get any further than that if I was to live forever. I don't take no stock in mathematics, anyway." Today that would be diagnosed as a distinct learning disability, "dyscalcula," the difficulty in dealing with numbers. (And let's not forget Huck's problem with "oppositional defiance.")

We have gone far beyond dyslexia, it seems, in finding things to diagnose in our kids. Section 504 of the Rehabilitation Act of 1973 (dealing with federal facilities) started it with a list of potential disabilities requiring help, including an "imperfect ability to listen, think, speak, read, write, spell or do mathematical calculations." There is even a diagnosis of "dysrationalia," according to a 1993 article in the *Journal of Learning Disabilities.* That would mean that a person lacks the ability to be rational (to accept new ideas, or reflect on his own beliefs) commensurate with his intelligence.

Whereas someone used to be dogmatic, ignorant or thick-headed, now he suffers from dysrationalia. Have we gained anything here?

DIAGNOSING THE PROBLEM

Newsweek magazine advised in an article about "tweenagers" in October of 1999: If your children in school are "trying hard but still not doing well, parents should talk to teachers about potential learning disabilities that may require special instruction."

It would be easy for me to laugh at this (as Perri Klass said, "Isn't anyone just bad at math anymore?") if I myself hadn't taken my son to a Manhattan neuropsychologist when he was thirteen for a $1,200 evaluation. The evaluation, which used WISC and "Trail-Making A and B" and "Digit Span Backwards" in order to prove its points, essentially fed back what I already knew: that I had a bright kid who was off the charts in some areas, like spatial reasoning, but who lost his way in complex tasks requiring him to remember instructions. He was easily distractable. The diagnosis: He had attention deficit disorder, without hyperactivity.

And you know what? It did make me feel better. I thought, You see? It isn't my fault. Unfortunately, since we are a fault-finding society, my son felt it was *his* fault.

I tried the analogy of needing glasses (some kids need glasses to see well) and crutches (some kids need crutches, etc.), but those explanations all seemed to involve telling my son that he was in some way defective. And no teenager wants to be defective. Try having a rational (nondysrationalia-ish) discussion with a thirteen-year-old about what is *wrong* with him. It might have been easier if he had been diagnosed as a child, but he had a silent form of ADD, and he had been a "good boy."

Because he was not one of those kids who jumped around in class, not one of those pesky boys who drive teachers bats, he had not been diagnosed in elementary school or junior high. Teachers adored him, and if his academic performance was inconsistent, they told me: "Wait, you'll see, he'll catch fire one of these days." He was a dreamer, he was *not* a troublemaker.

He sat in the classroom, gazing out the window from time to time, dreaming about cars and cartoon characters and Bruce Willis movies. Which is probably why he never knew what the homework assignment was. Even as a good boy, he was capable of creating chaos, losing house keys, backpacks, his lunch.

He was bright enough to do well in the early grades. He was bright enough to get into a selective high school, but once in the classroom, he seemed to lose all sense of purpose. From lost permission slips to lost ambitions, he was a kid who needed help.

Right from the start, his high school recommended that I put him in private school. But I didn't have a spare $16,000 a year. So instead I read books about ADD, many of which suggested that medication (mostly Ritalin) worked miracles. That and a little therapy and counseling would do the trick.

RITALIN, YES OR NO?

As *Time* magazine pointed out in its cover story on "The Age of Ritalin" in November 1998, long after I faced these issues, every parent agonizes over giving a kid medication: "Will Ritalin help? Will it change her personality? Is it fair for me to make the choice for him? Does it send the signal that she is not responsible for her behavior? . . . Will he have to take it forever? What if *all* children would be a little happier, perform a little better if they took their pills like vitamins every morning?" To that I might add: Is it right to medicate my child so he can perform up to my expectations?

A really lovely piece of reporting in *The New Yorker* in February 1999 by Malcolm Gladwell discussed exactly what it is about ADD and ADHD kids that makes them different: Among other things, they cannot control their impulses. They plunge ahead with the first response that comes to mind.

"Suppose for instance that you have been given a particularly difficult math problem," Gladwell wrote. "Your immediate, impulsive response might be to throw down your pencil in frustration. But most of us wouldn't do that. We would check those impulses and try to slog our way through the problem, and, with luck, maybe get it right. Part of what it takes to succeed in a complex world, in other words, is the ability to inhibit our impulses."

But, as he points out, the child with ADD, according to the official diagnosis, "often does not follow through on instructions and fails to finish schoolwork, chores or duties in the workplace." Such a child cannot regulate his behavior. His internal governor is turned off.

What Ritalin does, he explains, is provide an extra helping of dopamine (readily available with other stimulants, like cocaine and nicotine) to make kids with ADD somewhat "normal." By helping their restlessness and impulsiveness, he argues, Ritalin allows kids to take control of time. As he writes, "Time is about imposing order, exercising control over one's perceptions, and that's something that people with attention deficit have trouble with."

The reason ADD is being diagnosed now, he says, is that our modern society demands more education and higher levels of thinking and concentration. He concludes: "Modernity didn't create ADHD. It revealed it."

Unfortunately, Gladwell was writing in 1999, and I had to do all my thinking and struggling with these issues in 1994. At the time, I read a few books by doctors who claimed they had gotten through Harvard or Princeton or someplace equally daunting without ever realizing they had ADD. No wonder it had been so hard!

Well, please. I wasn't hoping for Harvard. That was like the mother who said that finding out her son had ADD was like planning a trip to Greece and discovering they were instead going to go to Amsterdam, a nice place but not what you had intended.

I worried: What if you had planned a trip to Greece but never got out of Newark, New Jersey? That's what it felt like, back in those dark days when public schools were reluctant to hear about ADD, and even more unwilling to do anything about it.

Back in my son's high school years, when nothing seemed to work—when my son continued to have trouble in school despite the charts on the refrigerator and notes to the teachers, the pleas that he sit in the front row in class, the hours we spent over the history of the New World, pre-Columbus, the time I spent taking him to the library and willing him to get some research done, even the taking of various medications—I had a mantra. At least I've got my health; at least he's got his health: *At least I've got my health. At least he's got his health.*

This went on for years while I consulted psychologists, psychiatrists, counselors and school advisors. Since my son's father (a well-known British psychologist) died when my son was a baby, I felt he and I both needed a lot of help. And I was determined to prove that I, as a single mother, could not only handle this but triumph over it. I set very high goals for the both of us.

I wonder today what would have happened if I had just said to my son: "Kid, it looks to me like you'd rather be working on old cars or television sets or air conditioners. How about throwing all these books out the window, and going to trade school?"

Wouldn't that have been kinder? What if he had been the smartest student in Transit Tech, instead of a struggling student at the second-best public high school in the city? What if he had dropped out of school, passed his GED and gone into the Army at seventeen? What if he had gone off to live in Spain, and gone to school there, where he could have become fluent in Spanish and fix Spanish air conditioners?

The road not taken.

In real life, I hired a Spanish tutor who came to our house once a week. Still, my son struggled with Spanish, a language his psychiatrist said he might never be able to learn (dys-*spania*). He would flunk biology, because he never handed in his lab reports, then sail through the biology Regents test. It was clear that Bronx High School of Science was *not* the right place for a kid like that, but what was?

And how was I going to prepare this kid for greater responsibility when he seemed so capable of making wrong choices: borrowing money and not paying it back, making friends with kids who were caught stealing cigarettes? I worried about his hanging out with the "wrong" kids. I worried about his *being* the "wrong" kid.

SO WHAT IS IT WITH THESE KIDS?

I was close friends with two other families as I was raising my son. We had a total of six children. Three of them sailed through college. Three of them (two boys and a girl) were diagnosed with

ADD and to this date have not finished college. Our ADD kids, we agreed, were certainly different, even at an early age.

John K. Durall is the program coordinator for the ADHD program of the Greater Long Beach (California) Guidance Clinic. During the summer, he directs Camp Oakes, which specializes in handling kids with ADHD (and what a fun place that must be). He wrote about some of the things he has experienced in the January/February issue of *Camping* magazine: "A person with ADHD may develop less *[sic]* competencies, make more mistakes, have fewer successes or be labeled as irresponsible or lazy. It is not uncommon for the child with ADHD to experience more pessimism with resultant passivity. It is not infrequent that the person with ADHD have or develop a coexisting problem of an oppositional defiant disorder, a conduct disorder, a depression disorder, an anxiety disorder, an obsessive-compulsive disorder, Tourette's syndrome or other disorders." Oh, great.

But Mr. Durall, who credits much of his thinking to Russell A. Barkley, director of psychology and a professor at the University of Massachusetts Medical Center in Worcester, Massachusetts, did say something that was encouraging. "Bear in mind," he wrote, "that the ADHD child is on average about 30 percent behind in age-appropriate self-control."

In other words, when my son was twelve, he was acting as if he was eight. Sending such a kid to college at eighteen is like sending a twelve-year-old, in terms of his judgment. More than anything, it would seem, what I should have done was just wait him out.

But that is hard to do when there is no way to get off the assembly line of grade school, junior high, high school. As much as I knew, and as hard as I tried, we seemed stuck. Things did not improve until I took a second job, diverted the insurance money for a tornado that struck our house in the country and, for his final year of high school, sent my son to a strict boarding school on Long Island, a coat-and-tie place called the Knox School that insisted upon, among other things, a two-hour study hall every night.

ANGST IN THE SUBURBS

"When he was young, nobody ever suggested a psychiatrist for him," a suburban New York City mom told me about her son, who is now grown. "They were supposed to have done tests on him in first and second grade. He was always a disorganized mess. His homeroom teacher offered to meet early with him to help him organize his work and his backpack. Nothing took, nothing stuck. You might as well talk to the wall. Like you were talking some other language. His backpack was a mess of papers, old stuff, new stuff. It was no wonder he couldn't do his homework. He couldn't find his assignment. He didn't have the book."

She stopped for breath. "Isn't there some kind of help for a child like that? Don't we know what that means when we see that? Nobody could help my son when he was young and would have accepted the help."

She can look back on ten years of doctors' opinions and feel she did not get the diagnosis she needed. "I feel now that we were completely mis-served by the mental health community," she told me. "I think that he has some kind of learning disability. But once he got older I wasn't able to keep taking him for tests, because he wouldn't do it. One psychiatrist said bipolar. Two others said ADD. Between everything there could have been some kind of treatment when he was younger."

Now, she says, she's dealing with a "kid in a man's body."

"His maturity level is so much less," she said, "it's hard to accept. It's easier to accept a precocious kid, but when it goes the other way people don't believe it or don't accept it.

"Barely a week goes by that something isn't broken. He breaks the window or cuts the screen to get in or puts holes in the walls in the basement. His room is a complete pigsty. And he has friends down there who all gravitate to each other, all kind of lost."

Like most mothers, she wonders if she is to blame. "I constantly was told 'Take him to private schools, small classes.' Yes, go ahead and tell a single mother that the best thing for her child is a private school. That will make her feel ten times worse than she already feels. At that time, I was just doing the best I could."

Hearing her anguish, it's hard to accept the point of view of Neil Bull, the counselor in Cambridge, Massachusetts. "ADD is a serious thing," he said, "but it is used as an excuse and it certainly is fashionable."

THE ADD DOCTOR

Dr. Edward M. Hallowell wrote *the* book on ADD with Dr. John J. Ratey in 1994, *Driven to Distraction*. The book is encyclopedic in its discussion of the child (or adult) with ADD or ADHD. The children described in this book could have been my son: distracted, doing sloppy work, not working up to his ability, frustrated and in need of more structure.

In *Driven to Distraction,* Drs. Hallowell and Ratey write about a teenager named Will who discovered he had ADD only when he was about to flunk out of college. "A part of him did not believe in the diagnosis," they said. "It was too good to be true. A part of him felt much more comfortable with calling himself lazy than with accepting the idea of ADD." Will, as it turned out, alternated taking Ritalin and not taking the drug because he worried that it was the drug that was succeeding in school, not he. Will eventually graduated from college, but the ordeal took a toll on his parents.

"They are no-nonsense Yankee types who all along thought Will was a creative, talented kid who just couldn't get his act together. They tried all the tactics parents of adolescents try: They yelled at him, they grounded him, they ignored him, they fought with him, they negotiated with him, they sent him to a psychotherapist, they hovered over him, they bribed him, they scolded him, they pleaded with him, they hugged him."

When I talked to Dr. Hallowell, I asked him, "Wouldn't it be easier, and better, if parents would not require their kids with ADD to go to college in the first place?"

"It's the elephant in the room that everyone sees but no one talks about," he answered. "We realize there is another way through life. That that linear track works well for a certain type of brain, but not so well for another."

He says he tries to convey the message to the families he sees at his "modestly named" Hallowell Institute in Concord, Massachusetts. "If you do have difficulty in school, you are not on your way to the slag heap," he tells them. But, he says, "people don't believe it. Teachers don't believe it. There is an inborn prejudice against any child whose brain doesn't operate on that track that gets them through school. Everyone ends up feeling guilty and ashamed. All the messages are, 'You're defective, You don't have what it takes.'"

There are a lot of class issues that need to be dealt with when middle-class parents have kids that just don't seem cut out for school. "A lot of people think, 'If my kid can't get through college, he has no life.' Gardeners can be incredibly creative," he noted. "There are people being shoehorned through college, and they're coming out with a 'can't do' attitude. One kid, his father was a Ph.D., and they battled in my office. The kid became an usher at the movie theater. Two years later, he was the manager of the entire chain."

He longs for a day when we put all those old labels (smart, stupid, dumb, lazy, willful and bad) in the trash can and just accept that there are different kinds of brains.

"It ought to be like a subject in school every year," he said. "You find out what kind of brain you have by sitting down and saying what comes easy and what comes hard. Then you learn how to manage it, which is more than 'just try harder.' "

As for hauling kids into doctors' offices for diagnoses, he says, "Very few kids deserve a diagnosis in a specific sense. I agree with Perri [Klass]: This diagnosis frenzy is ridiculous."

Dr. Hallowell is the father of three young children. He himself has ADD and dyslexia, he says, and took a year off from Harvard before coming back. His oldest child has ADD.

Yet even when he shares that with patients, they can have a negative reaction on being told that their child has ADD. "The most brilliant people in the world will say, 'You're telling me my son is a moron, or less than human.' It's almost like a death sentence. It's like the child no longer exists. It takes time for both the parents and the kids to get past that."

All of the special schools that work for kids with ADD, he says, combine structure with flexibility. "These kids are like toboggans," he said. "They need to be kept on track. It's like they have a Ferrari engine under the hood. Once they get into something they're good at, they become tenacious."

And it certainly worked for the better when my son was at the Knox School. To say he went reluctantly would be putting it too mildly. He loathed me for "shipping him off." But for the first time, I heard his excitement over learning.

The Knox School knew how to make kids succeed. When he said he could not learn a Shakespearean sonnet, his English teacher, who was also the headmaster, drove him to the beach at sunset and as the two of them walked the headmaster recited a line and then my son repeated it. Walking and repeating, walking and repeating. My son excitedly recited the whole sonnet to me in the car.

He wrote a sonnet, too, "My Dusky Beauty," although it was an ode to a car. And he learned Spanish, partly because he was in a class of six students. When he had to learn, he learned.

THIS IS YOUR KID
THIS IS YOUR KID IN COLLEGE

The University of California, Santa Barbara, posts this on its website: "In an academic setting, adult students with attention deficit disorder often exhibit many of the following behaviors on a persistent basis.... Often seems inattentive to details, and makes frequent errors in academic work; Has difficulty sustaining attention; May seem not to listen when spoken to directly; Has difficulty 'following through' on instructions, or fails to complete tasks; Has trouble organizing tasks and activities; Dislikes or avoids tasks requiring sustained mental effort; Tends to lose things necessary for tasks or activities (for example, keys, textbooks, assignment sheets); Is easily distracted by features of the environment (for example, background noise, light, or motion); Frequently forgets appointments and other daily activities; Fidgets or squirms restlessly; Has difficulty remaining seated; Often has subjective feelings or restlessness; Displays an inability to engage in leisure activities quietly; Is frequently 'on the go' or acts as if 'driven by a motor'; Talks excessively; Blurts out answers before questions have been completed; Has difficulty waiting in line; and often interrupts or intrudes on others."

Does this sound like a student who should be in college? But in fact this is a list of the kinds of things that universities must accommodate as disabilities.

The Disabled Students Program at the University of California, Santa Barbara, was founded in 1978. Diane Glenn, now director of the program, has been there since the start. At the beginning, however, the program was meant to help students with physical disabilities: the deaf, the blind, students in wheelchairs.

"When I first started I don't recall anyone disclosing learning disabilities," Diane told me. "In 1982 we had five or six. Now we have two hundred, and I'm sure there are others."

In 1982, before ADD became the dominant diagnosis, the main learning disabilities reported to UCSB were dyslexia or other processing problems. Ever since the Americans With Disabilities Act was interpreted to include ADD, the number of kids reporting ADD has grown.

A college student with severe learning problems may be entitled to the following "accommodations." They can have someone hired by the school take notes for them in class (which may seem revolutionary to those who have been out of college for a few decades, but many schools these days sell class notes through their student associations). Students with severe learning problems can also get their textbooks on tape. They can have extra time on tests. Sometimes they can have a reader in class with them, to help them interpret questions on tests. They can have someone help them organize their papers. They can ask a teacher to clarify a question on a test. If their learning problems mean they have difficulty spelling, they can have computers with a spell-checker in the classroom during essay exams.

So, I asked Diane, what does it mean when a student who makes use of these accommodations goes out in the world to take a job? Doesn't a college diploma indicate that someone can, say, read a book and follow instructions and spell?

"They need to be more careful in the way they choose a profession and choose their strengths," she said. "If they have a weakness in math, they can't go into statistics."

I'm glad that's settled.

"We consider our population to be bright learning disabled," she said. "They're usually above average. Maybe 15 percent say to us, when they come in, 'I'm not going to use any services; I'll do it on my own.' And that's not the best way."

Claudia Nicastro-Batty is a disability specialist at UCSB who works with kids with ADD and also with the hearing impaired. She sees what happens when kids with ADD hit a college campus and do not use support services. "In college," she told me, "students don't have reminders of structure. So they have a difficult time keeping appointments or attending classes, especially morning classes.

"If they're taking medications, they don't take them regularly. They have a very difficult time keeping track of assignments and handing them in in a timely fashion. They know they should keep a day planner. So they input the information but don't look at it."

Claudia sees that 40 percent of the students who come to the service with ADD also have other learning disabilities. I asked if other students ever complained about learning-disabled students getting unfair advantages in college. "I believe we're giving students equal access," Claudia said. "I don't think we're giving them unfair advantages."

Students are all held to UCSB standards, she said, although some learning-disabled students may have their foreign language or math requirements waived for admission.

"Once a student is here, though, when it comes down to substituting course work, there is a very stringent policy," Claudia said. The school will not substitute a psychology course for a math course to meet a science requirement, she said. And if a student has a problem with writing, tough luck on the required English courses.

"If a student has a written language disorder, and they are taking a writing requirement, we can have them use a laptop with spell-check and grammar check," she said. "But some students still have difficulty choosing the word they want. We can't ask faculty not to grade them for grammar."

Claudia is determined to make the UCSB program like the real world in terms of expectations. In the workplace, she said, "they can't just say to a supervisor, 'I can't get it done in time.' They need to learn *how* to get it done. Or else it really can become a crutch."

SO DO THESE KIDS BELONG IN COLLEGE?

Dr. Mel Levine, professor of pediatrics at the University of North Carolina Medical School, in Chapel Hill, says we should consider the concept of "educational readiness." We talk about it with kindergarteners, he says. But kids also need to be ready emotionally for adolescence and later for college. "And SAT scores don't measure educational readiness," he said.

"If you don't know how to delay gratification," he said, "then you don't go to college.

"There are some real pitfalls," he told me. "Kids who have had trouble acquiring vocabulary are lost in college. One big issue is how well you deal with abstract, decontextualized concepts. Things you don't use in everyday life." No wonder kids prefer classes in which they talk about whether Calista Flockhart is too thin.

Dr. Levine reported that he was giving a workshop for college professors on how to deal with learning disabilities, and a sociology professor got up and said, "I don't have any trouble letting kids who can't read get books on tape or finding another accommodation. But what do I do about the kids who can't understand sociology?"

That would be dyssociologia, no doubt.

A more typical problem, he said, is that students with ADD never make it to class. "In college you have more time than you've ever had in your whole life," he said. "You get temporal intoxication. These kids fall apart because they don't know how to manage time. I have a lot of kids who are totally in a time warp. They need a coach. The faculty has to expect for them to submit a time line of their work in progress."

And yet he, too, does not believe that kids with ADD all belong in college. "I feel terrible when high schools all over the country are gearing up to get kids into college and college has no idea what to do with them, except for the elite ones.

"When President Clinton says every kid has a right to a college education, I gulp," he said. "Maybe some kids have a right *not* to have a college education. You can become very well educated without a college education. There should be another option. Kids need a chance to ripen."

BUT IF YOU REALLY, REALLY WANT JASON TO GO TO COLLEGE

According to Ruth Shalit's scathing article in the *New Republic* in 1997, "Defining Disability Down," 40,000 high school students asked for special accommodations (mostly extra time) when they took the SATs in 1996–97. So lots of students with learning disabilities head off to college.

In fact, so many kids attempt college despite their learning problems, there are books written especially for them, like the 1996 Princeton Review book *Help Yourself: Advice for College-Bound Students With Learning Disabilities.* That book, for instance, has a chapter titled "I'm LD, Hear Me Roar!"

But some kids are not quite that ready to be, in the language of the enfranchised disabled, "self-advocates." For those kids (with wealthy parents) there is a college in this country that is set up entirely for learning-disabled students. Landmark, a two-year college in Putney, Vermont, opened its doors in 1985. Back then, ADD was rarely diagnosed. Instead, many of the seventy-seven students who came to Landmark that first year had dyslexia, difficulty with the written word.

"I would say a lot of those students probably had ADD as well, undiagnosed," Dr. Lynda J. Katz, president of Landmark and a noted ADD researcher, told me. "When I came to this school in '94, because of my background in ADD, the school acknowledged that a lot of the students had ADD."

In the fall of 1999, Landmark had 340 students in a program that costs (hold your breath) $35,000 a year. (Guilty with an explanation: no endowment to speak of, classes of around six students each and a three-to-one student-faculty ratio, although faculty members primarily have a master's degree.) Landmark offers students an associate in the arts degree (an A.A. degree), which essentially means they have finished the first two years of college. If the students earn between a 2.5 and a 3.5 GPA at Landmark, they will automatically be admitted as juniors to twenty colleges around the country.

But not so fast. Some of the students at Landmark are not yet at college level. "We have noncredit courses, and a lot of those courses are for students who have more severe language-based disabilities," Dr. Katz said. Landmark designates these noncredit courses as either "eighties" level or "nineties" level.

But, I asked, wasn't that stranding students in an institution in which they are paying a great deal for a "college" education but not doing college work?

"I think we've come to grips with that during the last several years," Dr. Katz said, "because it was taking some students so many years to get through even the noncredit program. Now if they are admitted, a student can only stay at one of those levels for a year.

"Those kinds of steps ensure that we're not doing what you just said," she told me. "We have no interest in seducing a child or telling a student you have the capabilities of doing this if that isn't the case. Sometimes they need those one or two years more to help with self-esteem so they can go off to a trade school or where there is a career orientation immediately. We kind of make that known up front."

In other words, for parents who are willing to pay, Landmark could create a plumber with a $100,000 associate's degree behind him. It all depends on what a parent thinks college is for.

In the past Landmark has attracted students who had already been unsuccessful at regular colleges. "Some of them have flunked out of four or five colleges," Dr. Katz said, "and you can imagine what that feels like." Dr. Katz finds that a number of students, especially boys, just need more time to figure it all out. "At about twenty-four or twenty-five, life kicks in and they begin to look at priorities, and things have meaning and importance," she said. "Around twenty-four, something clicks and they change. Then they're off and they're on their own."

BEFORE YOU ASK "WHO NEEDS THIS?" LISTEN TO *THIS* STORY

My instinct would be to say that parents who pay for a program like Landmark are delusional about what their children can accomplish. And then I talked to the charming and highly personable David Cole, who went to Landmark and is now a senior at Brown University. David grew up in New Hampshire.

"I was diagnosed ADHD very young, on Ritalin very young, very unsuccessful in grade school all the way through," he told me. "A miserable experience. They offered an assessment in seventh grade that I was bored with school. So I skipped eighth grade. Then I was totally unprepared for high school. I had no study skills."

David went to Hanover High School. "There was a very narrow model of success there," he said.

The city has a large medical school and is the home of Dartmouth College. "So there were lots of doctors' kids looking to go Ivy and the locals," he said. "It was miserable. I got heavily involved in drugs, dropped out at fifteen and ran away from home."

David spent time in San Francisco, living on the streets. But even that got old. "I kind of ran out of steam," David said. "That wasn't working either. So I came home, got sober." His parents put him in touch with Deke Smith, an educational counselor with offices in Cambridge, Massachusetts, and Portland, Oregon.

"He was dragged in by his mother," Deke told me. "And there was something in him that struck a chord in me. I thought,

'Here's a kid with obvious ability for whom school was basically a disaster.'"

At the age of sixteen, David was in love with metal sculpture. His grandfather was the head mechanic for the Mount Washington railway. So Deke needed to find a high school that would allow David to work with metal.

The Putney School, in Putney, Vermont, is the kind of place where students build their own classrooms and milk cows at 5 A.M. "What I like best about Putney is that it has a broad definition of success," Deke said. "*And* they had a forge. I said to them, 'Here's one you're going to have to trust me on. Take him.' And they did.

"His talents were recognized, and he also tied into A.A. at Putney," Deke said.

It took three years of C's and D's at Putney for David to get his high school degree. "That meant I was in high school for a total of six years," David told me. "I was probably twenty and change when I finished there."

But he still wasn't ready for "college" college. So he went to Landmark. "They really gave him the tools," Deke told me. "He may be their most successful student of all time."

I had to ask. Didn't this cost the parents, like, a fortune? David's father is a lawyer now, but was a late bloomer himself. David's mother had to work three jobs for five years to put him through law school. "I try to console them that I am high performance *and* high maintenance," David said.

"They spent a *lot* of money," Deke said. "I remember a meeting with his father. He asked, 'Deke, are these two years going to pay off?'"

They did. "I met a tutor at Landmark," David told me. "Frank Sopper, a new English teacher. Kind of like when smart money bet the other way, he kept going."

David has a hard time saying exactly what it was that Landmark did for him. "A lot of it was growing up. It was less about what they taught me," he said, "than the chance to be successful. There was also a process of self-acceptance."

After two years at Landmark, David had a 3.96 GPA, "close enough so I rounded it up to a 4.0," he told me. He applied to four colleges and got into all of them.

David now is a twenty-four-year-old senior at Brown with a

major in visual arts "with a focus on theory," he said. But David is doing more than that. With another Brown student, Jonathan Mooney (more on him next), he has written a book about college for nontraditional students to be published in 2000. And the two young men have started a special program they hope to take national.

Project Eye-to-Eye, based in Providence, Rhode Island, matches college students who have ADD or other learning disabilities with elementary school children with similar problems. "We work together as mentors in and out of the classroom," David said. "And get together to do art."

AND THIS YOUNG MAN COULD NOT READ

Jonathan Mooney grew up in Manhattan Beach, California, and Lakewood, Colorado (yes, that Lakewood), near Denver. He will graduate from Brown in 2000. But Jonathan did not learn how to read until he was twelve, and he still has difficulty with spelling and the written word.

His dyslexia was diagnosed in fourth grade, when he was performing at a first-grade level. At the time he was also diagnosed with clinical depression (you try being in fourth grade and reading at a first-grade level). The school told his mother about the dyslexia, but told her it would go away. No one ever told him about it.

"It was the eighties," he said, "so they said, 'Don't tell him and screw up his identity formation.'

"I grew up in a mixture of resource rooms and special-ed rooms and being kicked out of the class." He dropped out of school in sixth grade. "I *hated* school and I grew into school phobia. I would cry every single morning. So in sixth grade I stopped going completely." His family was already in turmoil. His father, a lawyer, was involved with the counseling center that represented the parents in the McMartin Preschool trial in California, a highly publicized case of alleged child abuse.

"So my parents were in the middle of it, and consequently I was, too," Jonathan said. "Reporters were jumping out of the bushes for eight years. That was part of it: dyslexia, depression and my parents weren't around a lot; they were doing that."

Nonetheless, he says his parents were always supportive of him. Always. "My mom used to read to me every morning. *Leo the Late Bloomer.* She used to read that to me every morning."

Jonathan the Late Bloomer focused all his energies on soccer. School was another matter. "I had developed enough coping strategies" about reading, he said. "To this day I don't read in a traditional sense. I can't sound things out. It's just sight cues. So if I come across a word I haven't seen before, I can't read it."

He got by on his prestige as a soccer player. Then his family moved to Colorado, where he entered his freshman year of high school. "That was a bad time for any kid to move. I hadn't yet had a chance to get an identity as a soccer player. I'd hide in the library. And I failed all my classes."

Come high school, he says, he began to piece together the fact that he had a learning disability. "I knew I couldn't spell, but part of me knew I wasn't stupid."

He was promoted to a sophomore. "My high school story is cheating a lot," he said, "a tremendous amount." He was surprisingly good at English, but he had to dictate all his papers to his mother to type. "That's how I got through high school," he said, "but kind of running congruent with that was a serious problem with alcohol."

He got a scholarship to Loyola Marymount University on the basis of his soccer playing, even though he says he was depressed, drinking and not doing that well in school. At one point in college he was arrested for public drunkenness at a concert.

And then he was injured. "I broke my ankle the first practice day, then hurt my knee," he said. "At the same time that soccer wasn't working I was coming to terms with my dyslexia. After my first semester, I pieced it together."

He had to fight Loyola to earn the accommodations he said he needed for an English final. He loved writing, even though it was hard for him to read and to spell. He had gotten through his English courses by faxing all his drafts to his mother so she could correct his spelling (which he says is on a third-grade level).

But for the in-class final, 50 percent of the grade was going to be scored on spelling and grammar. He went to his professor and asked for special consideration, but was turned down. He took the test, did badly and then protested his grade. After a fight

("I had to be proactive"), he was able to retake the test. "And the semester after that, I got a four-oh in all my English classes. This is the upturn of the story."

But what made the turnaround?

"I had no reason to believe that I could do anything other than play soccer," Jonathan said. "I couldn't spell, write. I just took a leap of faith. It was 'Fuck this! All those people who told me I was stupid—I'm going to prove them wrong!'

"And there was a *lot* of hard work. It borderlines on the absurd at times, the amount of work I do. I worked harder than anyone else I knew."

He decided to transfer to Brown, in Providence, Rhode Island. "Brown doesn't have a core curriculum," he explained, "so I don't have to take languages." Beyond that, he does not find that Brown is particularly welcoming to learning-disabled students. "They do the minimum that the law requires," he said. But he is allowed unlimited time on tests and can use a computer for spellchecking and grammar. "That's official and guaranteed." And many times he is allowed to take his essay exams home.

His biggest complaint: Brown does not allow him to have a reader for in-class tests, "because there are mistakes I could not catch, missing words."

Is it fair to other students who don't have a diagnosed disability, I asked?

"That's off-base," he said. "That's like saying 'Why give a ramp for someone in a wheelchair?' It's about making the environment accessible. If you give me unlimited time, it will improve my grade about 20 percent. A regular student will have a grade go up only 1 or 2 percent."

But that of course begs the question of what a college degree is supposed to stand for, if not the ability to read and understand questions and express oneself in grammatical sentences with words that are correctly spelled. Especially for someone majoring in Twentieth-Century Literature.

"What is one supposed to get out of a college education," Jonathan mused. "What I'm looking to get out of college is self-understanding of how I learn. I want to know my strengths and weaknesses. When I enter a career, I know I'll need a reader."

He said: "I ask people, 'Do you ever use a secretary? A spell checker? An editor? And most people will say 'Of course'."

And hey, he and David have that book contract, to write about their experiences of going to college. "Our goal is to attack the pathology, the idea that these kids are diseased," Jonathan said. "Our life stories are those of being labeled and segmented off as people who won't be successful. The end result is much different. We aren't defective."

WHAT IF WE JUST ASK THEM TO CONCENTRATE?

Jake Horne is an educational counselor in Washington Depot, Connecticut, who specializes in making a "structured year" for kids who are not ready for college. "I have a lot of empathy for people who have trouble focusing," he said. "But I think that kids can learn how to do it in the right environment."

The Fenster School in Tucson, a high school for learning-disabled kids, is just such a place. And while it tries to send its kids off to college, "we are very realistic," said Mike Lyles, the admissions director. "Our target is not Ivy League. Our target is Arizona State University, the California state universities."

He describes Fenster's students as "capable but underachieving," usually because of ADD, ADHD or other learning disabilities. Many of their students are identified as needing special ed. But the Fenster School does not focus on the particular diagnosis (which he describes as a "crutch") and does not make typical accommodations. For a highly structured boarding school, Fenster is remarkably affordable, $19,000 a year.

How do they turn kids around? The old-fashioned way. "We monitor academics," Mike said. "Our teachers are paid to identify students daily who need help because they are falling behind, because their grades are slipping or because they haven't turned in homework."

Classrooms are small: There's a ratio of eight students to every one teacher. "So our teachers can push and find the underachieving student," Mike said.

And there are plenty of them. It was the beginning of the 1999–2000 school year when I spoke to him. "Yesterday," he said, "of our one hundred students, we had forty-five who needed 'study table' in the evening. They lost their right to be in their room."

The point of a strict boarding school environment is that it can make a student internalize the structure so when he or she goes off to college it is possible to stay on track. One thing that separates Fenster from most other strict boarding schools, however, is its policy of keeping miscreants on campus.

"Like all schools we have reasonable rules," Mike said. "But unlike other schools we go every step of the way not to kick students out. When students make poor choices, they need to learn boundaries. If they make a mistake, they lose free time, or privileges." (And there's always that 150-acre campus to tend.)

Remember that strict boarding school I sent my son to, the one I took a second job to pay for? The school got him turned around to the point that he was accepted at the Rochester Institute of Technology. And then, six weeks before high school graduation, on the day of the senior prom, he got kicked out for doing something stupid and venal (the Bart side of him asserted itself).

No white pants graduation for him. While he was allowed to finish his course work at home and take his finals with a proctor in New York, he was not allowed back on the Knox campus. All the month of June, whenever I passed a mailbox with balloons tied to it and cars parked outside, I burst into tears because I knew that someone was celebrating a kid's graduation from high school. I never got to do that.

Mike said, "Many of our families are middle income. We deal with grandparents who sometimes have to step in and do something with the grandchildren because their sons and daughters cannot provide the appropriate structure. They reach into retirement funds. We have single mothers who are making every dollar count." As a result, he says, they keep the naughty ones in school, recognizing that acting foolishly is part of these kids' problem. "A lot of our students, if they figured out how to get out of here, they'd be gone," he said.

Mike at first said that any family could replicate what the Fenster School does, if they insist on strict guidelines. "It's very simple," he said. "All they need to do is take an active interest and provide that structure in the afternoon and the evenings that we used to have in this country. My wife quit her job to stay home, and it's been the most fabulous thing for our children. They're not being taught by strangers. You're not having Mom and Dad who are too tired, but say here's Nintendo, here's cable. It's the wrong message. You can take the time, and go over the homework. Discuss the day in school."

Oh, come on, I said. What about mothers who *have* to work? What about parents who try that, and it just doesn't take?

"Okay," he admitted, "sometimes there's blood in the way. It becomes a tug of war in the household. The secret here is that we're not related to the kid. And you can't provide the structure at home if it's not happening at school. Everybody has to pull in the same direction."

And sometimes kids just need to get away from their parents. The Fenster valedictorian for 1999 came to the school from Sacramento. When she arrived with her mother, Mike said, "She was wearing more barbed wire in the admissions office than we have here: a dog collar, spiked hair. She was this little fourteen-year-old girl, all Goth, with a spike through the tongue, her ears. Acting out. Mom was at wit's end."

She came to the school with a 1.5 grade point average at her college prep school. Fenster said it would take her as she was, spikes, boots, dog collar and all, but that she had to shave her multicolored, spiky hair.

"We told her, if you perform up to your potential and make good choices, you can be an individual on this campus," Mike said. "You can dress the way you wish. And so she got away from Mom and for three straight years she had a four-oh average. And she was accepted into Smith College. Artistically, she is the most gifted we've ever had. And when she graduated she was wearing skirts and had normal hair, a brunette. She was very soft on the inside, just a beautiful girl."

Sometimes it takes a tough attitude to make a soft girl.

The Fenster School does not believe in making special considerations for learning differences or ADD. "Because when he graduates from high school his employer doesn't care if he has ADD," Mike said. "I tell parents that on a daily basis. Our mission is to deliver that high school diploma so they can pursue college." And Mike's tough but refreshingly realistic attitude does not stop there.

"If they don't want to pursue college," Mike said, "if they want to take that minimum-wage job or pour espressos, that's great. You have to let them do it. And let them begin to figure it out. How will they get a car? Pay for the insurance? Let them figure it out."

Chapter Six

"I WANT TO GO TO ALASKA"

May the road rise to meet you
May the wind be always at your back
May the sun shine warm upon your face
The rain fall soft upon your fields
And until we meet again
May God hold you
In the hollow of His hand.
—TRADITIONAL IRISH BLESSSING

Take a look at that greeting again.

"May the road rise to meet you"—that's an odd blessing. If the road is rising to meet you, aren't you climbing a hill?

But maybe that isn't such an odd blessing, after all.

It's only by climbing a hill that we can get the long view. And it's only after climbing a hill that we feel a sense of accomplishment. So maybe that's the perfect blessing when sending our kids out into the world: May the road rise up to meet you. In other words, have a good, but not necessarily an easy, time.

Teenagers who have to be reminded five times to take out the garbage want to go off to Australia, to Ireland, to Hong Kong, to South Africa, Greece, India, Thailand, Bali. They want to backpack, hike, get a Eurail pass, stay in hostels, go kayaking. If all else fails, they want to ride their bicycles a hundred miles a day across America. Or at least go camp in Maine.

For those who don't aspire to travel abroad, Alaska always sounds good: It's far away from everything else, most people haven't been there, jobs pay well and for a place where people speak English, it's exotic. What is amazing is that, even if kids can't remember to do their homework, they will somehow survive these travels with a kind of resiliency and resourcefulness they seem incapable of at home.

One young woman I met, Anna Renterswürd of Bromma, Sweden, spent a year on the road, by herself, stopping long enough to work at odd jobs (bartending, cleaning hotel rooms) to make money for the next leg of her trip, which took her from Scandinavia to India and Asia, then to Australia and New Zealand, from there to Los Angeles and cross-country to Boston and New York. She visited with relatives in New York and then headed back to Bromma, where she planned to work just long enough to build up a kitty for another trip. College, she said, could wait.

Her American cousin, Annika Blau, worked as a barmaid in a pub in England, then used that money to travel. She took a train to Edinburgh, where she decided she would take the first bus that came along. That bus took her to St. Andrews, a place she had never heard of. An adult might wonder at the point of just hopping on the first bus that comes along, but that's because adults focus on the destination and kids focus on the journey.

"I got up on the second level of the bus," Annika said, "where you could see in every direction, put my feet up and just took it all in." St. Andrews, in Scotland, turned out to have a wonderful old cathedral with ruins that went down into the sea. "If I hadn't gotten on that bus," Annika said, "I never would have known about that. I still carry the picture of it in my head."

This same young woman, who grew up in New York City and dropped out of Wheaton College in Massachusetts after two years, has also traveled through Europe, gone out West with Outward Bound, and is now thinking of buying a truck and heading for Arizona. She has not yet announced that she wants to live in Alaska, but that may be next.

YOUNG PEOPLE, WHY SO RESTLESS?

The need for children to put some space between themselves and their parents is ancient. In evolutionary terms, it has probably ensured diversity of the species. Certainly there is precedent for it among our nearest relatives.

Among the macaque monkeys there exists something called the male-biased dispersal pattern: Females remain in their family groups; males around sexual maturity move to other groups. "In the wild, this event severs social bonds and exposes the male to new territories and social strangers and increases stress, potential predation, and aggression from conspecifics," the *American Journal of Psychiatry* said in June 1995. "As a consequence, the process of emigration increases mortality and morbidity for the age class of young sexually mature males."

No matter. In fact, macaques who were constitutionally inclined toward risky behavior left the family group at an earlier age. (Think of juvenile delinquents who begin running away from home at twelve.)

And, just as in humans, it's not always just the males who are bolters. "Red colobus monkeys are one of the few primate species in which both females and males leave their natal troop upon reaching adolescence," *Natural History* reported in October 1993. "A young female leaves voluntarily: Her instincts appear to be to mate and raise young in another troop. A young male, however, is forced into exile—he is bullied, mostly by older males, and expelled."

At the dawn of a new century, not many middle-class American children are bullied into leaving their communities. Most of them are eager to get away. Ethan Meers, nineteen, left for the first time at fourteen to do an expedition in the Bighorn Mountains with the National Outdoor Leadership School, based in Lander, Wyoming. Up until that point, he had grown up near Chicago, and the biggest responsibility he had ever had, he said, was making himself a grilled cheese sandwich.

When he graduated from boading school he applied to Princeton University and got in. But instead of enrolling immediately, he deferred for a year. "My college advisor said he wouldn't have accepted himself straight out of high school but he would have a year later," Ethan said. "My mom was especially supportive. It took a while to win my dad over. When I told my grandma I was taking a year off, she told me I was going to be drafted, and she wasn't going to speak to me anymore."

Suddenly he plunged into a NOLS Rocky Mountain semester, at a cost of close to $8,000. It started in early September with twenty-nine days of mountaineering in Wyoming. Then he spent seventeen days caving in the Black Hills of South Dakota, then went down to the canyonland in southern Utah and went back-packing for thirty days. At the end of the semester, he went back to Wyoming for fifteen days of backcountry skiing.

"Look at all this stuff I can do on my own," he said, "like nav-igate through the mountains. There were hard days and group conflicts that had to be resolved. To me it was all foreign. I'd never had to deal with that stuff before. And to deal with it in a suc-cessful manner; it was an incredible experience."

He signed up for a NOLS college-credit course in the nat-ural sciences, but later found out that Princeton would not accept it. Nonetheless, "we had classes every day," he said. "In the semester course, there was a natural history element and first aid and leadership. Classes on different elements of climbing, knots, anchors, lead climbing. I remember in the canyon lands we had a class in having outdoor classes."

But the most important part of the curriculum, he said, was something NOLS calls Expedition Behavior. NOLS sees itself as a school for outdoor leadership, just as its name says. It sends eleven kids out with two or three leaders and lets the kids sort themselves out. "If you have a problem with someone you have to resolve it, or it would have serious effects on our ability to get from place to place over ninety-four days," Ethan said. Initially, the instructors would point out conflicts and tell the kids to fig-ure out a way around them. In the end they were recognizing problems and resolving them on their own.

"It was such a great experience," Ethan said. "I came back ten times more mature." He even tried a solo. "The solo wasn't an official part of NOLS," he said, "but in canyonland we did forty-eight-hour solos and I fasted for seventy-two hours as a personal choice. I had expectations of some sort of vision quest, but in the end I was just cold and hungry."

Children in almost every culture either dream of leaving home or manage to leave home symbolically, in rituals that test them, separate them from their families or allow them to jour-ney inward. For devout Muslims, there is the hadj, the trip to Mecca. In Aboriginal culture in Australia, it's the walkabout, six months solo spent perambulating the outback. In Native American culture, there is the vision quest or the spirit quest, a ritual that involves a young man's journey to a remote spot, accompanied by nothing more than water and perhaps some psychedelic drugs. Among African groups, the rites involve young men going out alone with a weapon to track game. Sometimes the young man is handed a blanket and told to go sit at the top of a mountain and commune with his ancestors.

Whatever the tradition, the young man's departure is accompanied by a ritual "going away" party, since his leaving constitutes a symbolic death. And his return is greeted warmly, since the person who comes back is thought of as a new person.

In American society we do the same thing, but the ritual consists of loading the car with $5,000 worth of electronic gear and clothing and dropping the young man or woman off at their dorm. Worse, when we hear from them again, they have not been reborn but are asking for money.

Seriously, each generation needs to feel that it has a transforming experience. For many kids, college just does not cut it.

Moreover, it is the bad luck of the current American generation, those echo baby boomers born starting in 1982, to have grown up during two spectacularly featureless decades. Think of it. In this century every American generation—except for the current one—has been challenged by an era filled with adversity and adventure. Men and women born in the two decades from 1900 to 1920 survived a massive world war (to end all wars) and an influenza pandemic. The next two decades offered up the Roaring Twenties and the Depression. The next era was even more dramatic for the generation Tom Brokaw wrote about in his best-seller: the World War II generation that then saw the threat of communism and the rise of civil rights in the 1950s. Even the twenty years after that had some pizzazz: the birth of a generational clash in the sixties, a divisive war in Southeast Asia, a struggle for women's rights, the sexual revolution, and in the seventies, bad hair and worse clothes. For each of those generations, there was plenty at home to provide excitement. Teenagers didn't need extreme sports or a trip to Alaska to feel challenged.

But here we have a generation, being launched into a new century, that suffers from a lack of nothing, a surfeit of comforts. There aren't even that many political distinctions to argue about. For them, the biggest argument is IBM or Macintosh, the biggest moral quandary is paper or plastic, the biggest crisis when the cable goes out.

Is it any wonder that children born at the beginning of the 1980s might be ready for something more exciting than entrance into college? As one young man who barely graduated from Packer Collegiate, a private school in Brooklyn, told me, "I just want to get a ticket and fly as far away as possible. And then I want to work my way back." This young man said he had no intention of going to college. "I hate school," he said.

Colleges, of course, know all about kids and their travel jones; that's what junior year abroad is all about, an enticement to stick it out through the first two years of college. But some kids, constitutionally, can't wait.

For some of those, a couple of weeks in Outward Bound (www.outwardbound.org) over the summer will do. Outward Bound is one of those programs that grew up in the United States in the sixties, combining getting in touch with oneself and with nature. Most baby boomers didn't hear about it until the eighties, when corporations began sending executives to a short form of the program so they would learn to "trust" each other. But the program has roots back in World War II, when a German refugee named Kurt Hahn taught English merchant seamen survival skills for an attack at sea.

Hahn's course involved a lot of climbing walls with ropes and relying on each other, which gave the seamen better odds of being picked up after a torpedo strike. There are still ropes and walls (and an emphasis on teamwork) in today's Outward Bound courses, although the organization offers 750 different courses (some of them for college credit) in everything from sea kayaking to wilderness expeditions to white-water rafting. The courses are not cheap, running about the same as a private college, from $800 to $1,000 a week. Outward Bound's courses tend toward the lengthy; their rule of thumb is that someone needs to experience a two-week course to have a transforming experience. And much of the transformation comes at the end, when participants "solo" in the wilderness (remember the spirit quest?), fasting or living off the land for a day or two. For many of these kids, it's the first time they've been alone, without a Walkman, a TV or a computer to distract them. The effect can be powerful.

Around 10,000 people a year (both teens and adults) go

through Outward Bound, the leader in attracting young people, who, according to the *Wall Street Journal* (July 24, 1997), account for about $50 million to $75 million in revenue a year for adventure travel. The program has now seen itself overshadowed by a host of other programs that offer shorter courses, rougher courses or less hoo-ha about "personal growth" and more challenge to survive in a tough environment.

The National Outdoor Leadership School (www.nols.edu) was started in 1965 in Lander, Wyoming, by Paul Petzoldt, who had helped start the Colorado Outward Bound school. A public television documentary in 1969 helped propel the school into prominence, not just as a place where Outward Bound leaders could be trained but as a program that would teach outdoor skills and self-reliance to everyone. NOLS offers sixty different courses that last from ten days to a semester-long course that is worth from ten to twelve college credits. "We have eight hundred students doing a full semester with us," said Bruce Palmer, director of admissions and marketing for NOLS. "That runs about $7,500 to $9,000, depending on the course." The youngest age group they work with is fourteen to fifteen years old; at sixteen most of the more strenuous courses are open to teens. Like Outward Bound, NOLS is not limited to the United States. One NOLS program is in Kenya, another in Patagonia. The largest is in the Rockies, and there is also an Alaska branch.

Kelly Brown, eighteen, from Boise, Idaho, participated in a Rocky Mountain semester at NOLS, which she credits with helping her deal with what she perceived as a weight problem. "I went in and thought, 'In three months I'll know what to do with my life.' And I came out as confused as ever. I still don't know what I want to do careerwise. But I came out of it with self-confidence and so much self-assurance and a value system about what I wanted and what I could give."

She credits her peers and the camp spirit and also the simplicity of the concept: "All you have to do is survive. Get from point A to point B and survive. There were no other distractions going on in my head."

The result was that "for three months I felt pretty," she told me.

"I'm really short, under five feet. And I've always been athletic but never been skinny. I'd always been pretty hard on myself. For the first time I was eating for fuel, and not thinking about it. It was the first time I understood food as fuel. In winter camp we had to eat four thousand calories a day. You had to say, I *need* butter, I need peanut butter. It was very healthy."

Not only that, but Kelly, raised a Catholic, found a renewed faith in the wilderness. "Religion was beaten into my head, and I really despised it," she said. "I had always questioned my faith. I had wondered. Through the three months I definitely found that again. Some of the scenery I saw, the solitude, it helped me believe again, not necessarily in a god but as a link in our lives. I'm a lot more peaceful now. With the scenery and the wild animals, you can't help but believe in God," she said.

She said that in the high school she attended, "the idea of learning was totally stripped from me; I didn't think anything was interesting." After completing the NOLS course, she said, "I have a thirst. I'm excited for the education." She is attending Regis University, a small Catholic coed school in Denver.

But for some families there is one serious count against programs like NOLS and Outward Bound: the cost. There are young people who work for six months to save the $2,000 to $3,000 it would cost to take a short outdoor course, and yes, they might pick up three college credits. But that same amount would pay for an entire semester at a public college. For a lot of parents, a better option is something like six months or a year spent on a kibbutz in Israel. Today working on a kibbutz does not necessarily mean planting trees or growing figs; some kibbutzes specialize in building electronics.

Going to a kibbutz to refinish furniture or work in an electronics plant is, in some ways, like taking an apprenticeship. In the eighteenth century in Europe young people went on what was called the *Wanderjahr*—literally, the wander year. A young apprentice would travel from master craftsman to master craftsman, studying different techniques before settling down to work as a journeyman. (Even the word "journeyman" indicates someone who has spent time as an apprentice, traveling and learning a skill.)

Danny Siegle, a delightful young man who grew up in North Carolina, can credit his *Wanderjahr* with taking him around the world, and perhaps providing a career. But the fact that he was not going to go straight to college came as a shock to his mother, Kathleen Siegle.

Danny Siegle had attended the North Carolina School of

Science and Math, a very selective public two-year boarding school in Durham, that provided a first-rate education to those who passed a rigorous test. Everyone at the school was smart. And everyone at the school, Danny said, went straight on to college. That was expected.

Kathleen got the news that Danny did not want to go to college—yet—while walking along the Seine. No, the family was not rich. She had taken Danny with her to Europe to visit another son who was stationed in the military. "Danny and I had backpacked and were staying in a hostel, near the Eiffel Tower," she said. And that was where he dropped the bomb, that he preferred not to go to the University of North Carolina, in Chapel Hill. "Danny's one of five," his mother said. "We've always said we'll help with education, but they had to choose an in-state school. He was accepted to Hampshire College. He wanted a smaller liberal arts school, where you could choose your own curriculum. He got scholarships, but it wasn't enough."

Chapel Hill, he felt, was too big. He just didn't feel ready. Instead, he said, he wanted to go out and see the world.

I asked his mother what she said in response. "I was just listening," she said. "I knew he would be going back to school."

Most parents would not be so calm or so reflective. But one thing Mrs. Siegle has learned to do is listen. "I think there's this desire not to be in a path not your own," she said carefully, "and some people know that sooner. And take these brave steps."

She believes children should choose a life's work that is akin to play. "I tell my kids, go back and imagine what you did all day when you were five years old. I think you get some clues as to what kind of work you want to do from that."

It is with this laissez-faire attitude that she has piloted all of her children successfully through postsecondary educations, although several of them took unusual time-outs and detours, including her oldest son, Brian, who spent a year and a half playing drums between his master's degree and his Ph.D.

"My parents lived through the Depression," she told me. "I don't think they understand it. They might think kids don't know what they want. But ultimately, I think they are delighted in the way my children chose paths out of the ordinary."

So let's hear about this experience from Danny's point of view. "I went from a neighborhood with eighty-year-olds," he said, to boarding school in Durham, where he learned a lot and slept only a little. "It was one of the best things that ever happened to me," he said, but there was also pressure to get on with college. "In that sort of culture it's hard, because it's assumed that you go. I applied to five colleges, got into four. Carolina was my last choice. The others were small and private, but they were too expensive. It looked as if Carolina was a default option.

"So I decided to defer. I felt I didn't know enough about the outside world. I'd been in a very controlled environment."

Typical of the kind of Rashomon aspect of storytelling in any family, Danny did not remember his mother's reaction as being quite so benign. "My parents were concerned," he told me. "We had long talks in the living room. I knew I would go to college, I just wanted to take a year off. People were skeptical, and said, 'Oh, you'll never go.' And people worried about the international thing. I wanted to travel. I'd read about foreign lands. It was all seeing what the world was really like."

There was one hitch. He had no money. So he spent five weeks living at home in Winston-Salem and working as a pizza deliveryman. That gave him enough money to buy a plane ticket to Seattle. At that point, he didn't have much planned. Just: fly to Seattle, find work, maybe on a boat, see the world. Then come back in time to start school a year later.

That kind of open-ended plan, in the hands of an eighteen-year-old, would scare most parents to death. Kathleen drove her son to the airport. She found herself searching for just the right words to say to him, that kind of accepting, we-love-you and whatever-happens-happens kind of statement that leaves room for the eighteen-year-old to call in a few days and ask for someone to bail him out.

So here is what she said as she waved good-bye: "I know," she said, "that the same winds that blow you away will bring you back."

"For me to say those words to him," she said, and paused. What she felt at that moment was this: that even if he didn't come back, that was not a reason for him not to leave.

Danny picked up his story. "I needed money to travel," he said irreverently, "and didn't know anyone in the drug business."

So he went down to the dock in Seattle and got a job as a cook on a fishing boat. "Luckily they didn't ask me if I knew how to cook. They asked me if I *liked* to cook. I knew how to boil water."

He lasted four months, and worked, by his own calculation, a hundred hours a week. "So I learned a lot about the real world there." But working a hundred hours a week meant that in four months he had saved $10,000. When the fishing boat landed in Japan, it was Christmas, and the company gave him a round-trip ticket home. He flew back to North Carolina to assure his family that he was fine, then returned to Japan to begin the rest of his adventure. By his calculation, he had seven months before school started, and he had to stretch the remaining $6,000 over that time, while traveling around the globe.

(This is one reason why the young should go out and see the world; they can sleep in hovels and hostels, camp out, crash on someone's pool table and consider it a wonderful time. Never again will so little money stretch so far.)

"I spent a lot of time in China," Danny said, "and Tibet, Pakistan, Jordan, Israel, Greece, Albania (one of my faves), Serbia, Hungary. I went straight through Europe—Germany, Switzerland—then flew home from London a week before school started. And then I entered school just like I told everyone I would."

He concluded, "I could have taken a year off and been a pizza delivery boy, but that would have depressed me."

When he told kids at school about his adventures, "everyone said, 'I'd love to do that.' But they don't," he said. "They say, 'I'm not that brave.' I'm not brave either, but I backed myself into a corner."

Danny took time out from college to teach in Turkey and Scandinavia. For him college was an intermittent experience, and although he graduated from Chapel Hill, he sometimes sounds as though he wasn't sure why. "I wanted to go to college after I traveled because I wanted to understand things," he said. "But whereas I had a lot of experiences, in college it was a lot of sterile theories that didn't match the world I knew."

One of the problems, he said, was being at a big state school, with lecture classes of two hundred students and, as he put it, "classes where they just talk at you."

"Students there don't care about the education," he said. "It's whatever they have to do to get the piece of paper. They're not interested in learning."

He remembered taking a geography course in which the grade depended on how much "seat time" the students would spend with "really slow computers, fixing up their maps."

"The people who had all day would fix it one way and fix it another way," he said. "So it was whoever could sit there longer. The professor was really old and he didn't care. Those who would sit for eight hours would get an A, and those who would sit for six hours would get a B."

One thing that bothered him was the fact that students at Chapel Hill seemed obsessed with jobs. "They all wondered: How do I get this job? For them university was just a big job fair. No one was interested in the questions I wanted answered. I wondered why they were the way they were and why I was the way I was."

For a while he saw getting his college degree as, as he put it, "a stepping-stone to get a job I wouldn't want.

"It was just too easy to get a degree," he said. "It was a kind of fill-in-the blank degree, and at the end I said, 'I don't even want this.'" That was about two months before his college graduation. He got through that crisis by rationalizing that he needed the degree to get back on a fishing boat as an observer. And, he said, "I was afraid of getting into debt. If I didn't finish I couldn't get this job, and then it would take me a long time to pay off the debt and I wouldn't be as free."

And so Danny got his degree in biology in June 1999 and immediately bought a motorcycle and drove it cross-country to Seattle, where he began training as an observer for the National Marine Fisheries Service. The training lasted three weeks and he got a certificate as a groundfish observer, a job that paid about $100 a day. His contracts last for three months each, and the first one will pay off all his remaining debts from college. The second three-month contract will give him another $10,000. "If I put that in the bank, then I don't have to worry," he said. "Basically, it's a security thing. 'What if you get sick?' A million things could happen. So if I just put the money in the bank, I can fend off those arguments."

Danny said that he did not really need a college degree to be an observer on a fishing boat. "You just need to be a fairly intelligent person," he said. "I didn't know a lot about fish, and they train you to identify them." Halibut, salmon, pollack, Pacific cod, flatfish. If he wants to work through the winter, he said, he would have to get certified in Alaskan king crab.

Perhaps he was in a sour mood the last time I got him on the phone in Dutch Harbor in the Aleutians, the biggest fishing harbor in the world, where he had put in for a few days. But several months after graduation, Danny did not sound as if he was happy about earning a diploma. As he put it: "You go to class so you can get the answers to the test. And if you think you're smart enough, you don't go to class."

When employers ask for a college degree, he said, "it's just a way to weed out people and it signifies that you're able to put up with a lot of crap for four years."

Then again, he said, "I certainly wouldn't be the person I am now if I didn't go to college. I certainly wouldn't be reading the stuff I read now. Political philosophy issues."

For the time being, he said, he just wanted to read for a while. And if he gets bored, he says, he knows of a school in Kazakhstan where they need people to teach English.

"I'm not here because Alaska is an amazing place. It's an independent job and there's so much money. And there's no one above me ordering me around. And it just happens to be in Alaska." When I asked him about the danger, he said flippantly, "It takes a lot to sink a boat."

What's that old blessing? May the road rise up to meet you, Danny. And the seas stay calm.

Chapter Seven

THE COLLEGE CONUNDRUM

*Today's students represent a generation of pragmatists who want
knowledge that they can apply to their lives. They are looking for
skills and certification, and they view the professors' opinions
as interesting at best and annoying at worst.*
—ZACHARY KARABELL (1998), *WHAT'S COLLEGE FOR?:
THE STRUGGLE TO DEFINE AMERICAN HIGHER EDUCATION*

So what is college? Is it the place where we sort out the haves and
have-nots, one group to the Ivy League, another to state universities? Or is it community college, where "regardless of class, race or
even prior academic performance, any American citizen and any
immigrant living in the United States can attend college and earn
a degree," as Zachary Karabell says in his book *What's College For?*

Is a college defined as a place with professors who have Ph.D.s?
Then what about people like Fran Reiter, a college dropout who
teaches in a graduate school at New York University?

Is it the Culinary Institute of America, where students wear
their chef's whites as they run from "Breakfast Cookery" to
"Caterina de Medici Kitchen," one and a half credits each? (The
Institute offers bachelor's degrees in either Baking and Pastry Arts
or Culinary Arts.) Is it the Fashion Institute of Technology in
Manhattan, which offers a bachelor's degree in clothing design?

Is it Jones International University, which allows someone to finish a bachelor's degree on the Internet? Is it Ziff–Davis University, which also offers courses on the Internet, and then allows the student to print out a certificate for satisfactory work?

What about a school that gives liberal "life credits" for raising children (psychology and social sciences), travel (political science) or reading popular novels (literature). The procedure, which is a kind of benign selling of indulgences, attracts students to colleges. "It's a scam," David Denman, an independent educational counselor in California, said. "They charge for it. Many programs have their fee and if you want credit it's an add–on, for which the college does damn near nothing."

Is it Dell University, the corporate online program to train new employees at Dell Computer? If you say yes to that, then what about the university at Caesar's World? What about Hamburger U, the training facility for McDonald's workers? There were 1,600 corporate "universities" in 1998, which offer their employees programs from lifestyle management to foreign languages to M.B.A.s and computer courses; corporations offer courses because they feel that university courses are not specific enough for their needs. If an employee graduates from one of these programs, does he have a college education?

What about the Audubon Expedition Institute, which offers, with Leslie College in Boston, an ecology degree for little more than riding around on a bus and talking to the Navaho about dam building, and to fishermen about fish? Or Ryerson Polytechnic University in Toronto, which offers degrees in hotel management, journalism and chemical engineering, as well as a bachelor of applied arts in apparel production management or one in hospitality and tourism management?

Defenders of college education as a time of rigorous intellectual challenge are either thinking of elite institutions, which may or may not still provide a classic education, or they have not been on any college campus in the last several decades. In the thirty years since the baby boomers threw out the *in loco parentis* rules and the core curriculum, college has changed. And it has changed primarily toward the more practical. In fact, the cover of Ryerson Polytechnic University's marketing booklet touts "Education *and* Experience."

Meanwhile, liberal arts colleges are languishing (students

don't see the point). At universities, college students make it clear they are of a practical mind. They want to be entertained in class (and grade their teachers accordingly). They want good grades no matter what the level of their work (and harass a teacher who gives them low marks). They don't like writing papers (and make that clear in grading their professors as well). In class, before the professor can finish his sentence, the students want to know whether a fact will be on the test. If the answer is no, the pens go down. That is, if the students are taking notes at all, and not using the commercially prepared notes offered by the student association. (It's far more practical to listen in class—or wait to be entertained—than to spend the hour furiously scribbling in a notebook.)

The farther down the academic chain you look, the worse the situation is. I had a cabdriver recently who explained that he drove two nights a week to make $500 to supplement his salary at Queensborough Community College, where he taught philosophy.

"My students," he said, "cannot write a paper. If I assign something on Plato's cave, I know they will just retype what it says in the Cliffs Notes, no footnotes, no other sources, nothing. The ones who do a good job of typing, with only a few spelling errors, get the A's. The others get the B's. It's a joke."

With so many high school students going off to college, something about the college experience had to change. And it did. College became not only more practical, it became dumber.

"College has become a default decision. Tons of unprepared high school graduates are shoveled into four-year colleges," Kenneth Gray, a professor of education at Pennsylvania State University, said. "But they just don't know why they're there." He was quoted in a 1999 article in *The Christian Science Monitor* titled "Is College for Everyone?" The article, by Mark Clayton, made clear that the answer is no. It noted that critics of the current educational climate say, "the bachelor's degree is being oversold to many high-schoolers who do not truly want the experience, or have only a slim chance of attaining a four-year degree."

There is a growing body of opinion that college has become something of a sham. And the people holding that opinion are often themselves academics. Zachary Karabell has taught at Harvard University and Dartmouth. A friend of mine who taught

Latin at Harvard simply rolled his eyes at the notion of its elite student body. "They never wanted to do any work, and they would argue with me all the time about their grades," he said. He left teaching for the friendlier shores of journalism. Another friend who teaches film studies complains about his students' dismay that they are going to have to watch films "with writing on the bottom" (that is, foreign films) and not sit there watching *There's Something About Mary.*

"We take our best and our brightest out of the population for four years at the peak of their youth, and we put them in a holding place called college," Larry Griffith, dean of admissions at the University of Delaware, told me. "It is because of our economic success that allows us that luxury." That same economic success has allowed us also to send our second-best and not-brightest, as well as the students who would be far happier learning to build a chest of drawers, or how to made a good risotto.

Landon Y. Jones identified the reasons for the problems with college twenty years ago in his book *Great Expectations:* "The easing of admissions requirements, the new emphasis on retaining students in academic difficulty, grade inflation, the abolishment of required courses, the stress placed on vocational and professional studies, pass-fail, the promoting of 'popular' courses within departments to protect faculty staffing and so on."

Take a look at what college students are studying these days. It's not English or history or Latin or political science. Business was the number-one undergraduate bachelor's degree awarded in the most recent year profiled by the Center for Education Statistics. Second was the social sciences. Third was education.

What is interesting to me is that, while the kids are opting for practical degrees, they are in many cases aiming too high in their ambitions. Most of those business students will have spent years studying how large corporations work; those from lesser institutions are going to get work, at best, managing the local Safeway or toiling in a Kafkaesque insurance company somewhere. Far from being masters of the universe, they will be lucky if they are masters of their own desk spaces. (Some companies have learned to economize by assigning desks to whoever happens to be there that day.)

And then there are all those fluffy degrees—communications, marketing, media studies, theater, costume design—being offered within four-year academic institutions. Does it make sense to pay $25,000 a year for four years to study costume design?

YOU CALL IT COMMUNICATIONS, I CALL IT JOURNALISM

There is a debate in the academic world about whether journalism is too academic a course or too practical. Is journalism a trade or is it a profession?

"Essentially, an extensive amount of skills work in a university broadcast journalism program curriculum was viewed a decade ago as too 'practical,'" Andrew T. Ceperley wrote in the spring 1999 issue of the *Journal of Career Planning and Employment*. "Today, it is viewed as valuable for graduates searching for their first TV news jobs. However, most programs are still hesitant to implement an extensive lab experience."

Part of that fear is reluctance to be seen as offering a *trade* school experience instead of a university experience. While students are bored out of their skulls by theory and would far rather be making a music video, universities want to make sure that their courses are still academically rigorous.

And this despite the fact that news directors and editors, people in a position to hire new students, consistently placed experience above academics in hiring. I am sure there were shock waves through every journalism school in the country when the Thomson newspaper group announced in 1999 that it was going to train local people in Wisconsin (no experience necessary) to be reporters in twelve weeks. The program was modeled on a similar one used in England. The idea was to get people who already knew the local scene to cover board meetings and neighborhood news. Most of the first applicants already had college degrees; many had graduate degrees. When they completed training they would be working for minimum wage, and be committed to working for the papers for twenty-one months.

And yet when I tell a young friend who is studying English and wants to be a journalist that he will probably have to start on a small city weekly covering local news, he just looks askance. He sees himself as traveling abroad, covering international affairs. He doesn't believe that he will have to start somewhere and work his way up.

If students are media majors, they expect to be a newscaster, or at least a producer on a network television show. The creative writing students all want to be novelists. The journalism majors want to write reviews or personal essays.

Faced with the fact that, as Leo Buscaglia said, "the majority of us lead quiet unheralded lives as we pass through this world," these students would rather stay in school, where they can pretend they are headed for greatness, rather than go out in the harshly competitive world, and find out they are not.

According to a mass communications journal, in 1996 there were 149,256 students enrolled in journalism and mass communications courses in colleges in this country. Communications certainly seems to be the preferred career choice for Miss America contestants. But what do the rest of the enrolled students hope to do with their degrees? They may get low-paying jobs in television as gofers. More likely they will end up writing press releases for the Wallpaper Council, or becoming the "press office" (a one-person job) for a small company, earnestly writing about the upcoming employee dinner dance.

THE CANADIAN WAY

Ryerson Polytechnic University in Toronto interested me because it represents a middle way, a cross between a vocational school and an elite academic institution. I think of it as the Canadian Harvard of applied education.

Up until five years ago, Ryerson was limited to granting diplomas and certificates, not bachelor's degrees. Now, in a more liberal era, it has bachelor's degree programs in everything from aerospace engineering (bachelor of engineering, or B.Eng.) to midwifery (bachelor of health sciences, or B.H.Sc.).

It is a school whose brochure will list on facing pages industrial engineering (first year: calculus I and II, chemistry, digital computation and programming, engineering graphics and design, linear algebra, materials science fundamentals, physics I and II, statistics and liberal studies) and interior design (communications I and II, design dynamics, design technology I and II, history of design, interior design studio, philosophy of design, liberal studies).

Ryerson recently added a bachelor of commerce degree for a program in retail management and another in information technology management, as well as a bachelor of applied arts degree in disability studies.

I spent a day with Bill Lougheed, the former director of Ryerson's School of Hospitality and Tourism Management, and with Ira Levine, dean of Ryerson's School of Applied Arts, which includes journalism, a school of radio and television, theater (including dance, acting and technical production), interior design, fashion, graphic communications management (B. Tech.) and image arts (film, new media and photography). Ira had to pull out a brochure and check them off to keep them straight.

It was a sparkling fall day in Toronto, and the large campus close to downtown was brimming with kids hurrying through quads and between brick buildings to get to their classes.

THE NIGHT CLERK SOLUTION

The School of Hospitality and Tourism Management is located in, not an old brick building, but a hotel; in fact, during the summer it turns itself into a conference center, and students stay on to get some practical experience as desk clerks and other hotel workers. Bill Lougheed, who sports an imposing gray pompadour, picked me up at my own hotel and drove me to the school.

"We basically started as what you have referred to as a trade school," Bill said. "Originally Ryerson was set up that way, and then just gradually got into the diploma program in different areas," due to, he said, "the skills or the success stories, if you will, of some of the people that have gone into certain fields." He was talking about Ryerson's engineering graduates, who were found, essentially, to be running Ontario. First the engineers got their bachelor's degrees, then the entire school became accredited for the bachelor's degree.

Bill and I sat talking in a noisy cafeteria, where students not only ate but practiced their hospitality skills. The four-year Hospitality and Tourism Management program has more than five hundred students, with new minors in marketing and human relations and communications. Students need to fulfill liberal arts requirements, but, Bill noted, since Canada still offered a thirteenth year of school (what is called senior matriculation, an echo of the A levels in Britain), most of the students came well prepared.

Many of the students transfer in from academic secondary

institutions after two years. "They can see that they're getting jobs when they graduate from this school," he said.

His graduates have joined the Delta Hotel chain, the Four Seasons and other international chains. Some end up in managerial positions. Some become concierges for corporations. Some open restaurants, go into developing resorts or become consultants. An assistant hotel manager in America in 1996 earned an average of $40,000 a year. General managers averaged $54,000, and often earned bonuses of up to 25 percent of their salary. Sometimes they also received free lodgings for them and their family, as well as meals, parking, laundry and other services.

First-year classes include business information systems, dimensions of the food service industry, financial accounting, food and beverage management systems, lodging organization and operations, property management systems, service and professionalism, tourism concepts and liberal arts.

Students at the school are evenly divided between male and female. About 15 percent of the student population is Asian, and another 5 to 10 percent is from the Caribbean. Because many Canadians know French as well as English, they are popular in the international hotel trade. ("And they say we have a good Canadian work ethic," Bill added.)

But because Canada is a melting pot, Bill's school also offers job candidates who speak Spanish and Portuguese, Hebrew, Arabic, Mandarin, Cantonese and a dozen other languages. Graduates of his program may go on to master's degrees in hospitality at Michigan State, the University of Denver, George Washington University, the University of Toronto or Cornell, which gives Ryerson graduates credit toward a master's degree for courses they have taken in their fourth year. Tuition for Canadian students runs about $5,000 (Canadian); for American and foreign students it is around $11,000 a year (Canadian), which translates to about $7,500 American.

Because students are required to have 2,000 hours of related experience working for two different companies before they graduate, the hospitality school has a large job center, with about fifty postings a week. And because hotels are open twenty-four hours a day, many of those positions are at night, which is perfect for full-time students. "You do studying, you get a lot of that copying done and everything at night," Bill said. "The kids know how to work around that."

The biggest problem, Bill says, is that his school has such an excellent employment office, students from other parts of Ryerson come over and poach the listings. "You know, there's a gratuity situation, where they pass the bucks, and there are entrepreneurial areas that open themselves," he said. "My students aren't competing with other hotel students, they are competing with Ryerson's business majors for these jobs, and with kids studying to be doctors and lawyers."

THE CREATIVE ALTERNATIVE

Hospitality may have something of a ring of servility about it. Not so artistic areas like dance or acting or graphic design. A few blocks away, through a vaulted archway and away from the street, is the office of Ryerson's dean of the School of Applied Arts, Ira Levine, who has 2,700 students in seven programs, all of which offer four-year degrees.

"Ryerson is the only Canadian polytechnic, whereas both Great Britain and Australia have a whole secondary sector known as the polytechnic," Ira told me. "We actually have more in common with them than we do with a lot of the other universities in Canada."

He noted, however, that in Ontario there is a postsecondary system called CAATE, encompassing the Colleges of Applied Arts and Technology, which function more or less like the American community colleges.

"There may be more of those than there are universities," he said. The state-sponsored CAATE schools offer diplomas for programs that last from one to three years. "But they focus on applied skills, all sorts of electronics, you name it. It runs the gamut from the most blue-collar-type deals to advanced fields to advanced multimedia design.

"So there's a tremendous breadth of non-degree-based education," he said. "And this university used to occupy kind of a middle ground between the colleges and the university sector."

Now Ryerson has joined the universities in granting bachelor's degrees; it is launching master's and doctoral programs in the year 2000.

In Canada, he said, the pressure for more practical education was coming from the government as well as the students. "A lot of pressure is coming from the current conservative government and its particular ideology; one current is the growing emphasis upon applied education," he said. "Their emphasis is on targeted funding for hi-tech deals, and in particular computer science. But they are pressuring all the universities, including the most conventional and highly respected arts and science institutions like the University of Toronto, Queens University and others, to justify their programs. Justify their programs in terms of economics."

Ira told me that the notion of nonconventional students was "highly pertinent to an institution like Ryerson." He estimated that half of his students are over twenty-one when they come to Ryerson. "How do you know what you want to do at seventeen?" he said.

"Your basic thesis is our reality here," he said. "We have about thirty-seven to forty different professional programs; in order to get in students have to demonstrate a very strong commitment to the particular professional field. And most of the programs are quite competitive. Mine in particular. We accept one of fifteen or twenty students." Many of those students already have a university degree in an academic subject before applying to the journalism school or the School of Television and Radio Arts. Those students need only take a two-year course to get a second bachelor's degree from Ryerson.

The tuition for students who come from outside Canada is $11,500 Canadian, about $8,000 American, a year, which is reasonable, especially for programs that require a great deal of equipment, like film and television production.

"Admission is very, very competitive, partly because we have a very good reputation, and partly because we're the only game in town in many areas like radio and television," he said. "And we have the best journalism program by far."

One innovation at Ryerson is to put the more artistic side of computer technology with the arts schools. That means that web design resides under Dean Levine, not in the school of computer science. It also means that someone studying at the School of Television and Radio Arts could cut a CD in one of the school's recording studios, then collaborate with other students to make the CD packaging, stream the music up onto the web with MP3 technology, set up a website, then film a music video to promote the CD. That is done at Ryerson all the time. The idea is for the students to do hands-on work under professional supervision, almost like an apprenticeship. "That's exactly the goal, experiential education," Ira said.

"We have a lot of web-based work in journalism and radio-television as well," he said, "because of the conversions going on in those areas."

Needless to say, because of the demand in some areas, he loses students before graduation. "Attrition is very high," he said.

But, he noted, a school's retention rate is not always the best way to judge its success. Are the students staying because the degree is worth it, or because they can't get a job? "A retention rate may indicate something good about the school or it may indicate something bad about the school," Ira said.

I liked Ira's practical bent, which seemed so alien to much of American higher education. "We don't teach people how to write," he said. "We don't give people the talent to write. We do, however, extend their writing to different media.

"The film school," he said, "they go to that school to become film editors, filmmakers, cinematographers. They stay the fourth year, or leave after the third year, if they're good enough. Often the degree is there for those who *aren't* good enough."

Four 1980s graduates of Ryerson's acting program are now working in Hollywood. David James Elliott stars in the television drama *JAG*. Marc Gomes appeared as a detective in the television series *The Crow*. Eric McCormack is the costar of the television sitcom *Will & Grace*. And Marice Godin was on the sitcom *Working* and on *Seinfeld*.

As a technical school, Ryerson uses many teachers who are not themselves holders of advanced degrees; 60 percent of the faculty is full time, 40 percent part time. What counts in schools of applied education is ability and experience. Particularly in theater, he says, most of his faculty has a practical rather than academic background.

"It is a good thing that my own background transcends the conventional arts and sciences institutions, because I'm a product of them." (He worked as the general manager of a resident theater company at the St. Lawrence Center for the Arts in Toronto and also ran a modern dance company before coming to Ryerson.) Instead of looking only at degrees, he is also looking for at least twenty years of experience in his teachers.

"A new full-time hire is unlikely to be under forty-five," he said.

He offered to walk me around the Rogers Communications Centre, the school's laboratory for new media, journalism, television, radio and recording arts. "This is a complex that astounds everyone who visits from the educational sector," he said. "Students need access to our studios, and our computer labs, and our editing suites, often through the night." And indeed, there are kids everywhere, sitting at editing boards, in private suites, putting on web-based radio shows. The school has a couple of full-sized television studios, a set-building workshop, a props room, recording studios, computers everywhere, all within a coolly modern building with a two-story central hall.

One young woman he introduced me to, Liz Gesicki, attended Ryerson after working as a nurse. Now she is on staff as a full-time lab assistant. She constantly gets calls from people who need a Ryerson student, quickly, for a job editing film footage. "I'll go around to my best students to see if they want the job," she said, "but they've all already got jobs. If they're good, they're working professionally, even while they study here."

PROFESSIONS OR JOBS?

"There is the primary labor market, the jobs that have some stability and clear educational requirements, pay a decent wage and have fringe benefits and an opportunity for development and the salaries keep going up," said Kenneth D. Hoyt, University Distinguished Professor in the Department of Counseling, Education and Psychology, Kansas State University, in Manhattan, Kansas. "Those are the jobs people want."

Instead, he says, kids come out of high school with no skills, often having barely absorbed any of the academic fundamentals like writing and basic math. They are the ones who get the secondary jobs—"low pay, dead end, no fringe benefits, just jobs," he said.

Kids will take those jobs because they want fast money, but the jobs will ultimately lead nowhere. That doesn't mean that Ken Hoyt believes that everyone should go to college. Far from it. He is in fact this country's number-one proponent of career education, something he has been involved in since 1958.

I asked him if it ruffled any academic feathers that he was ensconced at a university while saying that people don't need to go to a university. "Other people get bothered by it," he said. "I don't. I say yes, there may well be a surplus of four-year college graduates. It's not the best thing for all kids to do. The best thing they can do is get *some* kind of postsecondary education."

Eight years ago, the DeWitt Wallace–Reader's Digest Fund gave Ken and his researchers $3.6 million to study career education in this country. "I have data on forty thousand cases, and I think you can say we've learned something in the last eight years," he said. "I'm writing it all up now." Primarily, he says, kids have a hard time knowing what training to get because they don't know what jobs are available, therefore they don't know what questions to ask. Witness the number of people in this book who finish one college degree only to turn around and start at a trade school to get the training they need.

I told him that when my son was eighteen, I just assumed he would go to college. "You're like 91 percent of parents in this country, who think their kids should go to a four-year college," he said. "Look at all the jobs that will be available between 1996 and 2006 and 70 percent of them do *not* require a college degree.

"I started researching this in 1958, when the National Defense Education Act said we should funnel all intellectually gifted students toward college. I was a professor at the University of Iowa, training counselors. And I objected to the National Defense Education Act from the beginning, because counseling is for *all* of the children. I started talking about counseling kids who don't go to a four-year college." In the 1970s, Kenneth Hoyt was director of the Office of Career Education for the federal government.

That office "was abolished during the Reagan administration," he said. For his new study, in which he looked at students in postsecondary career education in fifteen states, he first asked high school students what they wanted to know about work, then asked postsecondary students to explain what they were studying and how it could be applied. "Who do kids listen to?" he asked rhetorically. "Their *peers*."

He has issued his data on computer disks to school counselors in the fifteen states. "The Wallaces have been very nice to me," he said. "We distributed all those disks for free."

"If these kids are fully informed, they will make good career decisions," he said. "We don't emphasize so much *what* a person chooses as *that* a person chooses. It's the value of reasoned decision-making. What the kid decides doesn't matter, it's *that* he decides." That may seem a fatuous distinction, unless you, like me, have a child who is paralyzed by indecision.

Most children don't know what they want to do. They just know they want to make a decent wage, and want to be able to say what they do without being embarrassed about it.

Barbara Ehrenreich outlined their situation in her dissection of middle-class aspirations, *Fear of Falling*. "If you talk to them," she said, referring to students, "they will tell you with a frightening degree of similarity that they want to work in an area where they do not answer to anyone else, where they are free to make decisions and be leaders, where they are free to think and possibly help people and most important where they can earn a good living. In other words, they want to be professionals.

"Professions, as opposed to jobs, are understood to offer some measure of intrinsic satisfaction, some linkage of science and service, intellect and conscience, autonomy and responsibility. No one has such expectations of a mere job."

HOW DO YOU GET BEYOND A MERE JOB?

"The professors' and the parents' ideal of the liberal college education is not wrong," said David Denman, an independent educational counselor in California. "It's simply not what the kids have in mind."

Colleges and universities make it easy for students to feel disconnected from the learning process. "I worked with a kid last year at the University of Northern Arizona in Flagstaff, where the professor began the year by saying, 'You don't have to come to class. You can watch it on TV in your room,'" David said. "If the colleges are organizing education primarily on the basis of efficiency rather than excellence, rather than the way they ought to do it, then fine, sell the class notes. Kids shouldn't be in large lecture classes anyway.

"Education at the college level ought to be more active than it is. It's far too passive."

Passive education means sitting in class hearing professors lecture. Active education can mean a small seminar, in which everyone sits around, the way they do at Oxford, or in German high schools, where every student participates.

But it can also mean cooking school or computer school or boat-building school. Somehow over the years doing physical things, especially crafts, became the symbol of anti–intellectualism. Think of how many students announce that their course isn't *basket* weaving. Now, with the pendulum swinging toward making basket weaving part of a Ph.D. program, parents still aren't convinced.

Jake Horne, who runs Interpoints, a time-off program based in Washington Depot, Connecticut, acknowledges that the baby boomers have reverted to a more conservative attitude. "I was a flower child, I was politically groovy," he said. "And my friends have all retrenched. They're scared out of their minds about their kids."

As a result, instead of being open and accepting about their children's search for a path through life, baby boomers have become hysterical about grades and college admissions and careers, meaning professional careers. "We have this angst that our kids need to make money," Jake said. "And the only way to get there is to toe this line. These prep school kids coming down the line, they say 'I'm killing myself to get these SAT scores and doing things so I can go to Princeton and make some money.' The whole sensibility about what learning is, is lost."

Time off, he said, is a structured way to give baby boomers' kids what baby boomers knew how to do naturally. "It's hanging out, like we used to do—'Well, man, what's it all about?' Our kids don't have the opportunity to do that. It scares them."

HANGIN' WITH THE CAKE DECORATORS

Anyone looking for a beautiful campus would have to go pretty far to beat the Culinary Institute of America, in Hyde Park, New York, on the Hudson River. The school was founded in Connecticut after World War II by Katharine Angell and Frances Roth as a way to train returning servicemen.

It moved to a former Jesuit seminary on the Hudson in 1972. Today the school has added new buildings thanks to Anheuser-Busch, General Foods, J. Willard Marriott and Conrad N. Hilton. The day I visited, in midsummer, the school was in full swing. It admits a new class every three weeks and then cycles them through its program, made up of blocks of three-week courses, pretty much year-round. Every three weeks there is a graduation ceremony at the Culinary Institute, complete with a graduation banquet.

The Culinary Institute is accredited to offer a bachelor of applied arts degree, partly because it offers, in addition to its practical courses, a course in "culinary math" (weights and measures) and another one in "world literature," though that one, too, is taught in three weeks. (While some community colleges have not been able to get the coveted "edu" extension for their website, the Culinary Institute's web address is www.ciachef.edu.)

Other schools that give bachelor's degrees for the culinary arts include Johnson and Wales in Providence, Rhode Island; the New England Culinary Institute in Montpelier, Vermont, and Nicholls State University, in Louisiana.

The Culinary Institute of America charges about $16,000 a year in tuition for the first two years, then about $11,000 a year for the next two years (tuition includes two meals a day, and darned good ones, too). Graduates can expect, ten years later, to be making $50,000 a year (and all the Dover sole they can eat).

By comparison, the French Culinary Institute in Manhattan offers a six-month program, without a bachelor's degree attached, for about $23,000. That program, under the chefs André Soltner, Jacques Pepin and Alain Sailhac, says that its graduates, ten years later, are making an average of $65,000 a year.

But for parents hung up on their child's getting a bachelor's degree, the Culinary Institute of America may be the answer. For one thing, the math is easy. No calculus, only weights and measures. And parents will be impressed by the $7.5 million Conrad N. Hilton library (with 55,000 volumes on food) and the fact that Paul Bocuse sent his son Jerome to study at the school. Then there is the 150-acre campus, with class buildings that look more Ivy League than many Ivy League institutions and a number of residence halls. There are two tennis courts with underground watering systems. As the younger set would say, "Sweet!"

The difference between this and a normal college campus is that here the deferential term is "Chef," not "Professor." Even though everyone seems to be dressed in white tunics, a visitor can quickly pick out the ones in charge. Not only are the students obviously alert around them, but they are wearing the CIA's signature green and gold bands around their tunic collars.

The lecture hall where wine appreciation is taught looks like a television set, with steep seating and a lecture area that looks like a plasticized wine cellar in Napa Valley. The day I visited, wine was being passed around during a lecture.

"What do you do with the underage students?" I asked Jeff Levine, the media relations coordinator who took me around that day. "We have a special waiver from New York State for them," he said. The average age of students entering, however, is twenty-four; 12 percent already have bachelor's degrees in other areas.

One of the chefs I met that day was about to go into a cooled room to teach a class in fish butchery. He acknowledged that most of his students had more formal education than he did. He had worked his way up inside the kitchen, not the classroom. Yet the press officer flinched when I asked if the C.I.A. was really a trade school. "It's not a trade school," he snapped. "We give a well-rounded education."

Entering students choose between Culinary Arts, which is 75 percent men, and Baking and Pastry Arts Management, which is 60 percent women. We went into the baking building, where students worked their way through subjects like chocolate and confections and decorated and wedding cakes. The students spend hours working on their penmanship and decorative flourishes in icing. "And sometimes we check their spelling," the press officer said. "One day I walked by and I noticed a student had written 'Happy Birfday.'"

COLLEGE BEFORE MEDICAL SCHOOL, RIGHT?

Fran Lebowitz told me, "I want my doctor to go to college." Is this one place where we can agree that college is necessary?

Not according to Thomas W. Haines, head of the biochemistry department at the Sophie Davis School for biomedical Education (also known as the City University of New York Medical School). "Only Canada and the U.S. have this four year hiatus of college before medical school," he told me. Prof. Haines feel that the last year of high school is a waste and that "at present people should not be exposed to so much college."

He set up the CUNY medical school in 1972 for just that reason, he said. "The idea is that we take students out of high school and start them out with gross anatomy, first year." As for organic chemistry, the make-or-break college course for hopeful medical students, Prof. Haines thinks it is a scam. Organic chemistry, he says, is used to keep college students out of medical school. It predicts success in medical school, he says. "But that's because you have to buckle down. What it tells you is that someone can handle the gobbledygook."

Organic chemistry has very little use in medical school and even less in the medical profession, he says. "It does not tell you what will happen when they are out as a physician, or medical students or interns. Organic chemistry has nothing to do with biochemistry, or very little. What they need to know of organic chemistry, a very short, few-week session would do it."

Tom Haines's students at CUNY are primarily poor, ill-prepared immigrants. But he is a strong believer in open enrollment. "What you need is not high admissions standards, but high standards for the degree," he said. Even if students flunk out, he says, at least they had a chance. "I have failed students in biochemistry, and 90 percent of students who repeat get the same grade the second year. But 10 percent sail through—and you can't predict which ones will do it."

Medical students in his program spend four years at City University, take some of their medical boards, then transfer to a standard medical school. Places like Columbia and New York University Medical Schools get students who have proven themselves capable of succeeding in medical school and passing their boards. "They get minority students and don't have to remediate them," he said.

Tom is extraordinarily proud of his school's 1,000 graduates. "City takes immigrants and turns them into productive American citizens," he said. "I went to a graduation at N.Y.U. for the M.D.'s and all five of the graduates who are black were from our program," he said. "Immigrants are the engine that makes America. It's the third generation after that that is the problem."

Chapter Eight

THE MILLIONAIRE NEXT DOOR WHO NEVER FINISHED COLLEGE

Stockbrokers, lawyers, doctors, dietitians, hairdressers, computer nerds, dermatologists—it used to be their job to provide support for the rich and powerful. Now they are *the rich and powerful."*
—JAMES ATLAS, *TALK* MAGAZINE (SEPT. 1999)

And it's true. There are hair colorists who make a fortune and travel in the highest circles. "My hairdresser had a significant birthday," a woman in Toronto told me, "and flew twenty of his best friends to the south of France to spend a week with him there, celebrating."

Staci Linklater, twenty-seven, is a hairdresser in Las Vegas. She makes $160,000 a year (including tips) by working only three and a half days a week. She owns two homes, and puts the rest of her money into the bank against the day she starts her own salon.

Staci graduated from high school in Las Vegas with honors, "but I never did want to go to college," she told me. "I was watching TV one day and I saw a commercial for cosmetology school, and it was 'Oh my gosh, that's what I want to do.'" She has had the same boyfriend since high school, and he told her that she was too smart to waste her brain on cosmetology school.

"Now he takes back what he said," she told me. "He knows I am extremely successful." Her ads proclaim "Staci Hairstyles for the Hip."

She charges $45 for a wash and a cut. "But it's the coloring that makes the money," she said. "My average client spends $150 on color, and I do ten to fifteen a day. It adds up. It's not the $45 haircut. When I come home and add up my daily totals, it amazes me."

She started at one cosmetology school that closed down and finished at the Nevada Academy for Career Education, which also offered nursing and dental hygiene. "When I enrolled in school there I felt like it was taking my cosmetology career to the next level because I was going to school with nurses," she said. It took her a little over a year to put in the required 1,800 hours to get her license in Nevada. And then she passed her tests in hair and nails and doing faces. "You have to pass all three," she said.

Statistics show that only three out of ten cosmetologists make it through the first two years, she said, and only one of them remains in the field after three years. She knows a lot of kids she went to school with never graduated.

"I think it takes a certain personality to build your clientele and become successful," she said. "It takes people skills. I know I'm not going to be behind the chair ten years from now. I need to take what I've built to the next level."

That high school boyfriend is with her. "He's college educated," she said. "He went for seven years. We've been together for eleven years, and he's reading magazines and books and filling my brain with what he learns."

He took a degree in political science and started a small weekly newspaper in Las Vegas, which he sold. Now he works as a writer.

I asked her if she ever felt condescended to by his friends. "No, I don't feel that," she said. "There are people I come into contact with—lawyers and doctors—that speak in that college-educated sense that's too deep for me. I don't know if it's that it's too deep for me, or is it that I'm not interested in what they're saying? I don't ever feel they are condescending to me to my face. If I wasn't with the person I'm with, it might be a little different."

As Larry Griffith, the director of admissions for the University of Delaware, told me: "There's a snobbery in academia, but there are perfectly legitimate hair salon schools. Some people have a different path." There are hundreds of people out there who make millions of dollars from things like massage therapy, individual physical training, artisanal bread baking, high-end wallpaper hanging, running restaurants.

In this country there are 5 million millionaires, including a number like the media mogul Ted Turner, who was thrown out of Brown University twice, once for partying, and the second time for having a girl in his room. People who have their mojo working hardly need college to make them competitive.

OK, A LIST

Here are some people who did not complete college: Edward Albee (although his work is taught in college), Paul Allen (computers, you know), Woody Allen (did it stop him?), Wally Amos (well, it's cookies), Maya Angelou (poet, educator), Brooke Astor (she's old school), Jane Austen (and she had a chance), Dan Aykroyd (it's show business), Joan Baez (entertainer), Jimmy and Tammy Faye Bakker (duh), Warren Beatty (entertainer and presidential nominee?), David Ben-Gurion (politician), Sonny Bono (entertainer and congressman), Rick Bragg (Pulitzer Prize–winning journalist, but he's southern, and therefore gifted), Richard Branson (airplane and lifestyle mogul), Albert Brooks (another entertainer), Robert Browning (too long ago), Art Buchwald (an older guy), Barbara Bush (well, but she did attend *Smith*), David Byrne (musician—what did you expect?), James Cameron (director, ditto), Andrew Carnegie (started as a bobbin boy, but that was a long time ago), Whittaker Chambers (spy), Raymond Chandler (did he need a college degree to write tough-guy prose?), Coco Chanel (designer), Schuyler Chapin (dean of Columbia University's School of the Arts), John Cheever (writer), Konstantin V. Chernenko (not one of the major Russian premiers), Bennett Cohen (ice cream), Sean Connery (he was a milkman), Judy Crichton (producer of *The American Experience* on PBS), Walter Cronkite (he seems so erudite), Daniel Day-Lewis (even though he is the son of the poet laureate of England), Michael Dell (computers), Princess Diana (barely got out of secondary school), Leonardo DiCaprio (too young), Walt Disney (too old), Bob Dylan (too mumbly), Clint Eastwood (too actory), Thomas Alva Edison (an inventor), Lawrence Ellison (founder of Oracle),

Erik Erikson (things were different then), Philo T. Farnsworth (another inventor), Howard Fast (another writer), William Faulkner (drinking), Sally Field (another actress), Debra Fields (another cookie maker), Carrie Fisher (actress), F. Scott Fitzgerald (it was Princeton, and he was drinking), Henry Fonda (actor), Jane Fonda (it's hereditary), Shelby Foote (writer), Henry Ford (Fords), Ben Franklin (but he was a printer's apprentice), Buckminster Fuller (but he made a stab at Harvard, and the Navy), S. B. Fuller (Fuller brush), Bill Gates (but at least he dropped out of Harvard), David Geffen (fuller himself), Charlotte Perkins Gilman (busy being a feminist), John Glenn (astronaut/senator), Barry Goldwater (presidential candidate), Richard Grasso (head of the New York Stock Exchange), Arlo Guthrie (busy being a hippie), Alex Haley (writer), Pamela Harriman (ambassador), Ernest Hemingway (writer), Milton Hershey (it's *chocolate*), Al Hirschfeld (the artist), Dustin Hoffman (guilty with the actor's excuse), L. Ron Hubbard (did anyone think he *did*?), Robert Hughes (would anyone believe he *didn't*?), H. Wayne Huizenga (but he started with garbage), Tom Hanks (but he started in *Bosom Buddies*), Andrew Jackson (before our time), Peter Jennings (learned on the job), Steve Jobs (Steve Jobs), Kirk Kerkorian (billionaire media mogul, but he was born in a place called Weedpatch, California), Jill Krementz (author and photographer), Estée Lauder (makeup), Ralph Lauren (clothes), Richard E. Leakey (bones), Fran Lebowitz (the writer was expelled from high school), Doris Lessing (writer), Rush Limbaugh (ahem), Abraham Lincoln (he lived in the sticks), Charles Lindbergh (no interest), Clare Boothe Luce (ambassador), Madonna (entertainer), Malcolm X (no chance), Steve Martin (no way), H. L. Mencken (a maverick), Joni Mitchell (entertainer), Bill Murray (it was the seventies), Martina Navratilova (it was tennis), S. I. Newhouse (it was inherited), Jack Nicholson (it was ego), Florence Nightingale (it was the war), Anaïs Nin (it was the sex), Isamu Noguchi (too ethereal), Notorious B.I.G. (too street), Rudolf Nureyev (dancer), Rosie O'Donnell (entertainer), Yoko Ono (it was the seventies), Neil Simon (and we're beginning to think it shows), Gwyneth Paltrow (and she's still young), Gordon Parks (photographer), Suzanne de Passe (the recording business), Bob Pittman (founder of MTV), Edgar Allan Poe (it was the drugs), Alexander Pope (he didn't need it), Nathan Pritikin (so he's not a medical doctor), Wolfgang Puck (but Julia Child was a Smithie), Sir David Puttnam (British), Robert Redford (entertainer), John D. Rockefeller (with oil), Eleanor Roosevelt (it doesn't matter), RuPaul (entertainer), J. D. Salinger (writer), Margaret Sanger (birth-control education), David Sarnoff (media baron), Muriel F. Siebert (first woman to own a seat on the New York Stock Exchange), Erich Sixt, Jr. (a German car-rental mogul worth $800 million), Dawn Steel (media executive), Edward Durrell Stone (architect), Sharon Stone (entertainer), Barbra Streisand (it hasn't stopped her), William Howard Taft (president), Peter Throckmorton (underwater archaeologist), Leo Tolstoy (under the tzar), Nina Totenberg (legal affairs correspondent, MacNeil/Lehrer), Harry S. Truman (the wee haberdasher), James Truman (another Brit), Ted Turner (Ugah), Mark Twain (writer), Governor Jesse ("The Body") Ventura (Ugah-Ugah), Marilyn vos Savant (the "smartest person in the world" dropped out of college), George Washington (surveyor/president), Thomas J. Watson (founder of IBM), Auberon and Evelyn Waugh (too falutin'), John Wayne (the surprise is that he attended at all), Harvey Weinstein (Miramax), George Westinghouse (an inventor), Walt Whitman (a poet), Laura Ingalls Wilder (out on the prairie), August Wilson (playwright), Anna Wintour (another Brit), John Woo (action films), Steve Wozniak (computers), Frank Lloyd Wright (architect), Wilbur and Orville Wright (tinkerers), Will Wright (invented the computer game Sim City), and thousands of others.

UP FROM THE GROMMET FACTORY

Our country has always admired the self-made success, the person who pulls himself up out of poverty, or who reinvents herself. John Smith, who was chairman of General Motors, began working there on the assembly line. Edward Rensi, who is now president of McDonald's USA, began by working behind the counter. There is actually something called the Horatio Alger Association of Distinguished Americans, based in Alexandria, Virginia, that recognizes this kind of self-made billionaire.

Kirk Kerkorian, eighty, has wealth that Forbes in 1999 estimated at $7 billion, mostly from casinos and hotels in Las Vegas, cars (Chrysler) and the movie business. Nonetheless, he chooses to live in a one-bedroom guest house on his property in Beverly Hills. With two grown daughters, he now has a new two-year-old daughter with a tennis pro in her thirties, whom he married briefly.

His father made and lost money in farming in the San Joaquin Valley, and spent most of his life selling watermelons. Kirk grew up a ruffian, with dreams of becoming a professional boxer. After being sent to reform school, he dropped out at age sixteen, just after eighth grade. He held down odd jobs until he began boxing at age twenty. And though he was successful as a fighter, he was simply too slight. So he became a civilian pilot with the British Royal Air Force during World War II (someone forged a document saying he had graduated from high school), delivering bombers from Canada to Great Britain.

After the war, he parlayed his flight experience into setting up charter airlines and then parlayed the earnings from that into real estate in Vegas. I don't think "colorful" is quite colorful enough a term for someone like Kirk Kerkorian.

THINK, UH, DIFFERENT

While we assume that captains of industry might well get to the top without a college degree, by working their way up from the smelter or ferrying bombers across the North Atlantic, it is harder to accept that people who have an impressive intellect and erudition can succeed without a degree.

Of all the people in the list on pages 155–57 who did not graduate from college, the one name that seems to elicit the most shock is Peter Jennings. It somehow seems impossible to believe that a trusted newscaster, the person who tells us about Chechnya, could do that without having gone to college. In fact, Peter Jennings never even finished high school. Luckily, his father was in broadcasting, and Peter had talent as well as connections.

"People who make it big in money, power, prestige or achievement have always educated themselves in what they need to know, and they are still doing it today, whether they go to college or not," Caroline Bird wrote in *The Case Against College*.

It seems the droll observations of the writer Fran Lebowitz must have been honed at the *Harvard Crimson*. The *Washington Post* called her "a moralist, an elitist and a snob." Paul Rudnick, writing in *New Times,* said "she has followed the Noël Coward tradition of an intensely civilized, titillating frivolity. Her work is marvelously entertaining and intentionally superficial."

But Fran did not go to Harvard, though she has sometimes been to Harvard to sit on a jury for student architecture competitions. "I can't stand being there, even when I give a speech. I keep worrying that someone will make me go to gym. I don't even like being in Boston, because there are so many schools there."

She grew up in Morristown, New Jersey, and her parents, who deeply admired education, sent her to a private girls' school. She was expelled in her senior year, she notes, *after* her parents paid the tuition. And her parents did not put up a fight, as parents might today.

"It was 1969," she told me. "Schools had authority then, more authority than parents. My parents were very deferential to the school authority."

The exact reason for her expulsion was somewhat fuzzy, but Fran, forty-nine, assured me "it was nothing glamorous."

"I didn't set fire to the gym," she said, "and despite what everyone thinks I wasn't thrown out for smoking." (Fran is a passionate, career smoker, with a "What's the point of eating dinner, if you can't have a cigarette afterward?" sort of attitude.)

Basically, she was thrown out for sedition. "The headmaster told my mother that I was usurping his power and the other kids were in some way imitating my ways," she said. And then she added, acidly, "It was a deservedly small school, a remarkably undistinguished Episcopalian girls' school."

Those who know and love Fran's intensely judgmental nature—she once wrote a piece called "If I Ruled the World," and still aspires to be chief justice of the Supreme Court; "Someone told me you don't need to have a college degree for that," she told me, "so I'm still waiting. I am best at making snap judgments. We'd have the backlog cleared up in no time"—would not be surprised that what got her into trouble in high school was her surliness, "what my mother called 'that look on your face.'"

"Now you get thrown out," she said, "you go to another school. When I got thrown out of school my parents were very embarrassed. They still are. I really believe there are parents whose children murder people and their parents take it better."

So was it more embarrassing than getting pregnant in high school? I asked. "Being pregnant, that would have been bad," she said, "maybe *as* bad. But I'm not sure this wasn't worse. The thing my mother was concerned with was that people would know. So I was sent to live with her sister in Poughkeepsie, a sister who was married to an IBM engineer. That was my punishment. It was an incredibly strict family, with four children under nine. All of them took lessons. I was basically their driver. And I had to do certain things, like take piano lessons and the high school equivalency test."

"It was not very rigorous," she noted.

She even considered going to college, particularly Bard, which she said had a reputation for considering people who had not graduated from high school. "They didn't take me," she said. "Later, Leon [Botstein, the president] asked me if I'd like to teach there. But I'm the opposite of Groucho Marx. I would never teach at any college that did not admit me."

And so she went to work, in a series of menial jobs, since she didn't even know how to type. "I drove a taxi," she said. "I was a chauffeur. I sold belts on the street. I was a cleaning lady with a specialty in venetian blinds. I was a runner on Wall Street. I had kid jobs. I was a gofer on a set. I had all those kinds of jobs from eighteen to twenty-seven, when my first book came out. I did that kind of work for nine years."

She notes that she started getting her pieces published at eighteen—reviews of B (or worse) movies for Andy Warhol's *Interview* magazine. "But I made about two dollars a year at it until the book."

She said, however, that she did not object to the menial jobs any more than she objects to the idea of writing. She hates both. "I hate working," she said.

"I don't think I lost anything by not going to the schools I went to, or could have gone to," she said. "But I think a real education would be very beneficial. I do know a few people who are well educated, men about ten years older than me. And what they know, they really know in order. The best-educated people I know are the best educated.

"But the way that people view college education now, it's totally practical, it's money." And, she says, if you want to make really big money, college is not the answer either. "That's never been the path to wealth," she said, "unless you happen to have a roommate at Harvard whose parents help you get started. Otherwise, it helps you get to the middle class."

Has she suffered from never going to college? I asked. "I want my *doctor* to have been to college," she said. "I want to be sure he went to school. But it makes no difference in certain professions, not in this soft world of the media. For writers, I don't think it has a practical point.

"What really stuns me is writing school. It's the worst thing that ever happened. The scam of the century. You can't teach people to be talented, and the writing is terrible, truly deeply offensive. Almost none of these people should be writers. In a just world they would be deported." (Graduates of creative-writing programs note: You need be deeply concerned only if she makes it to the Supreme Court.)

"Gore Vidal didn't go to college. Neither did John Cheever. That's not bad company," she said. "I don't care. I think my parents still do."

BUILDING FROM NOTHING

It has always been the case that wildly successful people see opportunity where others see low-paying, no-interest jobs. They are often the people who, in the illiterate phrase from Apple Computer, "think different." And what are the chances of thinking differently if you plod through the same college courses and get the same business degree?

Wayne Huizenga, sixty, dropped out of Calvin College in Grand Rapids, Michigan, after three semesters. He went into the Army and then, with a little bit of experience in his family's garbage-hauling business in Chicago, he went into business for himself in Fort Lauderdale, with a used truck bought with $5,000 borrowed from his father-in-law. Within five years he joined that business with the family business in Chicago and started Waste Management, Inc., which he sold in 1984 for a bundle. He then rested for about five minutes and noticed that there were a lot of small video stores. Economies of scale must have leaped to mind, because in short order he created Blockbuster Video, with more expensive rental prices than many little guys and a narrower selection (he banned NC-17 titles, for instance); he nonetheless dominated with sheer size and numbers.

Then he sold that business in 1994 for $8.4 billion and got into entertainment and sports—the Miami Dolphins (football),

Florida Marlins (baseball), Florida Panthers (hockey) and sports arenas. Lately he has tackled the used-car business. In 1999, *Forbes* estimated his wealth at $1.7 billion.

I am waiting for Huizenga to figure out that the last great area in this country to be consolidated under one banner is the handyman. A national company of fix-its—people to change the washers on the faucets, clean the rain gutters, rehang the closet doors, fix the squeaky stairs and regrout the bathroom tiles all in one day—would make a fortune, and my son is available.

WHY GO TO COLLEGE?

The area in which education seems least relevant these days is computers. Or, as Brigid McMenamin wrote in "The Tyranny of the Diploma" in *Forbes,* "Bill Gates did go to college, but for only three years. He dropped out of Harvard to devote himself full-time to computer work. The time he saved from college—and additional years spared from grad school—gave Gates a head start in building what was to become the world's greatest fortune. It's not inconceivable that had he gone for a Ph.D., someone else today would be the world's richest person."

In her article, she also pointed out that college grads make more money, as a rule, only because the most lucrative professions (like medicine, the law, architecture) require a college degree. Nonetheless, she notes, "a hefty 21 percent of all degree-holders who work earn less than the average for high school grads." And she lists examples of jobs that pay well *without* a college degree: real estate agent, plumber, machinist, police officer, etc.

She could add "politician."

Harry S. Truman is the last president of the United States who did not go to college, and some people would argue the last great president. Governor Jesse ("The Body") Ventura of Minnesota did not graduate from college. A couple of years in the Marines and a background as a professional wrestler were all he needed for success. (And have no doubt about it: Professional wrestling has created more millionaires than the state business school.)

Fran Reiter is running for mayor of New York City after serving under Rudolph Giuliani as deputy mayor for economic development for three and a half years. "It was very exciting," she told me. "Selling New York was better than selling bad TV shows into syndication."

Fran, forty-five, attended Boston University as a fine arts major, but did not graduate.

"I left school for a number of reasons," she told me. "My roommate came from an upper-middle-class white suburban background, and she was functionally illiterate. She asked me to look at this paper she wrote for Western Civilization, and I couldn't read it. I said to myself, 'This is nuts.' And she graduated."

She says she went to school to become an educated person, but that college, even in the seventies, seemed like trade school. After two years she felt "it was time to go out and do it." She went to New York and wormed her way into a vocational class on television production. Then she watched daytime television to see which shows were produced in New York, picked up the phone and called the producer of *Money Maze* and asked for a job. He said come on down.

Yet she fantasizes about studying with an Oxford don—the whole bit, with cold student rooms and a glass of sherry with the tutor—and she still thinks about earning her bachelor's degree. "I sat down with people to figure it out. I had earned sixty credits, and if you put life credits in place I would have had very little to finish. Getting an undergrad degree would take a year. So I had to think, 'I can run for mayor or I can finish college.'" She decided to run for mayor.

Besides, she is already in a college environment. Despite lacking a bachelor's degree, Fran is an adjunct professor, teaching management of not-for-profits to graduate students at New York University. And she is working with the City of London to help them move toward electing their first mayor. "It's an interesting process to watch a place move into a new way of governing," she says.

"People can get very hung up on a degree. There are kids in college that *shouldn't* be there. It's become a status thing, like wearing a logo on your shirt. But that's what life is like in the year 2000.

"I think education is important, and I would never discourage someone from going to college who wanted to go. But it's not the only way, and it doesn't speak to becoming a successful human being. There are lots of ways of becoming an educated person.

"I've never lied about [getting a degree]. In fact, there is no college requirement to be deputy mayor. I look back and I have no regrets. It's been more exciting than I ever thought it would be."

I told her she was going to go into a chapter called "The Millionaire Next Door Who Never Finished College," and she laughed. "I just gave up a well-paying job to do this and all I do now is ask people for money. As they say in *The Godfather,* 'It is the business I have chosen.'"

DROPPING WAY OUT

Kevin Smith is the director and writer of the 1999 movie *Dogma* as well as *Chasing Amy, Mallrats* and *Clerks,* a low-budget exegesis on the lives of the kinds of people who work in video stores and convenience stores. Young directors who never graduated from college like Spike Jonze, thirty, who made *Being John Malkovich,* and Kevin Smith, twenty-nine, are merely joining a long, illustrious line of other movie directors who did not graduate from college, like Woody Allen and James Cameron.

"You don't really need it," Kevin told me as we drove around in his new Jeep near Red Bank, New Jersey. "When Bruce Willis gets an honorary degree, and you know those things are *real,* then that makes someone who spent $100,000 to go to college for four years say, 'What? Why did I waste the money?'"

So if your child proposes that she go to college so she can study filmmaking, consider the alternative.

Kevin Smith is Mr. New Jersey. He grew up in Highlands, and later moved to Red Bank. His father worked for the postal service. His mother stayed home with three kids, who went to Catholic schools. College was assumed. Kevin's sister got a master's degree from Temple University in Philadelphia and now lives in Hong Kong, where she writes for a style magazine. His brother went to Fairleigh Dickinson University in Rutherford, New Jersey, before studying to be a chiropractor and ending up installing high-end entertainment systems.

I sat with Kevin and his parents in the kitchen of the New Jersey home he bought them and talked about those days when Kevin started college. He has a close relationship with his parents, and calls them every day. At least twice a week, he stops by for a visit. They have the kind of easy, bantering relationship that can lead to an exchange like the following:

Kevin's mother, in an exasperated tone: "You talked about me on Conan O'Brien."

Kevin: "So I had to buy you a house."

Kevin, a flaming Bart, would be considered a "good boy" only by the most enlightened and understanding of parents. His films are often scatological, depict drug use, contain foul language and try to overturn the suburban apple cart. In them he plays a dour character named Silent Bob who is the ultimate slacker. Married and with an infant daughter, he still dresses like a twelve-year-old boy—hooded sweatshirt, sneakers, baggy pants. His consuming passion in life is comics.

After graduating from high school, Kevin was accepted at the Eugene Lang undergraduate division of The New School in New York City. "I cried when I left him there," his mother, Grace, said. Kevin explained to me that part of the problem was that there were six students sharing a New York apartment—not what a suburban parent was used to seeing.

"They had platforms built everywhere," Grace said. "And there was nothing but beer and Snickers in the fridge." She leaned close and confided, "These were *doctors'* sons."

Kevin did not spend much time studying at The New School. "He left after dropping water balloons out the windows, eight flights up," his mother said.

"Other kids were doing it, too, but they got tired of it," Kevin noted. "I didn't. There was this official letter—"

His mother: "Somehow we never saw it."

"—that said, 'If one more water balloon hits the ground...' so I moved out of the dorm and back home."

His mother interjected, fondly, "He said, 'My classes are taking less and less time.' We didn't know. We were just glad to have him home again."

He spent a brief time at the local community college, Brookdale, studying criminology and juvenile justice. It was "$50 a credit," he said. "No one goes on to the real college from there."

He did not complete even a semester. Then he talked his parents into bankrolling a sort of trade school in Canada called the Vancouver Film School. It was there he met Scott Mosier, who has produced and worked on all of his subsequent films.

"We were supposed to do a class project, twenty-four kids on four topics," Kevin said. "We pitched a documentary about a guy, a preop transsexual, called *Mae I?*. But we didn't get any work done. Mae dropped out. We had a week left. So we turned in a documentary called *Mae Day*. I don't even think we got a grade. And now they use it as a recruitment film—this is what Kevin Smith did *here*. The documentary is basically everyone complaining about us: 'They were unprepared, it was their fault.'"

His mom clarified what happened next, "They exited you."

His quiet father, sitting across the table, said, "He knew everything."

"They said you were too proud," his mother said.

Kevin explained: "I wanted concrete hands-on practice, a camera in my hands. They wanted to teach theory. If I wanted to talk about Goddard or Kubrick, I could do that on my own time. So I took the rest of the tuition money and went home and made *Clerks.*"

The 1994 black-and-white extremely rude movie, made when Kevin was twenty-two, cost around $28,000. His ever-understanding parents dipped into their "flood money," saved up because their part of New Jersey, on the "lowlands" side of Highlands, the "clam digger" side near the Atlantic Ocean, has devastating floods every decade or so. "Mom and Dad didn't condone the movie, but they never balked at it," Kevin said. "Mom went to the bank and took out $3,000 and said, 'Here it is.'"

The film was shot mostly at night with amateur everything. "It was a wonderful leap of faith on their part," he said.

Grace said, "I figured after he did that, he'd be on to something that would support him."

Kevin said, "She thought I'd fail, and that would be the end of that."

"It's all a blessing of course," his mother said. "God gave you a gift. You're a worker."

Grace even got called to come down late one night to play the woman who checks the dates on milk cartons.

"It was 11 o'clock at night. 'Mom, we need someone to come down,'" she said. "They didn't say for what. I thought they needed something. When I got there and they told me, I said, 'I can't do this, I'm not dressed for it.'"

Kevin: "I said, 'Mom, you're dressed fine.'"

Her biggest complaint: that he shot her bending down over the milk case and made her hips look big.

The rest of the story? The movie went on to become one of the biggest sleeper hits of 1994. And, Kevin says, "If I'd listened to the nattering nabobs of negativism, I wouldn't be here today. Well, I'd be here today, but I'd be living here, not visiting."

Does Kevin belong in a chapter on millionaires? You bet. Not only does he have a new two-movie contract with Miramax films, but ABC is putting on an animated television show based on *Clerks*. He also has a successful store in Red Bank called Jay and Silent Bob's Secret Stash, devoted to comic books and movie memorabilia.

Later that night Kevin invited me back to his house, not far from his parents', to meet his lovely new wife, Jennifer Schwalbach-Smith, once a reporter for *USA Today*, her mother and his producer-partner, Scott, and Scott's wife.

Kevin fired up the backyard Grillmaster and introduced me to their golden labs, Mulder and Scully, safely contained behind a fence in the vast backyard. Then Jennifer took me on a tour of the house and to meet their daughter sleeping upstairs, Harley Quinn. Let it be said that the house, while remaining unpretentious, has a three-car garage, six bedrooms and an indoor swimming pool, which was drained while they decided what color to paint it. (Kevin was voting for yellow, red and blue—Superman colors.)

In the two-story living room was the largest television set I had ever seen, with digital cable. There are original pieces of art from people like the cartoonist Matt Groening (yes, *The Simpsons*) as well as walls devoted to heroes, supervillains and action figures. Despite all that, and the sometimes shocking films Kevin makes, he and his wife seemed like intelligent, unpretentious folk who just happened to know and work with other people with names like Jon Bon Jovi, Alanis Morissette, George Carlin, Janeane Garofalo, Chris Rock, Matt Damon and Ben Affleck.

MISSING THE DEGREE

Sarah Williams, a marketing executive, says, "For me, my success was always overshadowed by the fact that I never finished college."

The day I spoke to her—she called from two consecutive car phones, hers and her husband's—was her last day as executive director of brand development at Unilever Prestige. She was about to take a new job as vice president of marketing at an e-commerce site called www.Jasmin.com.

"It's where the future is," she said. "Every company should start from the Internet and go from there."

Sarah was raised with parents she calls "total college heads." Her mother went to Smith, and her father went to Yale.

When she dropped out of college, her father was highly critical. "Now he thinks it's just fantastic that I did this without college," she said. "He's found a way to think it's great.

"I always felt that everyone must have overlooked this fact on my résumé as I continually climbed up the ladder," she said. "Today, though, I also see it as an important validation of one's intuition.

"I went to college in 1978, but I was already pretty much over the school thing way before that. I found high school in Greenwich, Connecticut, pretty boring and I applied to the University of Colorado, Boulder, just to get as far away from home as possible.

"Boulder is a total joke," she said. "It's too big, and all I wanted to do was go ski. If I had a great teacher I'd get an A, and if I was bored I wouldn't go."

By the second year of classes, she said, she didn't even bother to turn up for some of her finals. Instead, she went to New York to take theater classes at the Neighborhood Playhouse. To pay the rent, she went to work in marketing.

Today, she says, even though she didn't finish college, a company will hire her as a top executive. But in her corporate life, if she wanted to hire a marketing assistant, they would ask, "How many years out of college?"

"For many years I was completely haunted by it. When I am in a room with people with M.B.A.s, I feel that they have a greater foundation than me. It's like a nasty little secret that you didn't graduate from college."

At one corporation, she remembers a founder of the company pointing to an applicant's résumé. "Look at this," he said, "look where she went to school."

And Sarah responded, "Well, what has she been doing for the last ten years?"

"Once you're out there and you're working, the playing field is level," she said. "Either you have a natural ability to work quickly and hard or you don't. You need logic, but even more than that you need intuition. And you need creativity, which schools often kill.

"The thing I have found," she said, "is that overschooled people have lost track of their instincts.

"Today's supermeteoric leaders are not hindered about what *can't* be done. They went out there and didn't think twice about not moving forward. They didn't think twice about *not* doing it."

Like many of the dropouts I talked to, Sarah feels her college career was unduly complicated by the distribution requirements, the very thing that Americans most value about a classic liberal arts education. "I would never use 60 percent of what I needed in order to graduate," Sarah said. "Jobs want people who are specialists, not people who are well-rounded. I don't need calculus to get through life. Quicken does that for me."

Now she has children of her own. Does she urge them to work hard so they can go to college? "I want them to succeed for many reasons, to be in touch with what they're good at," she said. "Whether or not they go to college, I want them to have a passion for something. If they go, it's got to be a choice and not a knee-jerk reaction.

"Richard Branson said that no one should go to college because they're totally out of touch with consumers, with people. They talk about 'them' versus 'us.' They talk about consumers as if they're another race."

And when she hires? "My best success stories are people I've promoted right up from the bottom. Instead of these glamour queens who come in with an M.B.A., I want someone with a start-up mentality for the rest of their life."

LIVING IN FEAR

There are still people in this country who must hide the fact they did not graduate from college. A woman who asked to be called Irene says that she lives in mortal terror that she will be fired, even though one of the top executives of her company did not himself graduate from college.

Irene, who is forty-six, says that what did her in was the math requirement and that she was a "terrible student," and too busy doing drugs and fooling around in high school. "History, I liked. And English. I'm an excellent reader, but I can't do phonetics. I probably have a learning disability, but in those days they didn't test for that. I was just totally not into high school."

She did terribly on her SAT's, got tutored and with that got into a junior college. She did well enough there to make the dean's list, then transferred to another college and flunked out. "It was the math," she said. She tried another college, closer to home, but attended only two courses.

"I think the stress of college was too much," she said.

So she spent a year in secretarial school, and that was it. She worked as a secretary at a prestigious law school, and then began working in the nonprofit world. She tried a couple of other times to finish college, even took a paralegal course, "but I couldn't pass the math," she said. "Now I do budgets. You explain."

It was when she worked for a university that she began lying about her degree. But they found out and she was asked to leave. But once again she lied on her application about getting her degree and took a job in marketing in the clothing industry.

"I've been here fifteen years," she said. "They've never questioned me about my degree. But I *know* you can't get a job with this company without a degree. I always have it in the back of my mind that they're *going* to question me. Even the underlings have to have four-year degrees. I actually hired someone who didn't, and they fought with me about it.

"I'm good at what I do. And I always think about going back to school, and my husband is trying to encourage me. But I just don't think I could pass the math."

Her husband is a doctor. We were traveling together by car to a Japanese restaurant when I commented that it was hard to find people to talk about Proust in the rural area in upstate New York where I have a weekend house.

"What's a proust?" Irene asked. And I thought, oops, bad example when talking to someone who didn't finish college. But then her husband, who was driving, made it clear he didn't know what a proust was either. And she makes more than he does.

"I vacation internationally," Irene told me. "I'm well read. I collect antiques. I love my family. And I'm a good cook. But it's always been an issue with me. Someday, somehow I want to get that piece of paper. To show that I achieved it. I just want the piece of paper."

LIVING LIKE A MILLIONAIRE

Not everyone who becomes a success in life becomes a millionaire. Some people just live like one.

The kind of people who become millionaires and multimillionaires don't stop working just because they're rich. In fact, they work harder.

But the rest of us fantasize about becoming rich so we can retire, read *Forbes* on the beach, play golf, live with a view of the ocean and go sailing.

Alvah Simon, who describes himself as forty-eight years young, spends all of his time on his sailboat, a French cutter just shy of thirty-six feet. He runs it with his wife, Diana. "It's very strong," he says, "which allows us to go to so many extremes."

Alvah was born near Buffalo, New York. He is the only one in a family of nine *not* to go on to get a college degree; in fact, he never even earned his high school diploma. One brother is a lawyer, and there are several nurses.

"Everyone has some level of higher education but me," he told me by phone from a friend's office on the coast of Maine. "But they also know I found the right track and stayed on it." He had anchored in Maine over the summer to publicize a lovely book he had written, *North to the Night,* about spending the winter in the Arctic aboard his boat.

Alvah was kicked out of a well-known Jesuit high school in Oak Park, Illinois. Back in upstate New York, he completed four years of high school in three. "To get back up to speed I had to compress," he told me.

Halfway through his senior year in high school he was accepted into Hastings College in Nebraska. So, figuring he had the system aced, he quit high school. "Hastings never figured it out," he said.

He got through one year at Hastings, and was then put on probation. "I was working for $1.16 an hour to pay my own tuition and then skipping class the next day. I just wasn't finding anything there that I was looking for."

He came back a year later and again was asked to leave. "That was the end of it," he said. "I was a flower child of the late sixties, so it boiled down to 'I want to work with people.'"

He says there was a tremendous "sense of relief" when he

figured out that formal education was not right for him. "I have never once since that point applied for a job or been denied an opportunity that I wanted based on not having that degree," he said. "I wanted to be a social worker in Chicago and I did that, without the degree, because I had a street education. I wanted to skydive, and so I ran a business skydiving. I wanted to travel and sail and write." He's done all that.

"I've led a life," he says. "Not an easy life, but I wouldn't trade it with anyone I've met. I've never felt the degree denied me anything. And now I'm such an avid history buff. I read biographies. Back then they weren't shown to me in a way I could digest it."

He says he thinks he has always known what he wanted to do in life, but that society "tries to convince you otherwise." He loved "the Errol Flynn myth that you could lead a swashbuckling outdoor life." His father ("the trainer," Alvah calls him) would drop his children off in the woods and let them figure out how to get home. At eighteen in the Simon household, you were expected to be on your own. So there was always the impetus to move on.

"My plan was to go out in search of adventure," Alvah said.

His hero always was someone like Jack London, a stonemason, writer and social activist. "He did twenty different things," Alvah said. "As a sailor he was the first yachtsman to sail around the world for pleasure. He did just amazing things with native intelligence and courage, not education. He knew so much and could extrapolate from his masonry to other things."

Alvah has spent fourteen years circumnavigating the globe, twenty years outside the United States. "That's when I entered my university," he says. "That was my higher education.

"I started out smug, thinking I was going to make my way as a teacher. Very quickly I became a student to indigenous native people—all these native people we've dismissed as ignorant. We've taken our beliefs and made them into religion, and we take their beliefs and make them into myths and voodoo. I spent those years living with them. It turned into a longer and longer odyssey, and it's still going on."

Alvah has modeled himself on people who "live the life and walk the walk before talking the talk." And that's the kind of person he is. He is not done with adventures, even after his time in the Arctic. He headed down to Panama for the handing over of the Canal Zone in December of 1999. While there he expected to make contact with the five indigenous groups. "In their minds their country has been wounded for all these years," he said. He is particularly interested in the Kuna Indians, "because of their militancy.

"They didn't secede. It's not a Kurdish rebellion. They just wanted autonomy, and they've done it with a militancy that is shocking. They are not going to be eradicated." This time he planned to take along cameramen from the Travel Channel. Alvah and his wife, Diana, also speak frequently on college campuses about their travels.

We talked a bit about kids, and their obsessive belief that you have to get a college degree before getting on with your life. "I wonder if this is a modern version of the apprenticeship guild," he said, "working hard for four or five years so you can pick up the hammer. I think they fear the experience, and there's more of that now than there was in the sixties and seventies, when everyone ran away to Haight-Ashbury. Then you were supposed to find your passion and follow it, as Joseph Campbell said. Now we've lost that, because of the arcane degrees that people get."

And yet Alvah is far from being against education as a springboard for life. And he worries that this book will encourage good students to drop out. Or as he put it, "There will be a certain segment eager to hear your message. 'Twisted by knaves to make a trap for fools,' as my mother used to say." He did not mention Jesse Ventura by name.

On the other hand, he is skeptical of the number of people who really want to pursue a career in, say, business.

"Young people are brave to the point of stupidity," he said. "So when people tell them they will earn this much money over forty-three years, they go for it." Instead Alvah, the aging flower child, believes we must follow our passion.

"I met a wealthy family on a yacht in the Pacific," he told me. "They had someone on board to give Latin and Greek lessons to their children. And their youngest child wanted to be a fisherman. He was playing with these Indonesian kids and riding with his feet up on the gunwales. It was beautiful and they were horrified.

"We've progressed past the point where physical labor and craft have any nobility," he said. "To do what you do, that's the odyssey. It can sustain or protect, it can provide for your family."

Moreover, the old hippie said, "the cost of that education brings them out of it poorly educated, not prepared for an adult life and enslaved to debt. In Europe you automatically take one year off. You throw yourself into challenging yourself. Now when you come out of school you're $80,000 in debt. You can't go to Nepal. And that compound interest just digs you in deeper. Once they get on that slippery slope they come out of school massively in debt.

"At that point," he said, "they figure they're in so deep, they might as well buy a car. They burn so many bridges. It's the system"—right here, you can supply the word "man"; he didn't say it, but you can think it—"the institution. Now it's to the point they select their colleges for the chance to network."

Instead, Alvah has followed his own muse: the quest for knowledge without boundaries.

"That's what I was after, and the only place to find it was in the desert and the ice and the water," he said. "That's where the teachers are. I'm a rich man and I know it."

Chapter Nine

DO COMPUTER GEEKS
NEED COLLEGE?

Beware of all enterprises that require new clothes.
—Thoreau

Do kids who want to work with computers need to go to a four-year college? The short answer is no. Look at the numbers of kids who are making $30,000 or $50,000 or millions without a college degree.

But are these kids missing something? (Yes, if only keggers at the frat house.) Will they be hampered somewhere along the way? (Maybe.) And does it make a difference if they are systems analysts or website designers or local area network specialists? (Absolutely.)

Computers have changed everything. At the turn of the century, working in computers seems to be the quick and irrefutable answer for many young people. The need is obvious—there are 400,000 job openings that are going unfilled. And kids have been learning computer skills from the time they were in elementary school.

Most of the young folk I spoke to for this chapter learned more at home than at school, fooling around with the family computer. They almost always know more than their parents; they often know more than their teachers. In computers, a nineteen-year-old is an alpha.

Concerns are twofold. Are schools, in their rush to put a computer in every classroom, and perhaps on every desk, caving in to the demands of the business world and skimping on other things, like shop class, music and languages? (For a highly critical discussion of this question, see Todd Oppenheimer's award-winning story in the *Atlantic Monthly*, "The Computer Delusion," published in July 1997.)

The answer to the question is, of course, local, with each school district making its own decisions. White Bear Lake High School, in Minnesota, for instance, offers nineteen different music classes, from ninth-grade choir to music theory, five semesters of art, lots of classes in woodworking. All of its computer courses are offered under "business education," and include two courses in the Macintosh (including using Quicken, Macintax and HyperCard) and several in Windows (including building web pages and learning Microsoft Office).

Other schools have gone so far as to become partners with giants like Cisco Systems and are giving a four-semester course, in high school, that would allow a graduate to walk out the door, take a Cisco Certified Network exam and walk into a job as a network administrator. Cisco is offering its "Network Academy Curriculum" in five thousand schools, most of them secondary schools, though there are a few two- and four-year colleges. The curriculum covers everything from pulling cable to "subnet masking rules," whatever they are.

Just stop for a moment and think how strange that is. If this were anything other than computers, would schools be lining up to participate? Imagine a four-semester course in, say, telephone installation. How about a four-semester course in meat and fish butchery? I am not saying the Cisco Academy is wrong. I'm just saying it's a whole new world; somehow, without consciously making a choice to opt for vocational education, teenagers may be doing just that by taking computer courses.

Secondly, are kids who are leaping into lucrative computer jobs being denied the rich education they might otherwise get if they had gone straightaway to college? The answer to that assumes two things: that the only time to go to college is right out of high school, and that college is actually worth attending, or worth the cost of attending.

Certainly, people out in the working world see the advantages of knowing computers. "The Internet is the great equalizer," said Sarah Williams, a marketing executive who recently moved to an Internet start-up in New York City. "It's going to liberate a million and one kids who can't afford school or feel it doesn't work. You say to your kids, 'Why are we looking at college? What is the value added?' They want to take two years and program, and *then* think about it."

ON THE FRONT LINES OF
THE COMPUTER REVOLUTION

Here's where the rubber meets the road: Tanner Zucker.

I had admired the Flash animation on a new web site (www .rumpustoys.com); then I discovered that one of its creators was just out of high school and working full-time in Manhattan. Tanner, who turned nineteen in January of 2000, grew up in Gilford, New Hampshire. He got his first good computer in seventh grade. "I wanted to spend a million dollars to get the best," he said, "but there were limits. So I had to find out what would work well, and get the best system I could." He took to reading J&R Music World, which lovingly described different components. A month later, he knew every product in it.

It was 1993, and the family bought a Compaq DX266 "with the floating decimal point unit," Tanner said proudly. "It was fast for the time, a huge jump from what we had."

A few months later, the computer stopped working. (Or, as he puts it, "it was a useless box.") By then Tanner and his three sisters considered the computer essential to their lives. "So I fixed it," he said. "It was some software program. Spent endless hours on the phone with Compaq. A month later, they sent forty floppy disks. I installed all these drivers and it was working again. And now I was five hundred times more knowledgeable about it."

HyperCard for Macintosh was a standard program at his middle school, so Tanner and his friend Justin put one of their school projects on HyperCard, "to make it interactive." The next thing they knew, the computer director of their school was asking them to run a seminar for the teachers, to show them how to use HyperCard. Tanner was in eighth grade.

"So we find ourselves in front of a classroom full of teachers," he said. "I was daunted. I was afraid."

I asked what level the teachers were at with the computer equipment.

"Incredibly dumb," he said. "Half of them had no idea. And we were going around teaching them. I knew I knew more about the computer than my parents, but these were the teachers!"

As thanks, the teachers bought the two boys gift certificates at McDonald's, and thus Tanner got his first pay for his knowledge of computers.

From there the two boys were put on the technical advisory committee for the school board. And Tanner figured that was pretty cool. "It was enough for me just to go to that," he said. "I was living the life. Once a month, I was in the faculty lounge."

Tanner and his parents decided he should go to prep school. "At my school I could just go day by day and do no work and get A's. If you were well behaved they gave you A's, and there was no advanced curriculum. And half the class didn't care."

And so he picked Andover, partly because he wanted to play competitive hockey. "And hey," he said, "they had phones in the room and seemed pretty liberal." The choice was between Andover and Exeter. "I figured I'd get the same education at both. So I said, 'I'll take the phones with less rules.'"

At first he struggled with the more intense workload. By spring term he was on the honor roll, with a 5.0 average. (Only a couple of students every year got a 6.0, he said.)

"So I said, this wasn't so hard. I don't have to worry about this. So for the next three years I did a tenth of the effort. If I know I can be successful at something, why spend all day and all night to *prove* it. I know I can do it."

He attributes his merely good grades partly to laziness, partly to having other things to do. "I was not willing to give up my high school years to do homework. I ended up with a 4.0 and honors."

"I said, if I get a 4.0 and not do any work, why not? My parents were disappointed, and I got yelled at. And at the end of each marking term, the administrators would say, 'Take a year off, go back to Gilford.' And I said I'm learning just as much as the kids who are getting 5.0, I'm just not putting in *too* much time. They said, 'You're wasting your money.'"

"I barely passed Latin the last term. I hated Latin. I blew it off. It came right down to the wire. If it had gone badly I would have had to take a makeup test. It was close enough."

Shortly after he arrived at Andover, he discovered that sports weren't that interesting to him anymore. And, surprisingly, he did not spend all of his free time fooling around with computers. While other kids played computer games and went up on chat rooms, he enjoyed the social life at an elite New England prep school.

So how did he end up working as director of new media at Rumpus Corporation, a toy and entertainment company, right out of high school?

It started with another shopping trip, for a computer to take to Andover. "This time I had a bigger budget, and it was for me. I had ten different magazines every month. It was great. I was swamped. Completely immersed. I would spend any time reading magazines. Calling."

Eventually he ordered a machine from Dell, a machine that had all the extras he wanted. "Somehow midway through the year, my friends, the athlete soccer bunch, not the computer kids, they realized that I knew about computers. You know, the computer genius. So if they had problems with their computers, I helped fix them."

He also found out that if he added computer graphics to his assigned projects, the teachers were impressed. In one biology class the entire grade came down to the student's portfolio, and his looked showy because of the computer extras. In a social science class he helped his group do a multimedia presentation using his computer. The subject was "hunger and population." "Everyone said, 'Okay, do it on the computer.'" He used Microsoft Office and Power Point, pictures and music.

Show time involved getting up at 6 A.M. and lugging his computer across campus to the classroom. "That went really well," he said. "It was sort of the multimedia part with a news presentation. And we got a great grade and the teacher showed it to all the other teachers."

Even at a prep school in the late nineties, the teachers "thought you could just type on this thing," he said.

Same song, second verse. When he went back the next year, Andover asked Tanner and a teacher to head the technical development committee, though, he pointed out, both he and the teacher were so busy no one really got much of a program under way.

Tanner did take a couple of computer courses at Andover. He took a class in C++ ("That's something you can't pick up on your own") and he also took the advanced-placement computer course, though he found there that "everyone in the class was really a computer person, and I wasn't."

By that he means that the others were so conversant with programming they would do their projects overnight while he struggled to get it done before the next class meeting. "So that turned me away from computers."

It was only in 1997 that he learned a little bit about the Internet, when he helped a friend put some of the school's papers online. "We spent a couple of hours figuring it out," he said.

In his senior year, he says, he was using his computer only for basic schoolwork when someone on the school newspaper showed him how to make web pages. "That was my only web developing experience, right there."

As he approached graduation he applied to a number of colleges, without a great deal of passion, and settled on Boston University, because he had a sister there and it was close to family in New Hampshire. (When he was younger, he said it would be Harvard or bust; by the time he was in high school he had a new plan: enjoy life, go to whatever college would take him, put his nose to the grindstone for a couple of semesters and then transfer to Harvard or Yale.)

His parents were urging him to take a year off and travel. But he wasn't interested. "I'd say don't bother me, and then I found this job through the intern office."

There was a notice for summer work in New York City for someone who was interested in computers and web development. When he interviewed for the job, they told him there was a program called Flash that they wanted to use on their new site, which would sell children's toys, books and products, and develop branded children's characters. "They said get it and see if you can figure it out and send us something."

Of course, he had never heard of Flash. Nor did anyone on campus have a version of it. But he downloaded a trial version off the Internet and spent from dinnertime to 1 A.M. figuring it out. Then he worked up a little example for them and sent it off.

"It was okay," he said. "I accomplished the goal."

The next thing he knew, he was an eighteen-year-old looking for an apartment in New York, so he could start his job, which would pay him around $30,000 for a year's work. He wanted to move to 45 Wall Street, "an incredible building for young Wall Street professionals." But his parents wanted him to live near college students. So he got an apartment with an NYU student on Waverly Place in Greenwich Village. "It's *sort* of a two-bedroom. Or it's a real person's one-bedroom."

And while he's not crazy about living in New York, he is sticking with his job, which offers him not only a salary but options in the new company, "which I hope will be worth a lot."

The only problem is that he now must decide what he's going to do: go to Boston University after deferring for a year, stay at his present company or take an even more lucrative job.

"I've seen all these jobs posted," he said, "for $80,000 and $90,000. Do I plan for the future and do another year of Rumpus? Or do I make more money quickly? Go to school? There's no one to turn to for advice.

"All around me companies are looking for people to do things. My friends say, 'Cool, go do that and we'll take a trip to Florida. And my parents don't know what's shaping the industry. Their advice has no value. I feel like I'm all alone, and the decisions I make are affecting everything. And no one has any clue how to give me advice."

GETTING AHEAD OR LAGGING BEHIND?

In the fast-growing computer and Internet world at the turn of the century, studying computers in college can actually mean falling behind. New technologies are being introduced daily. Spending even a couple of semesters studying European history or Plato's cave, or taking a trip abroad to expand the mind, can mean missing out on a new development.

Josh Wray, who took a year off after high school at the North Carolina School of Science and Mathematics to go to Africa and set up websites in Senegal for a nonprofit program, found that even working in computers in a less-developed country can put you behind. "When I came back I felt like I had lost so much in terms of the computer industry," he said. "Like Flash was the big thing. I was 'Okay, man, I don't know any Flash.' I was cramming to learn it."

Josh notes, however, that he had no problem getting a job in Silicon Valley, even without knowing Flash cold. "One problem here is that there aren't enough employees for the job," he said. "They'll just hire anyone. There are not enough people to go around. I've asked about college degrees, and they'll say, 'We'll take anyone who can do the job.'"

He would like to think about joining the Peace Corps after he finishes his major in computers and business with a minor in French at San Francisco State University. But he worries about falling behind in computer technology again. "If I did two years abroad, I'd be so outdated," he said. "Things change so fast."

Right now he is working nearly forty hours a week at a start-up company that sells expensive jewelry on the web, www.miadora.com. He does HTML and graphic design for them, in exchange for a salary and, perhaps in the future, some participation in the company's profits. "I know that my experience here is going to be more valuable than my college degree," he says.

Another Miadora employee, who is eighteen, has already completed college and has a year's experience at Hewlett-Packard. He started college at thirteen. Josh, who is twenty, knows that he wants to finish his college degree, partly because he hears the thunder of younger kids, like that thirteen-year-old, coming out of high school right behind him. "In a few years, four or so, there could be a whole new group of college grads with computer skills," he said. "In a few years everyone is going to go into computers. It will become more competitive.

"If I can become independently wealthy by then, that will be good. And I do like learning, and I like what I'm studying, so it's not going to be torture to finish school."

And yet he also hears the siren call of money. One of his friends completed a year at Eastern Carolina University and knows everything about NT and Unix. He is working elsewhere as a network administrator and making $50,000, plus stock options. That leaves Josh pondering, "I wonder if I should do some full-time work and get a bank account."

WHERE DROPPING OUT IS A TRADITION

The year is 2004. You may graduate from college with a degree in computer science and find out that the computer industry is in the doldrums. Or that the Internet and all of its e-commerce has fallen flat on its face. Or you may get out of college and go to work as a systems analyst for $70,000 a year, but find that the billionaire who owns the company never bothered going to college at all, or dropped out early.

Bill Gates dropped out of Harvard after his third year. He is now the richest man in the world. Michael Dell of Dell Computer dropped out of the University of Texas at Austin after one year. He is now the richest man in Texas. Steve Jobs and Steve Wozniak, two college dropouts, founded Apple Computer. Lawrence Ellison dropped out of the University of Illinois and eventually started Oracle, a network computer manufacturer. He is now worth billions.

I asked John Heilemann, who is finishing a massive book on Silicon Valley, if kids today had to finish college.

"Do they have to go to college to get a job programming? No," he said. "Do they have to go to college to be a good programmer? No. Do they have to go to college to be a great programmer? Probably no, but almost all the genuinely great programmers have done so. (This distinction between good and great programmers is very important. There are lots of good hackers but few great ones, and the great ones are probably a hundred times more productive and important than the merely good ones.)

"But does that mean that programmers don't benefit from college in ways that have nothing or little to do with their wage-earning potential? Of course not. Since when is college about what happens in class, anyway?"

And that's an excellent point. Some of these kids are missing out on what is referred to as the "college experience," being young and often poor, hanging around with other eighteen-year-olds, wondering if you can scrounge up enough money between you to order a pizza into the dorm.

College means meeting other people who are, for instance, *not* computer programmers. It means developing social skills. Occasionally it also means going to a lecture, or a showing at the college film society. It means floundering around for a while, taking the core curriculum and trying to figure out what you want to do with your life. It even means going to class and being inspired by a teacher.

If these web billionaires do go back to college, they will be older students. They will never have the chance to run out of gas trying to get back from a concert, or the opportunity to go home for Thanksgiving weekend with a suitcase full of dirty clothes. Oh, wait. Maybe they can do that anyhow.

The point is that going to college is a rite of passage. But often kids do as Josh Wray is doing; they combine college with lucrative work. Or they start college and drift away before finishing. They are eating their cake and having some more cake.

ASKED AND ANSWERED

It is not unusual today to find kids who are written up in the *San Francisco Chronicle* for their exploits in the computer field. "Is it just me or was it not that long ago when kids lumbered through four or more years of college to get their degrees and then took a year off to traipse around Europe before sullying their hands with business cards," Mark Veverka wrote in April of 1999. "Not so in the Internet era."

His object lesson: Samuel Osborn, who had interned at the brokerage house of Bear Stearns while a sophomore at Berkeley. Samuel quickly became a fully licensed stockbroker, working from 5:30 in the morning until 1:30 in the afternoon.

Then young master Osborn would take in a few college classes. But eventually, he found, he wanted to jump into a web business. He quit stockbrokering, and quit school, to join two friends in starting up a new company selling and renting digital video disks online. In early 1999, another company bought his DVD business for 50,000 shares of stock worth $8 a share. And young Osborn, age twenty-one, and his friends were hired to stay on as executives in the company. With salaries and bonuses.

When asked what he and his partners thought about college, he replied, "We have no interest in going back to school anytime soon."

I asked Doug Coupland, who wrote the book *Generation X* and who has observed the computer world for some time, what he thought about computer kids and college. "In general, it depends on what they want out of college," he said in an e-mail. "If they want to be smarter, more fully rounded people, yes, go to college. As always. If they want money, they'll get it no matter what in computers, assuming their brains are rigged up to the level where they can do calculus. It's a refrain in the industry: Calculus Is a Filter. If you can't do it, best enter some other industry, because you won't cut it in tech. At all. And people will mock you."

Doug also notes that the people with the best chance of success are the ones who can combine their computer expertise with knowledge in another area. "Language theory is an easy current example," he said, "but the people I see who are happiest (and only incidentally making pots of money) are people who have fused their own personal interests with computer science."

A WEB MILLIONAIRE (WITHOUT THE CALCULUS)

"People who are really good at calculus are the ones who say you need calculus," said Scott Wainner, a recent web millionaire who quit college because he had trouble with that particular filter.

By the middle of 1999, it had become common for kids to become millionaires because of websites and new technology; their stories were in the technology press, even in *People* magazine and on television. Eventually the stories were only worth telling if the kid was very young, or the site sold for a great deal of money.

Wired magazine's wire service reported on two who fit that mold. Austin Heap, of Powell, Ohio, is very young. He is CEO of PureNetworks, an interactive website for the music industry, and PureRadio, which he hopes will connect radio stations and teenagers. *USA Today* voted Austin's website devoted to *South Park,* the foulmouthed cartoon series, the best on the Internet. NBC has profiled him. He has attracted advertisers to his site and made deals with the local radio station. For now, his mother writes his press releases. Austin is fifteen.

Justin Frankel, at nineteen, sold Nullsoft, his MP3 software and webcasting company, to America Online in a transaction worth approximately $400 million in stock. Nullsoft will allow other teenagers to download their favorite artists' music from the internet. Bye-bye, CDs.

When Scott Wainner, twenty-one, sold his web company in August 1999 to Earthweb, the news didn't even make the pages of the real *Wired* magazine. Instead Chris Gaither wrote him up for *Wired*'s spinoff wire service.

Scott told me he would fall into the "good SAT [1340], low motivation" category. He grew up in Dallas, the only child of a landscape architect and a graphic artist. "So I've got some creativity in me, but they're not analytical folks," he said fondly. "My mom got on the Internet a year ago, and my dad after that."

After Scott began having some success with his web business, he convinced his mother to quit her job and run a little posters-on-the-web business he set up for her. "That way, she could work from home and not have people barking at her," he said. "She's smart and creative, but she's not totally business oriented."

Scott went to Catholic schools in Dallas, and says he thinks he learned more in elementary school than in high school. In high school, he said, they didn't have any classes that interested him. "They had typing class, but I was faster than the teacher. I'd always been typing." That was because he had always been playing around with computers. "It was gaming and flight simulators," he said. "I got the computer when I was six, a TI99/4A, but it had a keyboard." Remember, he's talking about 1984, when home computers were something of a rarity.

"I enjoyed taking things apart. At ten I had a Tandy 1000 and my first flight simulator. But it didn't have the power to make the simulator seem real. It was too arcade-ish."

His future was set, he says, by "the whole upgrade syndrome."

"I didn't have any money, so I had to figure out ways to make my computer faster. I couldn't afford to buy a faster one. So I did overclocking, running your CPU at a faster speed than it was intended for. I started the website to create benchmarks to compare my computer with others."

Now, remember that the World Wide Web is only six years old. He was there right at the beginning, at age fifteen, publishing tips and how-to guides for the site, which essentially became a "my machine is faster than yours" kind of place. He called his amateur site SysOpt, for system optimizing. On it he wrote how-to guides, telling what he had learned.

He kept adding to it. Eventually his father said, "Why don't you put banner ads on it?"

"I didn't take it seriously," Scott told me. "There weren't any smaller sites that did that. I was kind of skeptical. But I e-mailed companies, and a few of them took ads."

He sold his first banner ad for $60. In the first year, he made $25,000. If I correctly caught the numbers Scott was throwing out, he says he made $175,000 the year after that. And four times as much a year later.

"So by last year I was making much more than I could possibly make if I'd stuck with college," he said.

Luckily, he has a couple of expensive hobbies. He likes racing bikes. And he flies planes. He went up in a small plane the first time at age fourteen. "The instructor was a total idiot. Said I wasn't old enough to get a license."

He started taking lessons at age sixteen and got his license over a couple of months. "At nineteen, I couldn't rent a car, but I could fly people around."

As always, it was a love of aviation (remember those flight simulators he started with?) that led his career choices. He decided to go to Texas A & M to study aeronautical engineering.

And that's when Scott encountered calculus. To be an aerospace engineer, he would have to take four years of calculus.

"Calculus is the worst subject," he said. "I did fine in math and algebra." He got a D in freshman calculus, and so he had to take it over again. Sophomore year he failed the next-level calculus. "So I had to take *that* again. I was fed up with it at that point. I was in my junior year.

"So it was a dilemma. Here I have this annoying, frustrating, time-consuming school that was costing me money. On the other hand I had this six-figure website. I just wasn't motivated in college—nothing excited me, classes bored me, I was just jumping through hoops and I couldn't even see the light at the end of the tunnel. That, combined with all the work I had to do on the website, spelled disaster academically."

He met with advisors who suggested he take a lighter course load, or take some time off. But he was also getting tired of life in College Station. His first year of school he had driven four hundred miles every weekend to see his girlfriend in Dallas. "I didn't do the whole college-dorm partying thing," he said, "but I did get the opportunity to experience a 'serious' relationship with a girl for two years. That didn't work out, but I learned a lot from it and think I'm probably a better person because of it." When the relationship, which had started in high school, ended, he was left with the social life around Texas A & M and College Station.

"There's nothing there but the college," he said. "It's a hundred-mile drive to get to anywhere. They're cowboy kind of hick people. Jeans are the dress code. They'd never heard of any drink except for beer. Not my kind of place."

Even the lighter course load didn't work. "So I decided to leave and work on the site. When I left I didn't intend to leave permanently. I intended to go back."

He speaks of all of this as if it happened decades ago. When we spoke, it had been less than a year.

A friend and business partner invited him to Portland, Oregon, to spend some time windsurfing. So he moved there and took an apartment with a view of Mount Hood. But a week or two after he arrived he had a bike accident, when a woman in a car drove by and broke his left hand with her sideview mirror.

"So I never did go windsurfing."

Instead, something better happened. A company contacted him about acquiring the site, which focuses on real gearhead stuff, motherboards, general computer components, technical support—and gets, hold your hats, about 2.7 million "page uses" a month with half a million visitors. When the company made an offer for Scott's site—"it's really hard to value something intangible," Scott said—he asked a number of people for advice.

"I asked my mom about it," he said. "At that point, the first company had offered me a very large sum of money and I was pretty happy about it."

But things got better. Another company, Earthweb, came on the scene. And since their offer was "seven times higher," as Scott puts it, he decided to go with them.

Scott is not being coy when he refuses to tell me what Earthweb paid for his site. For one thing, these days, he has four lawyers to tell him what to say. It was agreed that the purchase price would be kept a secret, to avoid a gold rush of higher and higher prices for small sites.

The deal was announced this way: Earthweb acquired Scott's companies—Sysopt.com and ResellerRatings.com—and another company, CodeGuru.com, for a total of $12 million with additional consideration to be paid based upon future performance.

Let's just guess that Scott got somewhere between $5 million and $10 million for his websites, and since he's given up day trading ("legalized gambling," he calls it) there is a chance he'll hold on to a good bit of it. The sale happened in August 1999 and he was twenty-one, old enough to legally drink the champagne that was poured to celebrate.

Earthweb moved Scott to San Francisco, where he rents an

apartment with a nice view of the Golden Gate Bridge. (This young man can afford a taste for views.) And he remains at www.sysopt.com as its editor in chief.

He drives a BMW, but a "base model," he says, a BMW 323CI, the new coupe. He has an American Express Gold Card and an Optima card. He is particularly annoyed at the payment desk on the Optima card, which is offered by American Express as well. He put $50,000 on his AmEx card and paid it off in full in a month. Then he reached into his wallet and used his Optima card for a $20 purchase, and forgot to pay it off that month.

"This creditor calls me on my cell phone and harasses me: 'Why haven't you paid this bill?!' It really annoyed me, because I had paid this same company 50K on time. But I didn't think to say that at the time. I just said, 'You'll get your money.'"

He has an accountant. His investment advisors are Merrill Lynch. "They have a pretty good deal when you have a good amount to invest," he told me. "You're a premier client and they call you frequently."

But he wants everyone to know that there have been costs. During the sale he was dealing with lawyers and advisors and regulations every day. "That was stressful."

And over the years, he says, "I missed out on lots of typical high school/college social activities because I was working on the site so much. I would likely classify my social development as stunted but not permanently broken." In fact, Scott, who says he used to be shy, is a perfectly charming young man, self-deprecating, full of good humor and quick, though in e-mails he tends to fall back on the geek habit of using emoticons. And anyone who looks at www.sysopt.com will see that he's a cute kid, too. That's his high school graduation picture he has posted.

Bottom line, his feeling about that college degree: "It just seems like a piece of paper. I think employers look at it as showing you can stick with something and learn something. But they want to see that you can do something, too. If you're twenty-one and you don't have work experience, you'd better have a degree."

BACK DOWN TO EARTH

There is a trade association for the information technology industry, the ITAA, in Arlington, Virginia. Harris Miller is its president. He says that for the core occupations of systems analyst, programmer and system engineer, the 20,000 companies his organization represents "have tended to use the four-year college degree as the major roadblock to decide who they hire."

Even though start-ups might grab anyone they can, he said, "while they're trying to make payroll and get the IPO ready, at IBM, they have a longer-term perspective." IBM has strict rules about hiring people with four-year degrees for jobs above a certain level. Bill Gates would never have made it there.

"And most people still given their druthers will look for someone who has a four-year degree. Writing program code or editing program code, 90 percent do have four years or better. But as the labor market has gotten tighter, and since the numbers of college graduates in computer science have lessened, they've had to turn to other sources."

Yes, folks. In the early nineties, the number of people entering computer science in college began to decline. As a result the number graduating at the end of the nineties was lower. (It's coming back up again now, and as surely as these things happen, there will come a day when there are too many people with computer science degrees.)

"The meat grinder isn't turning out enough people with degrees," Mr. Harris said. "In addition, four-year colleges and universities are not that flexible. They're not going to shut down the Spanish department and make computer scientists. So employers have had to look at other sources."

As a result, for-profit technical schools like the ITT Educational Institute or DeVry Institute of Technology are, he said, "ramping up" their training programs. These should not be seen as "vocational" schools, he says. A vocational school teaches a skill set that remains virtually unchanged over the years. In computer technology, a worker will assume that he or she has to be retrained, or get additional training, every few years.

The Information Technology Association of America says 63 percent of the jobs in manufacturing, financial services, accounting, consulting, communications and entertainment are technology-intensive. Mr. Harris notes that many of those companies as well as Internet start-ups will hire anyone with the skills. "They all need workers," he said. "And they are willing to go outside the four-year college system.

"But," he warns, "those who do not get a four-year education or more face limits as their careers progress. As you move up the ladder, other skills, reading and writing clear plain English, the ability to understand business concepts, become just as important."

He says he has students who come to him for advice as freshmen. "They say they're going to take all computer courses," he told me. "I say fine, if you think you still want to be a programmer. But for more diverse opportunities, hold your nose and take those other courses, the English composition, French. They give you more life options. The employers want the technical skills, but they want the rest, too.

"Some people are always going to want instant gratification," he said. "And thirty seems like an eternity away. But I think the vast majority of students do have good common sense."

That is to say, they'll hold their noses and take all those liberal arts courses that are supposed to make them more valuable employees.

Meanwhile, a number of certification courses have sprung up to allow people to prove that they know their computer stuff. A coalition of fifteen schools (the Virginia Foundation for Independent Colleges, or VFIC) has created the Tek.Xam, which they hope will someday have the same importance as the SAT. The exam, which lasts five hours and is given online, in a proctored computer lab, tests the person's ability to solve problems, create a website, use word processing software, analyze data and understand Internet basics. It also will, theoretically, test a person's knowledge of computer ethics.

In a practice version of the test, Virginia students scored about a 30 percent "pass rate," which is comparable to the pass rate for accountants on the CPA exam. Since these are colleges, however, it would be safe to assume that they see the Tek.Xam as an adjunct to a college degree, not a substitute for one.

THE WEB, NOT JUST FOR KIDS

One of the daunting things about the computer revolution is that it seems dominated by children, whose metabolism seems to keep pace with the speed of electrons. It was with great relief that I stumbled onto Kevin Krall, forty-two, on the web, and his web-page design company, Weblucent.

Kevin, like Scott and Tanner, pretty much taught himself all that he knows. But he did it after an outrageously varied career that took him from working in a warehouse to running a toilet-paper-making machine to being on the professional golf circuit.

Kevin used his savings to pay for a couple of years of learning about computers, pretty much on his own. "I spent my time online learning and practicing and trying and doing things," he said. "It's more than just knowing HTML. And nowadays it's virtually impossible for a one-man band to get a business going and to maintain it in the website design and development community." When I spoke to him, he was busy trying to raise money for a new venture.

"Right now in my spare time"—he laughed—"that's from midnight until two, when I get up because I can't sleep, I'm attracted to Flash. What people are doing with Flash is really exciting, because you can virtually make the website an organic thing. It almost looks alive."

Kevin's other venture besides his web-design business was a religious community on the web, although it took a couple of hours for him to get around to telling me that.

But let's start back a little earlier in Kevin's story. He grew up in Chicago. "Right out of high school I did try junior college," he said, "and almost made it through a semester. I was working full time at a plastic molding injection machine, and I cut off the top of my thumb. I was left-handed, it was my left thumb. So I had to quit school."

He was laid up for six months with splints and skin grafts, and when that time was up he had a slew of bills to pay. "The desire for learning has always been there, but I just never had the opportunity to consider college once I got into the workforce," he said.

He is not that certain about the value of a college education, anyhow. "All my friends out of high school went to college, and not one of them today is doing what they went to college for." When those friends finished college, he had been working at a warehouse for four years. And he had been promoted several times. Meanwhile, a friend who had majored in physical education was driving a truck. "It seemed pretty much a waste of time, college," Kevin said.

He spent several years at the warehouse and then he quit. "I will never work in a place I don't like. If I don't like it, I don't care if you're paying me $1 million, I'm out of there. No amount of money is worth the frustration of being at the wrong place. If you're waking up and dreading going to work, quit, because you don't belong there and you're hurting everyone else who *is* there."

He had saved some money, and in the months he took off, he met his future wife in church. The two of them moved to Tulsa, Oklahoma, to go to Bible school and Kevin got a job working for Quik Trip, "the Cadillac of the convenience store industry," he says, and at first I think he's being ironic. But irony is a stranger to Kevin Krall.

"They hire good people and pay great wages and their stores are immaculate," he said. The chain exists in Oklahoma, Mississippi, Kansas and Nebraska. He spent about a year working the night shift at Kwik Trip and going to Bible school during the day. But the schedule began to wear him down, so he quit Bible school.

The marriage lasted four years; the job at Kwik Trip, six. "Then I took another break," he said, and explained the pickup work he did for the next two years, erecting shelving (or "pallet racks") at warehouse stores around the country. "I'd spend three months in Santa Cruz and a month in Chicago, some time in Arizona all over the place."

But, he points out, he was divorced and "reaching the thirty plateau." "I was disillusioned at the time, didn't know what I wanted to do."

And then he noticed an ad that said that Kimberly Clark was about to build "the world's most technologically advanced manu-facturing facility in Tulsa." After a reading test, a computer test, a math test and a test of things like hand-eye coordination, plus three one-hour interviews, the company picked forty-three people out of the 15,000 applicants who flocked in. Kevin was one of them.

"And if you made it through that, you had a final one-hour interview with a facility manager," he said. "High school is a poor preparation for the real world. It's not a good foundation for what we experience in the real world. There should be more emphasis on testing for skills at an early age and training. We don't do any of that. We put [students] in a classroom in a group and say, two plus two is four. I don't want to get on a soapbox, but if it was up to me I'd do things differently."

The machine he helped operate for Kimberly Clark was four stories high, and run by a computer. He was trained for six to eight months before the plant went into operation. The machin-ery would make toilet paper, four tons of toilet paper every twenty-six minutes. "Two two-ton rolls, sixty-eight hundred gallons of water would come through our machine every second," Kevin said. "And it was loud."

Kimberly Clark intended to train its new workers from scratch to work in a team environment, with a very flat hierarchy. "We were running the company when we were on shift," Kevin said. "No one was a manager telling people to do this, do that. We worked as a team. That's what I liked. I'm a self-starter. I don't need people to tell me what to do. I don't *like* people to tell me what to do."

He liked the freedom and the machinery. For years he went to work, doing shift work, two days on, two days off, three days on, three days off. That meant that every other weekend was a three-day weekend. "And you know what that meant," Kevin said.

I was in the dark.

"Golf," he answered. "When I picked up a golf club, I was hitting two thousand golf balls a week. There were days I'd spend eight hours on the driving range. The pro golfers would have to come out and say, 'Take a break, stop, sit down.' They talked to me constantly about balance. But they were impressed with the speed, the rate at which my ability increased. Within a year I was playing with them.

"I started golfing at thirty-five; at thirty-eight I was carrying a four handicap. I won some local tournaments. It looked like I could do this. My window of opportunity was opening. I looked at it as, I could spend the rest of my life here or I could break away. If I didn't make the PGA tour or the Nike tour, I always had the long shot, the faraway deal of playing the senior tour. If I stuck with it for twelve years, I *knew* I could do the senior tour."

It was a decision that was a long time coming. "I kept playing golf and I kept getting better. I began waking up dreading going to work, and I loved playing golf. So that's what I did. I cashed out, took my severance pay, vacation pay, cashed out my stock and went golfing."

He almost made it a full year on the circuit.

"I ended up in Arizona for the last two, three months and I couldn't find anyone to sponsor me. Some people can do it; I wasn't able to."

He moved to Austin, Texas, because a buddy lived there. But when Kevin got there, the buddy took off. Kevin stayed. He says this next part as if it were a perfectly logical progression. "Now I was stuck in Austin, didn't know anyone, didn't want to be here. So I started doing graphic design work on a computer."

He explains. At Kimberly Clark he had learned Harvard Graphics and Lotus Freelance. And he had bought a computer at one point and started messing around with Microsoft Publisher and once made a business card for a friend.

In 1996, he got on the Internet. "Next thing I knew I was researching online education," he said. "A whole world opened up. I said, 'Hey, I can learn anything I want to learn.' There are no limitations. That's what struck me. I could do website design, or learn about gardening, or photography, or build a house."

What he discovered was Ziff-Davis University, which charged $4.95 a month for unlimited access to its course work. "I was broke and living hand to mouth. They were just starting out and had lots to do with computers and Internet stuff. So I started taking classes. In 1997, I honestly spent not less than an average of twelve hours a day with online learning, educating myself, finding out how to do everything.

"I took over forty classes online. They give you a certificate. You post your work and they comment, correct and adjust. There was no grade per se. I've never been one for grades. Accomplishment is my grade."

And while he took classes on the Internet, he began recording and organizing the information into ring binders. "I'm an organized guy. I like to have everything in place.

"I'm not going to do anything halfway. I'm going to do it to the best of my ability. My website, www.weblucent.com, that's the third website I've ever built." (It's impressive, I'll tell you that, very clean and professional, with some nice little innovations.)

"It's all in the preparatory work," he said. "It's just like painting a house. The real work is not the painting, it's the preparation, the spackling, the taping, the masking, the taking off the doors, getting the plastic sheets laid down and moving the furniture. All that's the work to do the job right."

During all those years that Kevin was working in warehouses and making toilet paper and playing golf and learning computers, he was also compulsive about one other thing. Over fifteen years, he translated three-quarters of the New Testament from Greek into what he calls "West Chicago."

"I don't know Greek, but there's a Greek-to-English literal translation, and a concordance and Bible dictionary," he said.

And it was only after telling me that that Kevin felt comfortable sharing his big idea with me, which is either silly or profound—and with the Internet, it's often hard to tell the difference between the two.

"I got this idea of doing this large-scale, online Christian community," Kevin said. "I drew it all up and ran into my business partner, who introduced me to this other guy. Last year he agreed to put up $50,000 to fund the community. The intention is: It's an open atmosphere. It does not convey any type of religious doctrine or belief. I wanted to create a community where everybody was equal and open regardless of creed or dogma or belief."

It would be a religious hub, a filter that would keep hate literature, pornography, racism, violence out of the range of the community it served. Kevin's Christian web community would allow those people who wanted to use the power of the web, but were afraid of what they might come across, to jump onto the Internet.

Let's put it this way: Have we calculated how many religious folk there are in this country? And as Kevin puts it: "You have all your other value-added services: youth groups, singles connections. You can find a doctor you want, or talk dogma with a Catholic, or listen to a radio broadcast.

"We control the filtering. Parents don't need to worry. If you subscribe to our community you can be assured that your kid does not have the capability to see hate websites or violence or abusive language. That's part of the environemt. A safe place for families and Christians and children to not be afraid of the Internet."

When I spoke to Kevin in the fall of 1999, he was in negotiations to get funding for his web community, www.Christian commons.com. "I stole that from the college I never went to," he said. "A place to meet and get together. My attention now is on meeting with venture capitalists and in developing business plans, cash flow." He predicted that his community would be up and running by June 2000.

"I'm not one of those who believe that those with the most toys win," Kevin said. "I believe the person who gives away the most is a winner. It's how much I can give versus how much I can get. I want it to be a benefit. That's my focus."

Part Two

LIFE, BEFORE COLLEGE

If you are convinced that your child should not go straight to college (that Jody has earned a break or that Jared has not earned the right to go to college), you now must figure out what your child should do.

Slacking around the house is not an option.

If your child is already making $30,000 a year or more working with computers (the turn-of-the-century paradigm), he may rightly tell you that he wants to work now and save college for later, if ever. But if your child is *not* a computer head, then you may have to help him or her come up with some ideas.

You can send the child off to live with a relative in another state or another country. You can indulge your child's need to travel (see Chapter Six) and finance a grand tour of Europe. You can let your child take a few courses at a community college, to see if he is ready for the full college experience.

What follows are some other ideas, and some stories about kids who have found success by taking a different course. Some of the more footloose may have a long and torturous journey, but you'll notice that almost all of these kids do end up going to college, after all.

They do that because they want to; they also do that because we have given them few other choices. As long as employers demand a college degree as the price of admission to the white-collar working world, kids will feel that they have to buy that particular ticket to ride.

Chapter Ten

WHY NOT BE ALL
THAT YOU CAN BE?

*Every human being has some handle by which he or she may be lifted;
and the great work of life, as far as our relations with each other
are concerned, is to lift each one by his or her proper handle.*
—HARRIET BEECHER STOWE

Listen up, baby boom parents: This is not the sixties and a kid
joining the military is not cannon fodder. Yes, the military will
see your son or daughter as a cog in the ongoing process of, you
know, defending democracy and things. But, in return, the
United States will take that child off your hands for three or four
years. The country will house, feed and clothe that child, teach
him or her responsibility, instill pride, inspire honor and offer
him or her a skill, from tank maintenance to military intelligence. The Army has two hundred specialties, including, yes,
computers and program analysis. Your son or daughter can even
study television broadcasting, or spend two years assigned to the
Army baseball team. All that and get paid roughly $800 to $900
a month. And get free haircuts. And thirty days' paid leave a year.

The catch? Basically, your kid has to be breathing and have an
IQ somewhere above that of an eggplant. Or to quote from the

government website: "Enlistees must be between the ages of 17 and 35, must be a U.S. citizen or immigrant alien holding permanent resident status, must not have a felony record, and must possess a birth certificate. Applicants who are 17 must have the consent of a parent or legal guardian before entering the service. Air Force enlisted personnel must enter active duty before their 28th birthday. Applicants must pass both a written examination, the Armed Services Vocational Aptitude Battery, and meet certain minimum physical standards such as height, weight, vision and overall health. All branches prefer high school graduation or its equivalent and require it for certain enlistment options. In 1993, almost all enlistees were high school graduates. Single parents are generally not eligible to enlist."

That's about it. "Everyone's not going to be a college graduate, this high-thinking-in-the-ether kind of person," General Lloyd W. Newton, a four-star general in the Air Force, told me. "We find our niche somewhere else in society."

Women and men, theoretically, are equals in the military, with women eligible to enter almost 90 percent of all specialties. So Jennifer can become a missile-maintenance technician or a heavy-equipment operator but not join the artillery or the infantry.

In return for those few qualifications, the military will pay up to 75 percent of the tuition for almost any college course your kid takes while enlisted. "You have to try really hard not to earn at least an associate's degree," one Army recruiting officer told me.

And, of course, there's the G.I. Bill, which is touted as paying up to $40,000 (even $50,000) for tuition after a kid leaves the service. In fact, the enlisted person contributes to this during his or her first year of service, to the tune of $100 a month. And no, it's not really $40,000, much less $50,000 for most recruits. The Veterans Administration matches the enlisted person's contributions at a ratio of 11 to 1, so the net result is around $14,000 to $15,000 with some bonuses. The Army pays the most (it has to, to get recruits; its contributions are added on top of the standard amount, for such things as reenlisting or driving a tank). The Marines pay the least. "We're famous for doing more with less," Chris Smith, a former Marine, told me.

And no kid should think that the government will simply hand him $14,000 in a lump sum to spend on education. The money is doled out in monthly payments of around $500 each for around thirty-six months of school, including trade school, enrollment.

Chris Smith, who went to Columbia University's School of General Studies to study anthropology, pointed out that the G.I. Bill did not stretch far in an Ivy League school. "I get $538 a month for every month I'm in college full-time, and a month costs me $5,000," he said. "Basically, it pays my rent."

But as you'll see later in this chapter, Chris got a great deal more than $538 a month out of being in the Marines.

THE WAY IT WAS, AND THE WAY IT IS

In the fifties and sixties, a kid caught stealing or joyriding was given a choice: do time or enlist. In fact, recruiting personnel used to loiter around the courts, letting judges know that the Army was there to take in a few good miscreants.

Going into the military was seen as a way of straightening out the lost, the aimless, the scamps who were not flat-out criminals and sometimes those who were. It was the handle by which society lifted a fair percent of its young men.

During wartime, when the country had the greatest need for soldiers, the military draft reached deep into the population for recruits, the rich as well as the poor. But the country also paid those men and women back. In 1942, the Army invented the General Education Development (GED) degree as a way to reward those soldiers who had dropped out of high school to fight. At a time when only 50 percent of eighteen-year-olds had a high school diploma, that GED degree had some stature. Moreover, it allowed the holder to attend college on the G.I. Bill.

But that was then, and this is now. Today a middle-class mother had this reaction when her son said he wanted to enlist in the Army: "I spent yesterday crying," she wrote me in an e-mail. "I never really thought of my son going into the military. It's not what you dream about. I'm not somebody who was ever pro military. I thought the military was for tattooed, wife-beating rednecks. My first reaction would be he'll be turned into this horrible killing-machine monster."

This mother is, of course, a baby boomer, and her knowledge of the military, she admits, is based on movies like *Apocalypse Now, Full Metal Jacket* and *Platoon*. When she says the military was not something she dreamed about for her son, she really means that she is horrified about an option that is beneath her son, who grew up in an affluent suburb and went to boarding school but ended up with a GED.

So for her sake and yours, let's take a look at today's military. The draft, as you know, ended in 1973. What we have now is a volunteer service, and to get volunteers the military has both had to pay more and in some cases expect less. Basic training runs are done today in tennis shoes, not military boots. "Boots hurt," said General Evan R. Gaddis, Commanding General, U.S. Army Recruiting Command in Fort Knox, Kentucky.

"We've learned an awful lot," General Gaddis told me. "We've changed an awful lot. We've studied and become sophisticated in physiology."

Today, 20 percent of military recruits are women. "They all have to go through the same training," General Gaddis said. "For physical fitness tests, we have different standards that go by gender and age. I'm fifty-one. I don't have to do as many push-ups or run as fast as an eighteen-year-old. There is a difference between males and females. A female has less upper-body strength, so we don't require as many push-ups. I wouldn't call that a lessening [of standards]. I call that a recognition that we should have had for a long time."

Ironically, most branches of the military will reject a kid who has only a GED. That's because the military discovered that the attrition rate over three years for enlistees with a GED was 45 percent, or double that of enlistees with their high school diplomas. Only the Army (the largest service) has tried to open the door to those without a high school diploma. A pilot program will attempt to provide enough remedial work to allow dropouts to get their GED's and get them to pass the military entrance exam.

Yes, there are entrance exams to get into the armed forces. There are even books to help Jessica ace the exam. And here's why she would want to do well with the ASVAB (Armed Services Vocational Aptitude Battery).

First of all, the exam is pretty easy. It consists of ten short tests covering word knowledge, paragraph comprehension, arithmetic reasoning, mathematics knowledge, general science, auto and shop information (well, it *is* the military, not Harvard), mechanical comprehension, electronics information, numerical operations and coding speed.

Each of those is scored separately, and then some of the tests are combined to yield verbal, math and academic ability. The four math and verbal subtests (arithmetic reasoning, mathematics knowledge, word knowledge and paragraph comprehension) make up the Armed Forces Qualification Test (AFQT), used in selecting some enlistees.

Sample questions from the numerical operations section of the ASVAB require operations like dividing 60 by 15. Note: The answers are multiple choice. Word knowledge would ask the future soldier to know that "variable" means "shifting" and not "mild," "steady" or "chilling." OK, the questions do increase in difficulty, but this isn't the SAT.

Scores range from 1 (and recruiters tell of candidates getting scores in the single digits) to 99 percent. A score of 31 is the minimum for acceptance by the Marines, but the Marines have enough recruits to afford to be picky; they are looking for at least a 50 from most of their enlistees.

And here's why Jared wants to study for the ASVAB: A score between 31 and 50 may get him into the Marines, but will label him a Bravo and send him straight to the infantry, the ground fighting forces; the higher the score, the more the service will want him and the better deal they will cut for him. Scoring at the 80 or 90 percent level (the Alpha level) will net him a signing bonus, a choice of assignment and a choice of training facility. If Jared is going in, let him be an Alpha.

Unless, like one Marine, Stephen Deitchman of Kansas City, Missouri, the recruit scores a 93 on the ASVAB and still requests the infantry. "No regrets," he said. "If I'm going to be a Marine, I'm going to do it all the way. The only all-the-way thing in the Marines is infantry, to be a rifleman. I can shoot, I can run, I can do all that stuff. It was awesome."

The Navy will take a high school senior with 31 percent, but expects older enlistees, those who have been working for a few years, to score at least 50 percent. Bashon Mann, who had completed three and a half years at the University of Virginia, did considerably better than that, scoring an 89. He threw himself at enlistment in the Navy after "bottoming out" in college, and he picked the Navy because of a celebrity.

"Look at Bill Cosby and what he's done in his life. I made a direct correlation. He was in the Navy. I admire him."

When he enlisted, he had already been put on academic

probation twice. "That was a maturity issue," he said. Petty Offi-cer Mann then said something so honest it nearly took my breath away. "I was in a situation where I wasn't paying for school," he said. "My parents were paying and I took that for granted."

Twenty-two days before graduation he had gone for a run to clear his head. He found himself running past the Navy recruit-ing office, and the next thing he knew he was saying, "Give me the papers, please!"

"She had to calm me down."

I asked if he, as a black man, had ever encountered any racism in the service. "Quite honestly, there are certain prejudices in our society, and the Navy is not separate from that society," he said carefully. "We reflect everything. You're going to have racism. Racism exists. The thing is to overcome that."

The Air Force requires a 40 on a specific portion of the ASVAB. The Army will take a 31 for a small number of high school graduates, but expects a higher score, at least a 50, of someone holding a GED (thus those prep courses).

Here's the problem for recruiters: In good times, like those at the end of the nineties, prospective Marines, soldiers and sailors who do well on the ASVAB can also do well on the SAT. Those kids are in college, and doing their beer drinking in the dorms. Or they are employed in a job that pays them far more than the Army can. Right now, military enlistment is way, way down. "There is competition for the best and the brightest," General Gaddis said.

Army statistics show that young men in the South are three times more likely to consider military service than those in the Northeast and twice as likely as kids in the Midwest and West. But in Fulton County, Georgia, in what could be considered the heart of the talent pool for the military, a whopping 84 percent of the three thousand seniors who graduated in 1999 planned to enroll in universities, colleges and vocational or technical schools. Another 7 percent were going to go straight to work. Some were undecided, but only 2 percent of its seniors listed the military as a choice. If the services are to meet their goals of 200,000 recruits a year, they need between 5 percent and 8 per-cent of the country's high school graduates. So, Fulton County, Georgia—not good enough!

That's why not even a felony conviction will keep someone out of the Army these days. General Gaddis told me that a few good criminals would be let in, but that it takes a general officer in the Army to grant a waiver for a felon. "The one most recently, a gentleman who was a hunter, I think, had a shotgun in the trunk of his car and the campus police arrested him because it was a felony to have a weapon on a college campus." The charge was reduced, and the Army let him in.

In these straitened times, even the demand for a high school diploma is being reduced. "We are now a high-technology Army, and we've found there are other measures of success besides the high school diploma," General Gaddis said. "There's trainability, flexibility and maturity."

Nonetheless, all of the services, except the Marines, are having difficulty meeting their recruiting goals. The Army (which is falling 9 percent short of its goal of 74,500) and Air Force (10 percent short) are having their worst recruiting problems in two decades. General Lloyd W. Newton, commander of air education and training, as well as officer in charge of all recruiting for the Air Force, told me, "I'm not having trouble at all getting officers, folks to fly things for me. What we're having trouble with is getting enlisted ranks, technicians."

The Navy was falling 12 percent short until Rear Admiral Barbara E. McGann, Commander of Navy Recruiting Command, stepped up advertising to reach generation Y. "We went to an approach a number of months ago of having real sailors telling their own real stories. No actors, no scripts," she said. "We launched that approach in both print and in an infomercial and direct-response TV campaign." Her advertising agency, BBDO New York, hired Spike Lee to direct her commercials, although she said that those rolled out "too late to affect fiscal '99," when the Navy met its recruiting goals.

And Admiral McGann has tried other innovations. The State of West Virginia, for instance, a landlocked state, one might add, has signed an agreement to give a free year of community or technical college to any state resident who is on active duty in the U.S. Navy. That is part of what the Admiral refers to as an "aggressive partnership with Tech-Prep," a program to offer technical studies to kids in high school and community college. The Navy, along with the Marines, also offers the Program for Afloat College Education (PACE), where civilian instructors live and teach on vessels as small as frigates for months at a time.

But Admiral McGann also sent a flotilla of recruiters out to do the door-to-door work it sometimes takes to get kids to sign up. "It's very much like billable hours in the legal profession," Admiral McGann said. (Her husband is a lawyer in Washington.) "It boils down to sharp recruiters, properly trained, telling the Navy story across America. We have enough recruiters out there this year. I think it's the sheer energy and hard work and dedication."

Admiral McGann reminds me of a particularly assertive piano teacher, one who only seems really military when she snaps out the word "outstanding." I asked her if she had ever encountered any problems of discrimination as a woman. (The Navy is 20 percent women.)

"I come from a large family of women," she said. "All professionals in the private sector. We get together on holidays and compare notes. There is a tremendous focus in our Navy on making sure that we worry about role models at all levels of the organization. As I compare notes with my sisters, it's interesting that there is not that institutional commitment outside the Navy. We've been approached by the private sector to learn about our diversity program. We spend an awful lot of energy growing officer role models from our enlisted ranks. If ever there was a place to learn tolerance, it's in the Navy or all of the services."

And she has her hopes up for the next generation of kids, whom she expects to be more welcoming of a career in military service. "From what I've been reading about generation Y," she said, "their values are more akin to their grandparents'."

Only the Marine Corps, which has a boo-yah reputation for being the toughest, easily attracted its full quota of 40,000 recruits. The Marine Corps, incidentally, attracts the youngest recruits and does so by touting values like honor, courage and commitment, despite (or perhaps because of) its reputation of being first in, last out of any skirmish. What is interesting about kids and the military is that the same child who has trouble with authority figures at home may crave the drill sergeant with veins popping out of his neck, a *real* authority figure.

I spoke on the phone with the young man who had decided (to his mother's distress) to enlist in the Army. This is what he told me about military discipline. "It's a little different from my mom yelling at me," he said. "We're talking physical intimidation. I know my mom can't beat my butt. I know she won't kick my ass, but this guy will. That's the difference. I'm looking forward to basic training. I think it's going to be fun."

But that doesn't help this kid's mom, whose peers spent their youth protesting the military (you know, "baby killers") during the war in Vietnam. During World War II, a popular and heroic war, 10,110,114 men were drafted, probably half of all draft-age men. But Vietnam called up only 1,766,910 men over nine years. In 1999 there were only 1.36 million people on active duty in all branches, a 36 percent drop from 1989.

Today, only one in ten Americans age sixty-five or younger has served in the military. Up until this generation, almost every person in America had someone in the family—father, uncle, brother, even mother or sister or aunt—who was a veteran. "In the past there was always someone sitting around the dinner table who could share their experience," General Newton of the Air Force told me. "I was just a little farm boy from South Carolina, and now I'll tell my nieces about being in the Philippines. They're impressed. But you don't get that much these days." Or the teenagers have already seen the South Pacific on a vacation trip with friends.

The low numbers of veterans sharing stories around the dinner table, and the fact that the military attracts primarily the poor, means that many middle-class kids never even consider the military and therefore miss the benefits that military life can offer.

Frank J. Milhofer finished White Bear Lake High School in Minnesota in 1993. "I wasn't the greatest high school student," he said. He went straight into the Army, "to figure out what I wanted to do in life and earn money for college."

Frank now works as a computer programmer and takes classes in community college. "I earned $25,000 for college with the G.I. Bill," he says. "I let the government pay for it. I haven't paid a dime out of my own pocket."

"One thing I don't understand," he said, "is when I go to school to register and see all these kids who are standing in line for financial aid or student loans to get money for school. Then they drop out and have to pay it back."

Unfortunately, not many kids think the way Frank does. The Pentagon frequently takes the country's temperature to see where the military stands. In 1999 only 26 percent of the sixteen- to twenty-year-olds surveyed said they would give a military career a tumble. And those people tended not to be members of the middle class.

"What young woman with an upper-middle-class background, graduating from one of the best high schools in Texas, would even consider the military?" asked Kristina Shevory in an article in the *New York Times* in 1998 about her decision to go into the Army after high school and to defer entering the University of Chicago. (Presumably Ms. Shevory was a high scorer on the ASVAB; she ended up in military intelligence, learning Russian.)

When I wrote an article about alternatives to college for that same issue of the *Times,* I listed the military as the first option out of six, much to my editor's consternation. She asked me to move military service farther down in the list, because "it's so far-fetched to tell *Times* readers to send their children to the military." I won the argument, but the prejudice continues.

A RELUCTANT MOTHER

The mother who believed that anyone in the Army was a redneck asked not to be identified in this book by name or by the city she and her son live near. So let's call her Elizabeth. She has a college degree. Her second husband has a master's degree. She is an expert on women in the workplace and lives in an affluent suburb.

She raised her son—he asked to be called Bob—in a middle-class environment. "Bob went to sleep-away camp," she said proudly. "He had music lessons. He took karate. He played baseball. I wanted him to have this good childhood, something more than what I had."

It didn't take. Bob managed to get himself thrown out of boarding school in ninth grade. He became what educators call an "in-school dropout" in tenth grade in public school, turning up only when he felt like it and doing no work. As his mother said, for him "homework was only a suggestion."

"It was so mind-boggling that an authority figure would ask him to do something and his response was optional," she told me on the phone later. "And that included his response to me."

His mother, then a struggling divorcée, spent a third of her salary on schools, psychiatrists and counselors. "I had him in therapy. The therapist said he was angry." She laughed, a sudden bark of pent-up feelings. The doctors also told her that Bob had

ADD, or was bipolar, or perhaps had a learning disability. She and her second husband signed up for Tough Love, a course that teaches parents to set limits for their children.

All to no avail. "He kept screwing up everywhere he went," she said, "and I kept trying to stay ahead of the latest disaster." When Bob, who was teaching himself Japanese, had to repeat the tenth grade, "that was when the wheels started coming off," she said. "He was missing things. I didn't see any work being done. He'd say, 'I did it in study hall.' You can't say, 'Let me check your homework.'" Actually, you *can* say, "Let me check your homework," but this mother was not up for the fights that would result.

And so Bob, a high school dropout at seventeen, spent two years in the basement of her middle-class suburban home smoking pot, drinking forties of malt liquor and listening to rap music. "This wasn't like a real mellow time," she said. "I had his friends' parents calling me. Cops showing up." But if she suggested Bob might seek employment or get his GED, he would scream at her for not being supportive. That's when she began worrying about Bob's collection of swords. She feared, as she put it, his "acting out."

"He was threatening to me," she said. "He used to scream at me. I had no control."

But once he enlisted, suddenly Elizabeth thought he seemed too young and tender to be going into the Army. Part of her distress was, in fact, a matter of class. She complained that the other parents at her son's school, in their affluent suburb, are "in the Ph.D. program of parenting. With a kid like this, you *so* don't measure up. We have a friend whose kid is up at the University of Chicago, with an internship. They're always going off on archaeological digs, and my kid is in the basement with rap music."

She and her second husband kicked Bob out of the house for six weeks to straighten him out. That brought him around to the idea of getting a job and taking his GED. But then he began talking about enlisting in the Army.

A week after I interviewed her on the phone I got another e-mail message from her: Bob had made the commitment. He was about to sign up for basic training at Fort Knox. But Elizabeth now complained: "He's not getting the same deal his friend is. They're taking him even though he only has a GED, and they're acting like they're doing him this big favor. He doesn't get a signing bonus like his friend does. He can't pick his location like his friend did. And he can't choose his training. They're going to spend two months training him how to load and shoot and maintain M1 tanks. I guess they think he's worthless and disposable, so they give him the worst sort of grunt job because he only has a GED. I'm afraid they'll treat him very badly, like a second- or third-class citizen, all because of the GED. I'm just not used to my son being treated *badly*."

Bob got into the Army despite his GED because he got a respectable 66 on the ASVAB, "without even trying," he told me. He signed on with the Army in part because he was looking for a world that would set some rules. "They're going to be yelling at me and screaming at me and getting me up in the morning," he told me. "I'm counting on having a problem with it at first. But I've already been away to boarding school, so it's going to be like that, or sleep-away camp."

Far from being intimidated by basic training, Bob was eager for it. "So they want me to go for a run? I can run," he said. "I used to run cross-country. Shoot guns? What's so bad about that? I don't have to kill anybody, not yet. I shoot guns, I do push-ups and I run. It beats going to school from 7:50 to 3:30 and being forced to go to church, like I was in boarding school. It's more fun doing physical things. I may not like to be following orders, but it's only going to be four months. I was in boarding school for a year and a half."

On the phone, Bob sounded like a charming, smart, typical nineteen-year-old, someone who, more than anything, needed to get out of the basement. While his mother was worried about what would happen to him in the Army, and troubles in Bosnia and East Timor, Bob was sounding as though the Army was a challenge that he needed.

"Anything they can throw at me I can do already," he told me. "I want to work with guns and do a lot of shooting, make the marksmanship team. I can't wait to get out of here. Aside from being sent to war, what could be bad about it? You know the benefits you get for this? You get the craziest benefits. You can have your own apartment for free, everything you buy is at a discount. You eat for free. Starting pay is, like, $20,000. How bad could that be?

"I'll be coming out when I'm twenty-four, twenty-five. I can start my life then. This is a good jump, especially for me. From where I'm at, this is a great jump."

And, he let me know, he expected to come out of the Army with a new physique. "I'm going to try to get the best out of this experience," he said. "I'm going to push myself as far as I can go, and I'm also looking to put on a few pounds. I talked to this one guy who came out of basic. He went in 145 and came out 165. And he was buff, too, he was cut!" he said admiringly.

One last thing, about Elizabeth and her concern that Bob might become a "redneck." Because the military is increasingly attracting minority applicants, her son is more likely to be subjected to "Latin American History Week" than a rigorous indoctrination in the art of squirrel hunting. Moreover, any parent of a college-age kid will tell you that their children change political orientation at least twice once they leave home.

When I asked one ex-Marine if he thought the service was more reactionary than the civilian world, he said, "The kids I knew coming out of boot camp couldn't spell 'liberal' and wouldn't know a conservative if they were sued by one. In my experience, these kids' ideological growth didn't come from the military institution, it came from their peers who brought their fetishes, fears and prejudices with them from home."

ONE FURTHER THOUGHT ABOUT THE GED

The GED Testing Service plans to replace the current exam in 2001 with a tougher test. And every few years the passing score on the GED is raised. (The joke is that it's not a matter of making the test harder, it's a matter of making it less easy.)

Right now, 750,000 high school dropouts a year take the GED, and two-thirds of those pass the five-part, eight-hour, multiple-choice exam in reading, writing, mathematics, social studies and science, and the short-essay requirement. They spend an average of thirty hours preparing for the exam.

According to an article in the *Phi Delta Kappan,* the average age of those taking the GED is twenty-five, and the test-takers have completed an average of ten years of school. Two-thirds are white. The sobering news is that one in six of the high school diplomas (or completion credentials) awarded in this country each year are GEDs. So getting an equivalency degree instead of a diploma is surprisingly common.

I know of a number of kids who dropped out of elite high

schools in New York and took their GEDs, an exam most of them could have passed in grade school. Let's face it: If you want to insult middle-class parents, about the best thing you can do is drop out of high school and take the GED. The only more shocking thing a middle-class kid can do is join the military.

HEY, EVEN BASIC TRAINING AIN'T SO BAD

Here's another thing to consider: Basic training has become a lot easier. A kid who goes through three months at the National Outdoor Leadership School will probably have had a tougher time. Some lifers are now complaining that the new military is producing a weaker soldier, a less ferocious sailor. "Even now I run into people who come back from basic and I say, 'My God, it's even easier than when I went,'" said Scott Bennion, a graduate of White Bear Lake who enlisted in the Army Reserves in 1993.

"And there are limits on what drill sergeants can do. They're even thinking of getting rid of the Smokey hats, because they made the brim hard, and they'd crack your nose with it and cut it. And I said, 'You can't get rid of *that,* that's a tradition!'"

I asked Scott what kind of physical fitness was required now for basic training. "As long as you can get out of a couch," you're okay, he said.

Scott's one complaint (he is now in the National Guard): sit-ups. "Every time I do them I get lower-back spasms," he said. "Doctors who work on the back say sit-ups are the worst thing you can do to your body. Military people need some way to test abdominal strength. What about pull-ups?"

Sorry, Scott, that would be unfair to the female recruits, who do not have comparable upper-body strength.

Certainly, the way the government describes it, Basic sounds like a college course in adventure camping. "Recruit training provides a 6- to 11-week introduction to military life with courses in health, first aid, and military skills and protocol," the Armed Services website says. "Days and nights are carefully structured and include rigorous physical exercises designed to improve strength and endurance."

The Air Force is even adding a week of what sounds an awful lot like the solo in Outward Bound to its training. That week, called "Warrior Week," will be "a little bit tougher," General

Newton allowed. Sounding a little bit defensive on the subject of push-ups and chin-ups and five-mile runs, General Newton said, "We set a standard of what we need our folks to do to be airmen. If you meet that standard, you're in. We know our niche."

Besides, he points out that his recruits are working with computers and airplanes, not running through the swamp (that would be the Marines). He bridled when one man commented that the Marines at Parris Island looked more military because they were doing their runs with rifles in hand. "Are you suggesting that if my airmen carry computers they're less prepared than Marines carrying rifles?" he told the man. "A rifle doesn't make you more Air Force."

Nor does running five miles. "Some people are ready to run five miles," General Newton said. "We only need a mile and a half. When we were in Kosovo, wherever we launch the planes from is right off the flight line"—that is to say, close enough so the airmen didn't have to run very far.

"I don't recall a single time when we've been in conflict and someone told me 'Your airmen are not prepared.' Not a single one has ever said we're not prepared," he said. "I rest my case."

General Gaddis, who says he ruined his knees in training twenty-two years ago, thinks the new form of training is far better than the old. "We train much smarter than we used to, and we don't hurt near as many people," he told me. "We have master fitness trainers. We know how to build endurance in the things that are really important to us. We used to work on just strength. Now we work on flexibility and endurance. I'd say we're making a better multifunctional soldier."

Flyboys have the cachet, sailors have the white uniforms, soldiers in the Army are, well, they're multifunctional soldiers. But the Marines continue to be the few, the proud. Their boot camp is longer—twelve weeks—and remains tougher than the others. Their branch is the smallest and the most avid. And what they do seems to work.

"I had a young man come in who had a 1.9 average in high school," said John Chopka, dean of admissions at Malone College in Canton, Ohio. This would not be a student that most admissions officers would welcome into college. But, he said, this young man had spent three years in the Marines. And so Malone College admitted him.

"I really think this young man is going to make it," Dean Chopka said. "The Marines gave him discipline and focus."

Or as General Newton of the Air Force put it, admiringly, "If you go into the Marines, they'll make sure your head is screwed on straight."

ONE MARINE'S STORY

Chris Smith was born in Tallahassee, Florida, into a family of six kids. When he was two, his mother abandoned an unhappy marriage to a man not Chris's biological father. She was thirty-two. Her youngest child was six months old. And all she had was a broken-down station wagon with a cracked windshield and bald tires. She loaded the kids into the wagon and drove to Oklahoma City.

"My mom was a night clerk at Days Inn," Chris told me, "and we kids slept in the car. She was thirty feet away and my little sister slept in a laundry basket in the front seat. I slept way in the back and looked up through the rear window at that ugly yellow sign, every night. I knew that something was wrong with this situation. It's so tangible, I could taste it. And I had this deadly fear that this was the most I would ever be. It was in the Marines that I found out that you aren't what you were, you're what you can make of yourself."

Even after his mother remarried and became a secretary, then inspector and eventually administrator of the state medical board, life was rough. The family lived in a Vietnamese neighborhood of Oklahoma City, and they were still poor. Chris worked sweeping the floors of the Catholic school he went to (and worked in an antiques store) in order to pay tuition. He began volunteering at nearby camps for children with muscular dystrophy and the mentally handicapped, just to get out of the house. "It was crowded. We were poor. I needed space."

He spent years working for the Red Cross disaster team. "At sixteen I was teaching all these adults in disaster relief," he said. "By the time I was eighteen, I was running disaster teams." For his last year of high school he transferred to what he calls "a really, really bad public school." And things got worse.

"I got kicked out of high school," for bad behavior, he told me. "They mailed my diploma to me. I made my mom cry, too, and she was a cop. I was always getting arrested and getting into trouble." He tried the University of Oklahoma, and that did not go well. He dropped out to manage a restaurant for a year.

Even though Chris was mature enough to have responsible positions, he says he had no confidence and low self-esteem. "Up until the Marines, I was a big loser in my own mind," he said.

"I followed the Dead for a while," he said. "Made jewelry to sell at the Dead concerts. I'd go back home, do a semester of college. Drove a van. Just things.

"Even though I was doing all these things, I still felt a big hole in my life," he said. "I was building a foundation, but I was never building upwards, just outwards."

He was twenty-one when he began dating a high school senior who would be the catalyst in his life. "She was in school and working and supporting her mother and her little sister," he said, "and she made me want to be a better person.

"I didn't see how I deserved this girl, so I joined the Marines. I joined thinking I had to join something better than myself. I went into the Marine Corps, thinking there I could find something more important than me and attach myself to it."

He went down to the local recruiting station. They gave him and a roomful of recruits the ASVAB. When the tests were graded, someone at the front of the room called out the scores. Some scores for kids trying for the Army were in the 20s, he says. Most going into the Navy and the Air Force were in the 40s or 50s. There were a couple of scores in the 60s. Then someone said, "Smith, 99."

"The entire room turned and looked at me," he said. "And my recruiter had that look in his eyes that said, 'That's right.' I felt twice the man I'd ever felt before in my life.

"They said that would qualify me to be a nuclear technician," he said, "and they wanted me for ten years. They offered me the quality enlistment program. A choice of duty station. And I said, 'Sign me up.'"

At twenty-one, he was 5 feet 10 inches tall and weighed, as he put it, 127 pounds "with soaking wet rocks in my pockets." He signed up for six years and went off to boot camp, where he had to be able to do a certain number of pull-ups, sit-ups and a three-mile run. In twelve weeks he went from six pull-ups to forty-two, from thirty-eight sit-ups in two minutes to ninety-two, and shaved nearly ten minutes off his three-mile run. "In just three months I realized my own potential," he said. "It wasn't something someone gave to me. I earned it."

He came out of boot camp near the top of his class and was assigned to the Marine detail at the White House. He lost the girl back in Oklahoma, but he became a sergeant in less than three years. "The Marine Corps never gave me anything I didn't have to begin with," he says. "It was like I had a toolbox inside of me. And they showed me how to use the tools."

One thing he learned to do was accept responsibility for all the things that had gone wrong in his life. "When I was in the Marines, I woke up one day and said I was responsible for my mistakes and had to claim that or I'd never move ahead. It was a moment of freedom."

He even learned the point of military discipline after watching an instructor put a recruit's head through a plasterboard wall. (The recruit, who was not hurt, was then told to plaster and repaint the wall before the next morning—and he did.)

"At the time, you think this is so stupid," Chris said. "And then you realize there's a hell of a lot of a reason for it. You learn to fix your mistakes. You learn to be a team and to fix other people's mistakes.

"They say, 'Don't tell me it's impossible.' They want to hear, 'It's done, sir!' And somehow you would get it done. I'd realize there are no limits. You are only as limited as you allow yourself to be. It's so empowering. You can be the lever that moves the universe. I learned all of this in the Marines."

While he was posted at Eighth and I, the Marine headquarters in Washington, he spent his spare time playing guitar at clubs in Washington. It was there that he met college students from George Washington and Georgetown Universities. Then he noticed that when he hung out with the college students, and *Jeopardy!* was on, he was the one getting all the questions right.

So he began a correspondence program at Penn State, in the independent learning program. It took him months and months to finish one class, because each homework assignment had to be mailed to the school, then graded and mailed back. He continued taking classes, even when he was trained in intelligence work, even during the three years he was stationed in the South Pacific. He was such a dedicated student, he said, he did his homework one time on a helicopter carrier in the middle of a storm. "Everyone was in a bunk," he said. "And I was in an office tied to a chair with my computer tied to the desk."

And then, after six years, he left the Marines. "I knew I had gotten everything out of it," he said. "I loved being a Marine, but I did it. And now I wanted to go explode upon the world."

He applied to Columbia University, to a program called General Studies, which was set up after World War II as a program to absorb returning soldiers. Today it appeals to nontraditional and older students. (It is the school that gave me my degree thirty years ago.)

Chris is president of the student council. He graduates from college in June 2000 with a bachelor's degree in anthropology and recently decided to pursue a Ph.D. in anthropology, focusing on modern nomadic cultures. He has a literary website and plans to start a publishing company. He supports himself by writing about acoustic music for popular music publications. And he's the coproducer of "Cutting Edge of the Campfire," one of the hottest acoustic music festivals in the country.

"I can do these things because I went back to school and made the connections," he says. "I can make these dreams happen."

BUT ISN'T IT DANGEROUS?

Every parent I talk to mentions the threat of war, deployment and the possibility that their child will somehow be hurt, crippled or killed in the military. The *Boston Globe* calculated in 1997 that 29,000 active-duty personnel had been killed since late 1979 in accidents, homicides, suicides and illnesses while in the military—55 percent of them in accidents caused by motor vehicles. Within the same time, fewer than six hundred were killed in combat.

So here's the answer to that question: Don't worry about Jedediah being killed by a sniper in Bosnia. Worry about his going out drinking with his friends and then driving back to the base afterward, just as you do now about him riding around with his friends on a Saturday night.

I'm not saying there is no downside to the military. But so many of us try to protect our children to the point that we are keeping them from having the kinds of experiences that would turn Chris Smith from a college dropout in Oklahoma to a successful college student at Columbia University.

Chapter Eleven

A THIRTEENTH YEAR

*Teenagers are people of whom too much
is asked and too little expected.*
—THOMAS HINE, *THE RISE AND FALL
OF THE AMERICAN TEENAGER* (1999)

Outside of New England, the notion of voluntarily spending
a thirteenth year in a private school is nearly unheard of. The
postgraduate year, offered at a number of New England boarding schools, has often been the place where rich kids regrouped
after failing to get into the college of their (or their parents')
choice.

But even that seems to be changing. I found one young
woman who spent a year at Exeter "just for the Exeter experience," even though she had already been accepted at Princeton.
She deferred. I found poor kids who had a chance to go to prep
school after they graduated from high school. Athletes who
needed another chance. Kids who had newly diagnosed learning
disabilities, who needed time to figure that out before hitting
college. And while I did not find anyone who said that the post-

graduate year was an end unto itself (they were all headed to college), there is no reason to assume that a postgraduate year could not be the culmination of someone's education.

Even schools that do not have formal postgraduate years may offer a thirteenth year. One school I queried, in Hawaii, said, "Here, as in many other places, it is common for an entering student to be asked to repeat the previous year." Jim Rizzuto, director of college counseling at the Hawaii Preparatory Academy, told me, "The repeat may be called for because of deficiencies or because the student has potential that was not fully realized in the previous situation."

And yet the notion of schooling beyond high school and before college remains somewhat strange outside of East Coast prep school circles. "Even 'independent school' is a foreign concept in Oregon," said Deke Smith, who does educational counseling in Portland. "You're a bad parent if you send your kid to a boarding school here, like 'What's wrong?' We have very few boarding school clients."

A PARAGON OF VIRTUES

Deke also sees kids at his office in Cambridge, Massachusetts, and it was there that he encountered Jedediah Purdy, a paradigm for unconventional education. Purdy was home-schooled until he was thirteen, spent a few bland years in a high school in West Virginia and then needed a bit of a polish before college, which he got at Phillips Exeter Academy in Exeter, New Hampshire. "We do have more and more kids applying who have been home-schooled," said Tom Hassan, director of admissions at Phillips Exeter. "They want the socialization." Some of those students are what Exeter deems "one-year seniors," who may already have high school diplomas, or may have, as Tom puts it, "maxed out" where they are attending high school.

Both Tom and Deke talked glowingly about Jedediah, who completed a sort of educational trifecta. First he attended Exeter, then Harvard, and is now at Yale Law School. Oh yes, and at the age of twenty-four, Jedediah Purdy wrote a book, *For Common Things,* which got a great deal of media attention and not a little criticism for its cornpone threnody to earnestness.

"Jed Purdy was my client," Deke said. "He came to me in August. I called Exeter. I said, 'Take this kid, give him a full scholarship.' I told them, 'This is Bertrand Russell.' He is just an extraordinary fellow. The most brilliant student I have worked with ever, barring none. He wrote so beautifully, even as a high school senior. I still give out his college essay. It's so intimidating."

A PLACE FOR LATE BLOOMERS

Well, yikes. Most kids who end up in a postgraduate year are not Jedediah Purdys. They are, according to Carol Loewith, president of the Independent Educational Consultants Association, based in Fairfax, Virginia, typically "the late bloomers, the ones who haven't erupted yet." Her organization of 230 counselors will charge from $500 in Shreveport, Louisiana, to $2,500 in New York to help groom a kid for admission to a good college. That grooming process can involve a postgraduate or thirteenth-year at a prep school.

"There are several different profiles," Carol told me from her office in Westport, Connecticut. "One might be a student with academic promise who hasn't reached it yet and needs to mature. For that student a postgraduate year is wonderful. Another batch of students for whom a PG year is appropriate is kids who haven't emotionally or socially matured into what college is about. They want to leave home but are not ready for the freedom of college. They can take it in a half-step."

What a boarding school offers, Carol points out, is the kind of *in loco parentis* supervision that colleges no longer provide. What a prep school cannot do, she and others point out, is straighten out a kid who is over the edge. Frustrated parents often think that a strict boarding school will be able to curb a seriously wayward child.

"There are so many parents in denial," Deke Smith said. He and his wife, Nancy, who also counsels students, know that a parent has a problem child when they get a call saying, "I'm looking for a military school."

"That's usually the tip-off out here," Deke said from Oregon. Once a child reaches eighteen, those options are seriously diminished. For one, Deke said, "your kid has to be willing to go."

ONE ATHLETE'S STORY

The third kind of student who thrives at boarding school is the athlete who either ignored academics or needs another year to mature physically. Sometimes those kids are trying to up the level of scholarship they are offered; sometimes they are trying to parlay a year at a boarding school into acceptance at a better college.

Alex Okosi came to this country from Nigeria to better his chances in life, but he is not the first person you would think of attending an elite boarding school as a postgraduate student. For one thing he had no money. For another, he was a fairly casual student.

The youngest in the family—his parents remained in Nigeria—he found himself bounced from school to school, and living with relatives. His one passion was basketball. "In high school, I wasn't really a good student," he told me. "I had the ability, but I didn't exert myself. School wasn't my first priority. The focus on education was out the window."

He describes himself as a "pretty good basketball player," however. "I could have gone to *most* schools, but not the top schools in the country," he told me. Between his junior and senior years of high school, Alex found himself traveling with a mentor on an AAU all-star team trip in New England. The mentor had, without Alex's knowledge, arranged for an informal interview for Alex at Exeter.

"It seemed very stuffy, very upper class," Alex said. "I wasn't exposed to the level of education and the level of wealth where the kids are coming from." He went home and didn't think any more about prep school. He was about to enter his senior year at a high school in Rochester, New York, he had the basketball season ahead of him and he had a number of colleges clamoring to recruit him.

Then he got injured.

"Consequently, all the schools that were interested in me, because of basketball, suddenly . . ." His voice trailed off. He found himself in an impossible situation, particularly because he hadn't concentrated on academics. Moreover, because he was here on a student visa, the only way he could remain in America was if he went to college. "Suddenly," he said, "college was not going to be a reality."

He had some offers from what kids still call "junior college," but he knew he did not want that. It was, he said, a dilemma.

And then Exeter came to the rescue. His mentor told him that the school would give him a second chance, although he would have to take out a small loan (the rest of the tuition would be covered by a scholarship). Most of Alex's friends didn't even know what prep school or a postgraduate year was. "Why are you doing this? There was always that question," he said.

"But Exeter was probably the most valuable experience I had," Alex told me, and clearly, from the way he talks about it, Exeter remains more important to him than the college he eventually attended.

"When I got there on the first day, I was pleasantly surprised," he said. "It was more diverse than any other place I went to." (The schools he had attended in the United States tended either to be black or white, or as he put it, "either urban or suburban, very extreme.")

"I was also surprised by how much education was emphasized," he said. "And for the first time in my life I was exposed to African-American students who were doing really well. It was an eye-opener. I had to write papers—things I barely did in high school." At the beginning he put in his share of all-nighters.

"It was," he concluded, "the first time I felt I was part of a learning environment. They respect you for what you do, not who you are."

With the push toward academics, and recognition for his intellectual ability, Alex's interest in basketball began diminishing. "Before Exeter," he said, "I was used to everyone coming to the games. But at Exeter, people were practicing their own thing or studying. Exeter was for the smart kids, not for the athletes."

Because of that, few coaches came through Exeter dragging basketball scholarships behind them. But Alex did get a scholarship from St. Michael's College in Vermont, and, as he says, got to go to college for free, studying business and economics. Today he works in Manhattan for MTV, coordinating sponsorships and group sales.

And he remains a huge fan of his prep school, recently attending his fifth reunion. "When I go back there," he said, "I still get goose bumps."

LEARNING DISABILITIES, TOO

Essentially, then, a postgraduate year works for kids who require more schooling for academic, social or athletic reasons. There are also a growing number of schools who will take a postgraduate (PG) student who has unresolved learning disabilities. Schools like Maplebrook School in Amenia, New York, take kids up to age twenty-two who have learning disabilities, attention deficit or bad study skills. Such kids can take a PG year in a school with classes as small as six to eight students. (This can be especially useful if a child was diagnosed late in the game and has not had a chance to accept the disabilities or cope with them.) Instilling an acceptance of evening study halls—a boarding school staple—helps a lot.

None of this comes cheap (unless there is a scholarship). Parents should assume that a postgraduate year will cost about the same as a year at a very good private college, around $20,000 to $25,000. It is possible to save money by doing the search for a boarding school yourself (there are helpful lists on the Internet and an increasing number of websites, run by places like the Princeton Review); that would allow you to skip hiring a private counselor to get Jacqueline or Jessie into a good boarding school. But if you're going to pay $25,000 for tuition, room and board, you might as well toss in another $1,000 for a counselor's expert advice (and all-important connections).

Those counselors will outline all of the choices, which range from the old-line prep schools like Choate-Rosemary Hall to academic-year-abroad programs like The American School in Switzerland (TASIS), schools in Britain that will offer college credit, even the National Audubon Society Expedition Institute in Sharon, Connecticut.

Jean Hague, an independent educational counselor in Atlanta, Georgia, admitted that taking a thirteenth year was still somewhat rare in the South. But she was particularly enthusiastic about the possibilities for "superior students with an outstanding record, who want some fresh air before Harvard or whatever."

Her favorite offshore program is called Ithaka and is located on the Isle of Crete. "It's a wonderful program for bright students who want to clear their heads a little bit," she said.

But most kids who land in postgraduate years are more likely the slow starters, especially boys, who did not focus early enough on academics. No matter how good their last two years of high school were, college admissions officers look at their grades in ninth and tenth grade and see "slacker."

PG AND ONLY PG

The Bridgton Academy, in North Bridgton, Maine, is unique in that it is set up to deal *only* with postgraduate students, 179 of them in the 1999–2000 school year—all boys.

"We operate more like a college than a high school," Lisa Antell, director of admissions for Bridgton, said. "Our mission is to make sure our guys leave here with the discipline and confidence to succeed, as well as the time-management skills."

She finds that although the school draws students from as far away as California, the concept is still new in much of the country. "Once you get out of the Northeast, people haven't even *heard* of a PG year," she said.

Recently the school took a student from Birmingham, Alabama, who had been expelled from a boarding school in Asheville, North Carolina, for drinking. This student had spectacular SATs—an 800 verbal, 750 math. But he was an average student who procrastinated getting work done and who now did not even have a high school diploma.

That's a rare exception. Most of her students have their diplomas. They got by in high school, then woke up and realized they couldn't get into the colleges they wanted. "Occasionally they've had older brothers and sisters who went to college and struggled and failed. And so they say, 'If he did that and struggled and is so much brighter, then what's going to happen to me?'"

She also gets calls from the service academies, to take on promising recruits who need another year of high school. Bridgton is considered a "foundation" school for the U.S. Naval Academy. In this case, it is shape up *and* ship out.

Bridgton, which charges $24,000 a year tuition, offers ten college courses for credit. And in many ways it feels like a college. The kids do not have to sign in or out. They have free periods. They can leave campus on weekends. But there is a dress code ("they have to look presentable"; translation: no baseball caps), and there is a two-hour study hall every night.

"Most of these kids aren't used to it," she said, referring to the enforced study hall. "But they know you need it. I can't imagine what it would be like for these kids to go to college with the *lack* of preparation they have."

One strong suit at Bridgton is writing. "We focus on writing even in math," Lisa told me. But self-advocacy is emphasized, too. "These kids don't know how to go after everything they need in college," she said. "You have to approach a professor if you need extra help, and you need to know how to access the resources—you have to get into a class you need at the registrar's office."

Her biggest problem with parents, she said, is that they tend to baby their children, even lingering on campus during orientation. "We tell them, 'Go home,' and the parents say, 'You've got to be kidding me!' But it's for the best. The kids have to learn."

Bridgton limits the number of ADD and LD students to twenty a year, because that is as many as they can handle. Bridgton also sees older kids who had opted out of the college track, worked for a while, and found a renewed interest in school. Seeing those kids become excited about learning can be very gratifying for the staff.

"A big reason I've stayed here," she tells me, "is that it's a really rewarding place to be. The sense of confidence that these guys graduate with!" Her response to their success is, she says, "almost maternal."

AN OPTION NOT JUST FOR THE RICH

At the Northfield Mount Hermon School in Northfield, Massachusetts, one program brings ten to twelve poor or disadvantaged students into the rarefied prep school atmosphere. Pamela Shoemaker is director of the program, called Transition Year. The school has a total of 1,100 students from fifty countries in grades nine through thirteen, including seventy postgrads.

For the general postgrad population, she said: "There's an odd, predictable curve, where they say, 'How did I get here?' They work harder than ever before, and still they don't get the grades. There's a dip of morale, and they're getting C's and D's. And gradually they pull out of that. Some do it by the end of the fall term. Some it takes until the end of the winter. Usually by midwinter something has clicked and they get a better sense of themselves. They get that confidence."

One distinct problem for older students is the school's curfew—10:30 most nights, and 11:30 on Saturday. "That seems like a loss of freedom to a nineteen-year-old," she said. "I always ask them: 'What are your goals for the year? How do you keep your sights on your goal?'"

The Transition Year program is a subset of the postgrad population. The program began sixteen years ago with seed money from the Geraldine Rockefeller Dodge Foundation in New Jersey. The kids who are selected run about one-third Latino, one-third Native American and one-third black; they receive full scholarships, including the $24,000 tuition, travel, books, even health insurance.

"If the child is the first to graduate from high school and has done well *there,* the idea of doing another year of high school is just so weird," Pamela said about the kinds of kids who come to her through the program. "It's hard to say, 'I'm going to high school for another year, because I've done so well, and they're paying me to do it.' It's so weird."

What Pamela stresses with Transition Year students is the ability to assess who you are and how you got where you are. "If you can do that, you will do fine in college," she says. "I think that's more important than the math concepts. If you learn both, that's great."

THE REALLY BAD APPLES

You know how every child at some point fantasizes that his parents are not really his parents? (That his parents are, instead, prettier, smarter, richer?) There are some children who cause their parents to fantasize that these are not their children. (That their real child is, in fact, sober, reliable and working hard at school.)

"The scariest ones are the ones who get to be eighteen and you know they are antisocial," Carol Loewith, the college counselor, told me. "And you want to put them in a therapeutic program. You know there's a worthwhile member of society in there." When parents of this kind of kid say they want a college "with a lot of structure," she says, "I know this kid is going to run away."

"If I see a student who is in the worst-case scenario, with a one point GPA and involved with substance abuse, a bad crowd, doing petty theft, truancy, staying out a lot, but whose family is straight-arrow and not willing to throw in the towel, it's those kinds of families I would encourange to look at Northstar," a low-level therapeutic school out West. (Therapeutic, in this sense, means a lot of psychologists and trained social workers, a great deal of supervision and an attempt to reshape the kid's thinking.)

"There's a *huge* financial commitment," she said. "Sometimes families are just angry, or maybe they've already invested a great deal of money in a student in court cases. So when it comes to recommending a very costly therapeutic environment, they will say, 'What guarantees that this will work?' Sometimes frustration comes out sounding like anger."

If a kid is stealing, doing drugs, running away from home and not listening to his parents, a postgraduate year will probably not be the solution. If the parents have the wherewithal, they can try for a school like Northstar, which will take kids over the age of eighteen but can charge between $50,000 and $80,000 a year, including transportation and therapy. Therapeutic schools are great for kids who have serious behavior problems, but the good programs require cooperation from the kids involved. (How many wayward students does it take to change a lightbulb? Only one, but he has to *want* to change the lightbulb.)

A warning: Parents should beware of some programs that kidnap teenagers in the middle of the night, hold them incommunicado outside the United States and charge upward of $50,000 for "counselors" who have almost no professional credentials. These programs do exist; they advertise; they have glossy websites.

But a responsible parent would be advised to check out all programs carefully. Teenagers can be frustrating and sometimes parents are frustrated by what is fairly typical teenage behavior. When I asked David Denman, the college advisor in Sausalito, California, what kinds of things might land a teenager in a good therapeutic school, he listed contentiousness. "Of course, there are degrees of that," he said. "When it becomes too contentious to deal with, that's the lowest level. Then drugs, alcohol, problems with the law. Promiscuity. Or precocious sexual activity. Either having sex too young or having sex too much. That covers it."

One mother, he said, brought her daughter in, "and she really quickly in front of the kid rattled off a list of the kid's short-comings and said, 'I want you to fix her.' I almost said to her, 'It's not like spaying a cat.'"

In terms of therapeutic programs, the ideal, he feels, is one that is open-ended, that does not require a kid to stay a set period of time. He often recommends the Montana Academy in Kalispell, Montana, "which has a superb psychiatrist as the clinical director," he said.

But he noted that none of these programs will do much for a child's education. "You've got to keep your priorities straight," he said. "If you've got a contentious, druggy kid, send her away and then start worrying about the academics. You've got to get the big problem straightened out first."

The better-known programs are up there in the $50,000 to $80,000-a-year range, including transportation and extra therapy for child and family. Some programs even charge extra for parent seminars. I asked Dave what parents could afford that, and he answered, like a shot, "Marin County and Bloomfield Hills and Westchester County. You know the places."

Dave sat in one of the most expensive therapeutic schools having breakfast one morning and began talking with a young man seated near him. "I introduced myself, and he introduced me to his brother and they told me that their sister was in the affiliated school in California," he told me. "I figured that was $200,000 a year after taxes, right there."

But if your child is over eighteen, most of these therapeutic programs will not take him. And there are other, far more affordable options that will give a child a chance to grow up. Read on.

Chapter Twelve

A YEAR IN WORCESTER, MASSACHUSETTS

*The best time to take action toward
a dream is yesterday; the worst is tomorrow;
the best compromise is today.*
—ALVAH SIMON, *NORTH TO THE NIGHT* (1998)

David Sohl was one of those kids who did not apply himself in high school, in his case, at the Watkinson School in Hartford, Connecticut. "I was very unfocused and slacked off a bit," he admitted. "I didn't have the good background for the colleges I wanted to get into."

David, who wanted to work in the theater, decided to put off going to college for a year and do something he loved. He could have tried to get work in local community theater, but he took a slightly different approach. In 1997, he applied to what seems a unique institution: Dynamy (www.dynamy.org), a residential internship program based in Worcester, an old industrial city of 170,000 in Massachusetts.

"Your future's not a black-and-white decision," Dynamy's brochure says. If Aaron Spelling were looking for a new television show to replace *Melrose Place* and *Beverly Hills 90210,* he could do worse than pay a visit to Dynamy. Consider the dramatic possibilities. Every year Dynamy gets a group of thirty to forty kids who don't want to go to the colleges they got into, or who didn't apply to any colleges at all, or who went to college and hit a wall after a semester. (The breakdown at Dynamy is roughly three-quarters kids just out of high school, one-quarter kids who have some time in college.)

Some of them are misfits. Some are gay. Some are rebels. Some simply can't stand school. Some want a break from the routine of classes and homework and tests. Almost all are from middle-class families who expect them to go to college. And at the end of the year, almost all of them do.

Here's how Dynamy works. First of all, it is not a "therapeutic" community, the term of art for an institution for mixed-up kids who need heavy supervision for psychological problems or problems with drugs or alcohol. Instead, Dynamy is a kind of womb, a safe place where kids can grow and test themselves for a year. "Our program is designed to help young people make connections to the world around them and themselves," said David Rynick, the executive director of the nonprofit program, "to base their lives on things they care about. We ask them, 'What do you want to learn this year?'"

The theory goes something like this: Put a kid in a situation where he is away from home and expected to do real work, where he is treated like an adult and helped toward his own goals, but has expert advisors keeping him on track. With a year like that, a kid can regain his interest in school, or find the missing focus in his life.

The young men and women in Dynamy (there are slightly more males than females most years) live in Dynamy-owned apartments with roommates, and work at three unpaid internships during the school year. The program offers all of the freedom and fun of school with none of the studying. "They buy their own food," Mr. Rynick said. "They are free to stay up at night, as long as they get up for their jobs. They need to learn from their own experiences."

COMMUNITY COLLEGE WAS A BORE

One young man I met in Worcester, Dave Hartman, was twenty-one when he came to the program. Dave is a big guy with a beard, and looks older than his years, which already put him on the old side of the program. Dave has a kind of gentle solidity that makes you think fondly of a phrase like "big galoot." He is immediately likable, and his year at Dynamy was considered a roaring success. But when Dave arrived in Worcester he had no confidence in his ability to do much of anything.

Dave, who grew up in Rochester Hills, Michigan, had a mother who had gotten a master's degree in education and a father who had dropped out of college. Dave had tried community college, but felt he was not getting anywhere there.

"I was drained from going to school consistently," he told me. "I was going through the motions. The community college courses just seemed dull and drawn out. I felt like I'd just done it for four years. Every step forward would be two steps back."

He had been thinking of taking a year off and working as a waiter. Then he stumbled on the Dynamy program, which costs $10,850 for tuition and another $3,800 for rent for nine months. (Food money and spending money are on top of that and run about $70 a week.)

"My father didn't want to see me dropping out and doing what he did," Dave told me. He was sitting in the basement of the school superintendent's offices at the Worcester public school system, where he was interning. It was a place that had all the charm you might imagine. He tipped his folding chair back and continued. "So they were both extremely supportive. I had expressed to them the problems I had been having with college. And my mother wanted me to do what's best for me."

In fact, his mother, a former teacher and president of the school board, has begun making it her mission to help other kids find options other than college. "They didn't have much information if you didn't want to go to college or technical school," Dave said of his school's guidance counselors. "My graduation class was three hundred fifty, and we had five or six counselors. I figured, like everyone else, that you went to college and did your soul-searching after you graduated."

Dave came to Dynamy even though he wasn't sure it would work for him. And he was worried about the expense. "I hadn't been real successful in college," he said. "Was that going to happen here?"

He began the year by setting some goals for himself under the direction of his advisors: budgeting his money and his time and improving his organization. He found that the demands of working in the real world helped get him organized. "I've had to find a way to spend fifteen minutes instead of an hour on something," he said.

Once-a-week sessions with his advisor helped him stay focused on his goals. I have the same kind of admiration for Dynamy's counseling staff that I once had for Louise, the patient black woman who handled the two-year-olds at my son's nursery school in New York. Every year Louise took a handful of toddlers and got them out of diapers and through potty training. I used to marvel at Louise's patience and forbearance. Who could do that kind of job year after year? I wondered.

Now I know. There is a special breed of person who just loves taking kids through rites of passage. And who doesn't mind doing it year after year. Most parents wouldn't want to tackle potty training again, and few parents are equipped to deal with a confused eighteen-year-old who is out of step with his peers. The people at Dynamy seem to relish taking on a new crop of young adults who have chosen another path.

THE DYNAMY YEAR

Every year, Dynamy's counselors deal with kids asking themselves who they are and what they want to do with their lives. The counselors also deal with eating problems, issues of identity, depression, acting out, kids who don't get up on time for their 6:30 A.M. job feeding the animals at the zoo. They have kids who rebel even at working in an anarchist's bookshop, kids who get into trouble drinking (rules strictly forbid it) or who can't get along with their roommates.

The counselors I met there seemed like combinations of priests, college residential advisors and camp counselors, with miles of experience on their meters. They all seemed like good, decent folk who had chosen as their life's work dealing with the kinds of frustrations and soap opera problems that would make most parents go gray. And, they admit, there are times when a child's problems are simply beyond them. I asked if any of the young people in the program had ever committed suicide and the program director, Fred Kaelin, twenty-five, looked stricken.

"No one has ever committed suicide while they were here," Fred said. "But I worked at a camp where a thirteen-year-old hanged himself. It's something I worry about here. We're not clinical. We're not counselors. But we pay close attention to some of those most extreme ways that young people call out for help, and we can get there earlier here because we work so closely with them."

It's these counselors who keep the kids in the Dynamy program from doing what parents fear young adults will do when they leave home: staying in crash pads or sleeping in the streets and doing drugs. The Dynamy year is carefully structured, a blend between freedom (to fail or succeed) and responsibility (to do what they say they will do).

It begins with three weeks of Outward Bound at Hurricane Island in Maine. Like Outward Bound and the National Outdoor Leadership School, Dynamy is a product of the sixties; it was begun in 1969 by Bruce Berquist.

"Thirty years ago, we were the only game on the block," Mr. Rynick said. "You either went to college, went into the military or got a job or came here. That was it."

After three weeks together in Maine, the kids choose roommates. Then the real work begins. The admissions director, Jono O'Sullivan, forty-two, tells them, "This is not a year off."

They meet with counselors to begin discussing goals. The counselors know the only way the year will work is if the kids are following their own dreams, not someone else's. Talk is encouraged, with the girls usually having an easier time of that than the boys.

But talk they must, because as soon as one of these kids says, "I want to learn about glassblowing," they will find themselves signed up to work at a glassblowing studio, and have to be there every day. Their word is their bond, and sometimes that bond is too tight.

WHEN TROUBLE STRIKES

The organization's guidance counselors are very careful to avoid those "I told you to X; why didn't you X?" kind of accusations that parents throw at kids.

"It's so easy to say, 'Because I say so.' But that's not the way here," Fred said.

Or, as Jono put it, "We say, 'I'm not playing the role of your father. Why are you playing the role of the child?'"

The ace the advisors hold is the gentle reminder that "this is what you said you wanted to do," and "we made a contract that you would do this for nine weeks," said Jono.

"We want them to figure out how to get around their problems," David Rynick said. "Our approach is to let them try their own solutions."

But the counselors are strict in enforcing the rules about drinking, drugs and fighting. "With the drug and alcohol policy—that's where we have to be more authority figures," Fred said. "One thing we talk about is the difference between use and abuse of drugs or alcohol. Three violations and you're kicked out. We are very up front with them. Lose control and if there's a fight, you're out of here."

As many as five or six of the interns leave for some reason before finishing the year. "There's no magic here," Jono said. "It doesn't work for everybody. There are dropouts."

And sometimes the program dismisses students. "We tell them that the process isn't working," Jono said. "And that can be for a whole host of different reasons: a clear lack of commitment in making the internships work, usually around issues of attendance. If someone's making it to work but struggling on how to make it work, we can deal with that. But if they're not even trying to go to work, we can live with that for a while and try to help them find the focus. But after that . . ."

Failures fall into three broad categories, he said: interns who need a much higher level of support for emotional or developmental problems; kids who don't have enough focus and maturity or energy to make it through the program; and those who violate the drug and alcohol policy.

But for the ones who remain, the process seems to work. Dynamy offers internships in almost anything kids want, two hundred different jobs, Mr. Rynick said, except for big-time broadcasting and architecture. ("That's a hard one," Mr. Rynick said, "because graduates of architecture schools will take unpaid internships. Why hire an eighteen-year-old when you can get a trained architect?")

Because Dave Hartman, the kid from Michigan, was interested in teaching English, it was decided that his final nine-week internship, ending in May of 1999, would be at the Worcester school district. Before that, he worked at U.S. Congressman James McGovern's office in Worcester, and did his winter term as an intern at the Civil Liberties Union of Central Massachusetts. In all three jobs, as it turned out, Dave was asked to do a lot of research, much of it on the Internet.

"It helped me a lot, because research had always been one of my weak suits," he said.

In Congressman McGovern's office, he also wrote letters of recommendation, or, as he described it, "this person is a good person blah, blah, blah." He learned how much time elected officials spend on things like securing World War II medals for constituents. "Just finding out a different side to government," as he put it. All of which helped him decide where he wanted to go next.

FRED AND DAVE

Fred was Dave's advisor. One of the youngest counselors, in his first year in the program, was working with one of the oldest kids. Fred, who had taken a master's degree in teaching at Tufts, had tried teaching in a small-town high school. But, he says, he didn't fit in. A freethinker, he was told, in essence, "Keep your mouth shut." Coming to Dynamy, a bastion of freethinkers, seemed like a great move. But still, Fred was only twenty-five years old.

"My relationship with Fred . . ." Dave began, and then trailed off. "In the beginning of the year it was really difficult. I mean, he's someone I could have been in high school with. So at first I was like, 'Ahhh, I'll talk to him about this,' but I'll talk to Michael"—another counselor—"more about things like he was a parent. But slowly I was able to open up to Fred."

By the end of the year, Dave said, he considered Fred more a friend than an advisor. "It's really unique" is the way he put it. What is remarkable is how Fred, only four years older than Dave, was able to bring Dave along.

"When Fred and I went in, we set some goals there," Dave said. "And if you go down the list, I either accomplished them or I had to put them on hold because something else came up. I don't feel that I failed in any of them." He paused and looked me straight in the eye. "It's the first time in a while I've had that kind of accomplishment."

He pointed out as well that these were real accomplishments, "not like I sold the most summer bulbs."

That, my friends, is worth any amount of money a parent has to pay.

Dave finished the year thinking about international business, or lobbying for unions in addition to teaching. With his Dynamy year behind him, Dave planned to attend a small college in Michigan for a year—one thing he learned at Dynamy is that he likes things small—and then Wheaton College, another small school, near Providence, Rhode Island.

"Most of our graduates go on to college," Mr. Rynick said. "About 75 percent go and complete college within six or seven years of graduating from here."

Robert Gilpin, the founder of Time Out Associates in Milton, Massachusetts, has great respect for the staff at Dynamy and their program. He usually sends at least one client to Dynamy every year. "There are hundreds of therapeutic programs, but there's only one like Dynamy," he said.

Bob Gilpin understands that kids need to be put in a situation where they succeed at something real. "What I've discovered is that someone whose high school career has been checkered with failure can spend two years going out learning and still not being educated," he said.

But put them in a program like Dynamy, "they are so turned on and motivated, they want to go back and get an education," he said. "What a lot of people don't realize is that there is a large world of alternative education that a lot of college guides don't mention."

On the other hand, Jake Horne, an independent advisor based in Washington Depot, Connecticut, believes that Dynamy's program has a serious drawback. "My kids are not Dynamy kids," he told me. "My belief is that kids need to go out and try different things. They do at *least* three different things a year in different places. A kid will head off to Ecuador in the fall to work in a small school for three months, come back at Christmas, shift gears and head off to Nepal or Australia."

Mr. Horne's clients are drawn almost entirely from the prep schools around him. But Dynamy finds that its interns, who are as likely to come from public schools as from private ones, are content to live in Worcester for a year.

Gayle Reardon, another independent counselor in Newton,

Massachusetts, said, "It's a matter of what you're looking for—do you want to live in an apartment in Worcester and have internships? That's Dynamy.

"There are a lot of questions that have to be asked," she said. "Are you looking for something that has travel and college credit? That would be Audubon Expedition Institute. I'm not saying Dynamy isn't a great program, but there are programs that have more structure."

A TESTIMONIAL

One woman who was among the first Dynamy interns is Senator Chellie Pingree, majority leader for the Maine State Senate. She met her husband during her year at Dynamy. Recently, she sent her daughter through the Dynamy program. Chellie says that she herself "was a troubled high school student" in Minneapolis in 1971.

"I didn't have learning disabilities growing up. I'm very smart," she said. "But conventional education was not right for me." Back in those days Dynamy accepted kids who wanted to complete their last year of high school in a nontraditional setting, a program they are considering again.

"It was truly one of the best years of my life," Chellie said. "It changed my life." In the seventies Dynamy required all of their students to work in a political campaign. "I had very good experiences and in each one got a lot of confidence in my ability to do good work," Chellie said. After Dynamy she moved to Maine with her husband. She spent several years running a farm and raising children on an island off the coast of Maine with only 350 people.

When Chellie decided to start a business, she remembered a lot of things she had learned from women she had worked for in Worcester. "It all came back to that year, when I was told, 'You can do anything you want to do.'"

And when she got into politics, the Dynamy experience came in handy again. "I said, 'Oh yeah, I remember knocking on doors.'"

Her first daughter was very successful academically. Not so with her second daughter. "She had some learning disabilities in high school and was not academic," Chellie told me. "She found her skills in sports." When that daughter got out of high school she said, "I can't bear another academic year."

She split her year off between Dynamy and traveling in Europe and came back a different girl. "It completely changed her choices for college," Chellie said, "and when she went to college she was a phenomenally good student. She still struggles with the challenges, but she has lots of confidence and poise."

The Dynamy experience, she says, has shaped her thinking about Maine's education policies. "I am supportive of all those programs that are practical, where kids are having these experiences. We make such unreasonable demands on young people and take the fun out of learning, and the success out of it, too. I say, 'Follow your passion.'"

THEY BELIEVE IN DYNAMY

"They say 50 percent of kids who start college do not get any kind of degree within eight years of entering," Mr. Rynick said the first time I talked to him on the phone. "All those kids who have spent all that money and have nothing to show for it."

"What we provide is access, support and community. And we can give all kinds of internships: radio stations, video, law, medicine, government, small business, education, social service. A real range of what people do."

I went to Worcester to visit Mr. Rynick, Jono O'Sullivan, the director of admissions ("Jono can tell a good kid from a bad kid," Mr. Gilpin said admiringly), and Fred, the young advisor, in May of 1999, at the end of the internship year. The men had gathered in Dynamy's office, in a house on Sever Street in Worcester, a residential neighborhood that in one direction shaded off fairly quickly to a down-at-the-heels commercial strip, in the other toward pleasant side streets.

I came at a busy time. There was a board meeting scheduled for the afternoon. Interns were dropping by to use the copy machine. There were plans afoot for an end-of-the-year camping trip and then graduation. The house had the air of a well-run fraternity.

Even though it was already May, Dynamy's phones were ringing with parents trying to find out if there was room for their kids the coming fall. "We see a bunch of activity from November to January," Mr. Rynick said. "And then more after April 15." That's when most kids find out if they got into the college they want. Clients are primarily middle to upper-middle class.

In truth, most of the Dynamy interns I spoke to didn't apply until sometime in July or August for the term starting in September, having dallied around trying to face college and then finding they just couldn't do it.

Those who believe in Dynamy—and the people in this room this day are hard-core believers—treat it more like a cause than a year of internships. But perhaps it takes this level of belief to make a program work. Mr. Rynick, who was formerly head of the Hammenassett School in Connecticut, at various times tells me:

- Dynamy is "like entering a foreign country. The rules, the language. It's a transition between being externally oriented to being inner-directed, and finding what's important to them."

- Dynamy "is a place where young people get the opportunity to dive deeply into their own lives—to come up against their limiting beliefs and behaviors about themselves and the world."

- "Challenging experiences . . . impel young people to abandon easy answers and look deeply into themselves."

- It's "experiencing our lives as a creative enterprise" and "seeing the possibility to be the architects of our own lives."

In a less expansive mood, he admits, "Some kids can pack a suitcase and take off. Others need the support." And that's what Dynamy offers: support, especially for kids who have been told that going to college is the only acceptable answer.

"We see that pressure to go to college all the time," Mr. Rynick said. "If you're a good girl or good boy, you go to college. We get the question askers." He laughed. "They are not always the most coherent questions. Sometimes it's just, 'I want to find out.'"

He also gets open-minded parents who say, "Why wasn't this around when I was eighteen?" ("Some are more positive about it than their kids," he confided.) On the other hand, he gets parents who feel they have been boxed into a corner by children who just won't get with the college program.

"Some parents figure, 'Oh, they refuse to go to college, and we don't want them to hitchhike across the country.' So this is a middle ground."

Later, when Mr. Rynick and I were having a modest lunch at a restaurant nearby, he talked about some of the problems he sees in our culture. "We've become an increasingly information-rich and experience-poor country. The ages sixteen to twenty are an idealistic time of life. What better time to have them out there, in the community?"

But he also said, "So many of our children are protected by their parents. One of the attitudes is: Fix our son or daughter."

FLOWER CHILDREN, REVISITED

Jono O'Sullivan was in the Peace Corps in Papua, New Guinea, before coming to Dynamy. "In the twelve years I've been here," he said, "I've seen a switch. It used to be that the kids were willing to come and the parents were reluctant. Now I see the parents are eager and the kids want to do the conventional thing. The parents beg, 'Why don't you give this a try?'

"I think a lot of kids wouldn't even consider Dynamy," he said. "Kids talk about going home and having to explain to the aunts and uncles who say, 'Are you taking English 101?' And the kid has to say 'No.'

"We don't fit into a neat box," he concluded. "In one way, what we do is make the world accessible and create a safe space for them to find their own path.

"Our culture offers an extended adolescence with continuously structured experiences to try to keep people on track," Jono said. But some kids need to break free of that kind of structure. "So I think that there is a growing acceptance that people of this age need something different. Not structure imposed upon them by someone else. Our applicants say such interesting things. They say: I don't want to go off to college without knowing who I am."

I asked an obvious question: Why Worcester, a city that does not inspire thoughts of introspection, even with Walden Pond only forty miles away? "Worcester was not a mistake," Mr. Rynick told me. "Frankly, size was one of the attractions of Worcester. Almost every person can find a job that would interest them here."

Jono and I talked for a moment about the idea of the walkabout, of the notion that eighteen-year-olds are burning for some kind of adventure or initiation into adulthood. "Most of those traditional initiation ceremonies," he said, "all involved some kinds of elders in the course of the challenge. That's how I see our program. I want to hire people who themselves have had journeys, who haven't just done high school, college, master's degree. I look for interesting people who have made choices for themselves."

Part of that thinking brought Fred in as one of the advisors. When Jono became frustrated with the kids who repeatedly failed to show up for work on time, Fred, who had worked briefly in the public school system, said: "Jono, you have to understand. In school they're allowed to be late 20 percent of the time. This is an expectation that's been set up. If you're a kid, you can choose to go in late on Friday because you have a test."

The two men decided to make absence at school versus work a topic for one of their weekly meetings with the kids.

Jono said, "Our viewpoint about life and education is: You can only be who you are; difference is unavoidable; the present moment is the best teacher."

AT WORK IN WORCESTER

Jono was honest about the problem the team sometimes had in securing internships. There was great difficulty "if they've had a bad experience with one of our interns, or an intern from another program." That's one of the reasons the Dynamy advisors are adamant about the responsibilities their students have. At the Ecotarium, the former New England Science Center, I met Jesse Anderson, the senior design engineer there, who had been sponsoring Dynamy interns for ten years. This spring term, his intern was a charming, self-possessed young man named Eric Heller.

"Here we treat interns as unpaid staff," Mr. Anderson told me. "We know that we have an obligation to them, as well as that they have an obligation to us.

"Interns at the Ecotarium have the same requirements as staff in terms of dress and hours," he said. "And they go through the same disciplinary process as staff if they fail to do what they are supposed to do."

Like most of the people I met who were connected to Dynamy, Jesse combined practicality with a zealous belief in young people. Having interns, he told me, allows the Ecotarium to do things it couldn't do otherwise, because of lack of staff. "But it's also part of our mission, to educate informally," he said.

The Ecotarium sponsors Dynamy interns in positions from public relations and marketing, to computers, to helping lead school tours and constructing exhibits. Some Dynamy interns are drawn to working with the live animals that are part of the Ecotarium.

"It looks like it would be a really fun job," Jesse said. "But people don't realize it means getting up at 6 A.M. to be here at 6:30. And then the first thing you do is start scrubbing animal poop out of cages. And you wash the dishes, prepare the food."

Dynamy's eighteen-year-olds are no different from your own. They don't want to get up at 6 A.M., especially during a Massachusetts winter. If an intern is late, first there are verbal warnings. Then written warnings. Then they are fired.

"Sometimes it just doesn't work out," Jesse said. "And it doesn't do the intern any good to keep them on. If you do, you build up the expectation that once they get out into business, they don't have to follow the rules."

Jesse's intern, Eric, was hunkered down over a computer terminal when I found him deep in Ecotarium's administrative offices. ("Our website can always use work," Jesse said.)

Eric is the kind of charming nineteen-year-old whom you think could be mayor someday. Real intelligence in the eyes. A willingness to listen. He's a born politician, the kind of student you assume colleges would be jumping up and down to recruit. What was he doing at Dynamy?

"I filled out college applications," he said, "but I didn't send them out. Just when all my friends said they were making decisions, I felt I didn't have a decision I wanted to make. I liked parts of high school. Some of it was too easy. Some of it was too annoying.

"My father is a physics professor at Harvard," he told me, sitting at a Formica table at a 1950s diner, part of an Ecotarium exhibit. None of the schoolchildren idling past seemed at all perturbed by people sitting in the exhibit, talking.

"And my mother's got her master's degree. I grew up in Lincoln, Massachusetts, and the whole school system there is based on getting their kids into the Ivy League. I just wasn't ready."

Eric says this in the kind of way that alcoholics stand up and announce that, yes, they are alcoholics. It comes with practice and with spending a year with a group of other kids who were, like himself, not ready.

What he was ready to do, he said, was something involving law. But when he asked around the law offices in his town, no one would take him. Even for an unpaid job.

"Every place said 'Sorry, we only take law students,'" he told me. "I was under a lot of pressure to find something for the next year. It was late August. My guidance counselor recommended a few programs. But Dynamy was the only one that had a legal program in it.

"My parents weren't all for it at first," he said, by which he means his father had reservations. "As far as the whole taking-the-year-off thing, my mom was for it as soon as she heard about it. That's the way my mom is. Anything I do is basically okay in her book."

And Eric did get his internship in a law office, during his winter term at Dynamy. Before that he worked at Worcester Common Ground, a community development corporation that finds houses, fixes them up and sells them to first-time home buyers. There he did property research on the computer and went to the county clerk's office looking for maps, "the usual intern things," he said.

"I think the first job didn't have much to do with my interest," Eric said, "but the work was so positive and community oriented, and you came home every day and felt good."

And now, at nineteen, Eric says he is ready to go to college, at the University of Maryland, as a political science major with a computer science minor. After that, he's thinking of "higher-level" law enforcement, by which he means the FBI.

Even Dad came around. "My dad was hoping I'd be a scientist," Eric said. "But after a while he's taken a liking to the idea. Both my parents are very pleased with what's happened in my personal development.

"Dynamy—it's incredibly difficult to explain what you're doing," he said. "An internship year, taking a year off. It's a very unfamiliar concept to most people. But after I explained it to my friends, they all thought it sounded like a pretty neat idea."

INSIDE A DYNAMY APARTMENT

If all this sounds too good to be true, the real shock I experienced was visiting a Dynamy apartment. While most college freshmen are crammed into hideous boxes called dorms, the kids at Dynamy live in spacious suites in old Victorian homes. Natalie Carpenter, who came to the Dynamy year at seventeen from Glenview, Illinois, a suburb of Chicago, had decorated her apartment in a large Victorian house on Cedar Street, which she shared with two other young women, with a very convincing-looking plastic platter of deli food. But that was the only false note in a gracious place with high ceilings, original woodwork, even stained glass in the bathroom.

Natalie, who had come out as a lesbian in high school and preferred to be called Nat, had heard about Dynamy from a high school teacher who knew a previous student who had done it. "It was a last-minute decision," she said.

For her, college had not ever entered the equation. For one thing, she said, how many people end up doing what they study in college? What was the point?

Nat spent her year working in political organizations, an HIV-prevention program, a rape crisis center and that anarchist's bookshop. She had also started learning how to blow glass at an artisan's workshop in nearby Sterling, Massachusetts.

"I don't want to go to college," Nat said. "My parents are very supportive. They know that I was really struggling in high school. They know that I'm a good kid." When Nat says she's a "good kid," you can see that she has done some thinking about it, and that she's pleased with the person she has become. "They know I'm not going to waste my life away."

She planned to move back in with her mother, play drums in a rock band for a while. And then get an apartment with her girlfriend and perhaps look into glassblowing. Nat had the kind of grounded attitude that you would feel lucky to encounter in a twenty-five-year-old. She had recently turned eighteen.

One last thing about the Dynamy program: If parents still hold out hopes that, unlike Nat, their child will go to college and get a four-year degree, Dynamy offers, for an additional fee of $500 for each four-credit course, up to twelve credits in seminars like "Race, Class and Gender" that carry college credit from nearby Clark University. In that way, and in many others, the program lives up to its founders' notion, that it would be what David Rynick calls "an urban Outward Bound."

Chapter Thirteen

SOMEWHERE BETWEEN
BEING A MISSIONARY
AND A GOOD PERSON

Never doubt that a small group of thoughtful, committed citizens can change the world; indeed, it's the only thing that ever has.
—MARGARET MEAD

In the summer of 1997, I sat in a crowded railroad car headed north out of New York City, annoyed at having to share the seats with some dirty and boisterous teenagers. Lots of things ran through my mind about where these kids had been (camp? hiking?) and why they looked so wild and bedraggled (drinking? drugs?).

It wasn't until I started talking to them that I found out they were a church group, on their way back from Fargo, North Dakota, where they had worked for a week helping the townsfolk dig their stores and homes out of the mud left by a once-in-a-century flood. They were in high spirits despite the fact they hadn't bathed in several days and had spent the previous night sleeping in a train station. (A rail accident out West had complicated their return trip.)

Which brings us to volunteer work as an alternative to school. As Jean Hague, an education counselor in Atlanta, Georgia, said, so many kids feel restless inside a classroom. "Young people are impatient with sitting through a history class," she said. "They don't see the practical nature of what they're studying. They want instant answers and maybe are not quite so willing to go along with core requirements." All of which flies in the face of their parents' expectations that they will become well-rounded and get a broad education—by sitting in a classroom.

GOOD WORKS FOR COLLEGE CREDIT

For parents who are insistent on their child's getting a degree, it is possible for a kid to get college credit for doing good deeds. The San Francisco Urban Program offers up to eight college credits to students at Westmont College in Santa Barbara for such things as working in a homeless shelter or helping at a children's theater. Steven Schultz, director of the program, said, "Part of the idea behind the experience is what I call civic education, learning about different kinds of issues our cities are dealing with and what things are being proposed for poverty or racial discrimination. That's an important part of their learning."

But, I asked him, why should students pay tuition to volunteer in a homeless shelter? "One of the important things about experiential learning is that it's well structured," he said. In his own program, the school and the student set goals; students come in every week to talk about their work.

"They have regular opportunities for reflection," he said. "One of the reasons that people have been critical of experiential learning is that when it's done poorly, kids have the experience but there's no reflective component. Experience for its own sake, as John Dewey said, can be miseducative, too."

John Dewey or not, experience, in my book, is always a great teacher; in the broadest sense of the word, even trying heroin can be an education. The question is not the experience, it's what someone does with what was learned. And while I admire the notion behind Westmont's program, I think any kid in this country can get that experience without paying college tuition.

ONE YEAR OF SERVICE

Some countries require their eighteen-year-olds to give a year of service. Here, there is Americorps, the voluntary program founded in 1994 for kids between the ages of eighteen and twenty-four. Americorps sends kids out for a year of working in schools or day-care programs or removing trash.

During the year, the kid gets a stipend; at the end of the year, there's $5,000 toward school tuition. One offshoot of Americorps is the National Civilian Community Corps, which focuses on the environment and disaster relief. (A precursor might be the California Conservation Corps, which sends kids off to live in a barracks and to work with nature.)

Other options open to eighteen-year-olds include Habitat for Humanity (you know, Jimmy Carter); Volunteers in Service to America (VISTA), which sends kids to all fifty states, Puerto Rico and the Virgin Islands to help the poor and an organization called Public Allies. Founded in 1991, Public Allies offers internships in nonprofit organizations and public agencies in Chicago, Illinois; Durham, North Carolina; Milwaukee, Wisconsin; Washington, D.C.; and Wilmington, Delaware.

BUT PROBABLY NOT THE PEACE CORPS

An eighteen-year-old could conceivably enter the Peace Corps. "Most Peace Corps volunteers [95 percent] have college degrees, as most of the countries we serve have that requirement," said Dana Topousis, who works for the Peace Corps. "We do have Peace Corps volunteers serving who may have many years' experience in a particular field, thus making them eligible when approved." What she means is that if some eighteen-year-old has years of experience in raising pigs, or knows computers, there is a possibility that that kid could go into the Peace Corps, but it is unlikely.

The Peace Corps will reach 10,000 volunteers by 2003, the highest it will have been in a generation and a 50 percent increase over the 6,600 it was in 1999. Sarah Parsons, who graduated from White Bear Lake High School in 1993, got her B.A. in political science from the University of Minnesota at Morris. After graduation, she enlisted in the Peace Corps and was sent to Turkmenistan.

"I think it's the ultimate independence from parents," her father, Rolf Parsons, told me. "She's literally on the other side of the world. She's having to put up with circumstances that we can't help her with."

When he saw her in London after she had spent a year in

Turkmenistan, she was scrounging for soda pop bottles to take back, because containers of any kind were in short supply. Power and running water tended to go off for three days at a time. It could be months between phone calls.

When she came back to White Bear on leave, she went to the kitchen, turned on the tap and said, "This is the best thing about this country."

Her father told me about Sarah's passion for public service. "She's always been interested in international affairs and service to people," he said. And, he confessed, "she's looking for a ticket into working at the State Department."

Note: An altruistic spirit is not the only thing that sends kids into the Peace Corps. The *New York Times* reported that some go-getters are using their Peace Corps experience in international banking and finance to promote their careers at home. "You can get real international business experience without having to slave in an office for a number of years," one young man told the reporter. About 850 of the 6,600 Peace Corps volunteers in 1999 worked in finance rather than in a wheat field for their two years of service.

MY OWN PRIVATE PEACE CORPS

Kids can also make up their own version of the Peace Corps, a year or more living and working in a foreign country. And since kids these days have extraordinary computer skills, they can do more than help cut sugarcane.

Josh Wray graduated from the North Carolina School of Science and Mathematics in May 1998. He applied to seven colleges and got into most of them. "But I wasn't really excited about the colleges I got into and could afford," he told me. His cousin, who ran a nonprofit center in Yoff, Senegal, about fifteen miles from Dakar, suggested he use his knowledge of computers to help her run the organization's computer center. All he would have to do is pay for his round-trip airfare, and he was welcome to come help. In his case, he would even be paid about $200 a month to cover room and board.

"My friends tried to talk me out of it," he told me. They all felt he should go to college first. But, he said, "after college I'll have debt and have to pay that off. I'd lose my life and never be able to do this again."

Josh's mother died when he was nine and he had been responsible for making his own spending money as a teenager. He worked at a local computer company in Durham, North Carolina, testing software for $10 an hour. He was prepared to work his way through college as well, but he didn't want to do it right away. He, like many other kids I spoke to, felt he had "lost his focus."

"I want to be enthusiastic and work hard," in Senegal, he said just before high school graduation. "I haven't been at school."

A year later, we talked about what he found living in Senegal. "I didn't have any money left when I finished paying for my plane ticket," he said. "And here I was in this six-hundred-year-old fishing village.

"When I first got there the heat was bad. I couldn't imagine doing anything at two in the afternoon. It cools off in the evening, luckily."

His job (in cooperation with Unicef) was to set up a web page and train a local mayor's workers in Microsoft Office. "The pilot went really well, and we sent web masters to the other mayors' offices, so I was one of the lead teachers to come up with the course to teach the web masters."

He did a lot of hardware training, showing people how to build computers. And that led to his trying to form a company to import computers from Taiwan, for half the price of what the Senegalese were paying. "I was not at all happy to buy them for that cost."

His salary made it possible to pay for room and board; he stayed at the family compound of one of the organization's technicians. There was a central courtyard and each member of the family (and Josh) had rooms off of that. The matriarch cooked for everyone: Josh, the technician, the technician's two grown brothers (and wives) and a sister and her husband and assorted children. "That's a pretty small household for Senegal," Josh said.

Because it was a fishing village, the menu was fish and rice: "fish, prepared a hundred different ways with rice prepared a hundred different ways," Josh said. "And they like hot stuff, hot peppers.

"It was a really great experience," he said. "I became fluent in French. In fact, I'm probably at least going to minor in it. And I'm doing really good in school now. I've gotten my focus back."

While he was in Senegal he applied online to San Francisco State. "I'd always wanted to be in Silicon Valley," he said. And he is working for an Internet start-up between classes.

"I'm taking French and African development and economics," Josh said. "I really like economics and all the money stuff."

So what had been the problem for him in high school, I asked. "Science and Math were really hard," he said, "and maybe not doing well in my classes discouraged me. And I was distracted by the dorms. I kept getting slacker and slacker and was barely getting by."

Now he is definitely thinking about international business. "Most Americans have never been out of the country," he said. "Maybe for a week or two in Europe. I spent ten months there," he said. "It makes for good conversation."

GOING ON A MISSION

Churches and synagogues send out thousands of kids every year, to places as near as your local soup kitchen and as far away as a kibbutz in Israel or a mission in Guatemala. No doubt the largest of these programs is run by the Mormon Church, whose volunteer force is six times larger than the Peace Corps will be at its peak. At any one time, there are approximately 60,000 Mormon missionaries working around the world, most of them young men between the ages of nineteen and twenty-six.

About 60 percent of Mormon men spend two years as a missionary. Young women are not required to go on a mission but still make up about 25 percent of the volunteers. Rather than receive pay, or tuition assistance, Mormon missionaries are expected to pay all of their own expenses if they can, a burden that usually falls on their parents.

At one point I had trouble reaching Scott Bennion on the phone. He had graduated from White Bear Lake High School in 1993, joined the Army Reserves and then somehow figured out how to do his two years of missionary service in the middle of his Army service. He had come back from his mission in St. Petersburg, Russia, and was now studying at the University of Utah in Salt Lake City.

Why had I had trouble reaching Scott? He was in Vegas, baby, gambling. "That was the college student kicking in," he said.

My kind of Mormon. One with a sense of humor.

"You're not supposed to drink," he said. "That's a commandment for all members of the church. I go to Vegas, but I go to have fun: ride the roller coaster, catch comedy shows. I don't go to the

Palomino. I don't drink. Gambling is discouraged, because it's an addiction. So I only take sixty dollars. I know I can afford that."

We discussed how he ended up a missionary in St. Petersburg. "Every now and then I question why I did it," he said. Right after high school he had wanted to go to college, but he didn't have enough money. So he enlisted in the Army Reserves and scored more than a 90 on the Armed Services Vocational Aptitude Battery, which opened up a lot of possibilities for him.

"At the time, I thought it would give me a direction for a career," he said, "but that was a recruiter line. I was thinking about becoming a doctor, maybe a dentist or surgeon."

He asked the recruiter what kinds of positions would allow him to get hands-on training to become a doctor, and the recruiter said the biological and chemical corps.

"I thought it was part of the medical corps," Scott said. "It turns out it's chemical and nuclear defense and weaponry. Like what was used in Desert Storm. Like biological weapons."

He did, however, get a big bonus for signing up for that one, and the financial opportunities he was looking for. "And I actually did enjoy it."

What he figured out was that his contract with the Reserves required him to be an "active reserve" for six years and "enlisted reserve" (ready to be called up) for two. So as he was hitting the age of nineteen, the age at which Mormon men take their missions, he put in for and received permission to jump from active to enlisted duty for two years.

When someone applies for a missionary post, the paperwork asks if he or she would like to be outside the United States and what foreign languages they have. Scott had had six semesters of German at White Bear Lake High School, and had lived as an exchange student for a year near Düsseldorf. He thought that if he was lucky, he would go to Germany.

He came home from work one day, and his mother was, as he puts it, "all giddy." The letter had come from the head of the Church of Jesus Christ of Latter-day Saints. "We ripped it open, and it starts, 'Elder Scott Bennion.' I hear my mom scream. And I read it, and it said I'd been called to Russia, St. Petersburg. I said, 'Holy shit.' Not the right response from a good Mormon boy."

His parents contributed to the fund to send him to Russia, as did members of the church. And he prepared himself for the rigors of missionary work. "Abstinence from coffee, tea, movies, TV—these are worldly distractions that keep you away from the work of being a missionary," he said. "And in a way it's kind of like basic training." He would work six days a week in St. Petersburg and be given one day off, to write letters to family and friends, do laundry, go grocery shopping, see the sights. "And we could get permission to see a ballet or an opera, take in some of the culture," he said.

"You couldn't go to bars and clubs and dance halls," he said. "That's a very distracting element to get involved in if you are a missionary, especially if you're a nineteen-year-old boy and these European girls are ooing and aahing over you."

I thought he was joking again, because the uniform for a Mormon missionary makes him look like a very square vacuum cleaner salesman, or a secret agent from *Men in Black*.

But Scott was serious. "Most of these guys are smoking, drinking, and here's these clean-cut college guys, with polished black oxfords, black suits, white shirts and ties. It was very exotic and different. Apparently *Playgirl* has this poll about what was sexiest. Number one was Chippendale dancers, and the next was LDS missionaries—big, strong, clean-cut guys."

"Are you sure about this?" I said.

"I've never *seen* that magazine, of course," he answered, "so maybe it's a myth or a legend."

The missionary apartment in St. Petersburg was spare: no television. And modern music—Scott said, "Green Day, Nirvana"—was forbidden. "Because if you were preaching church doctrine, you couldn't have 'La Vida Loca' going though your head. You can listen to the Mormon Tabernacle Choir, Copland, Mozart, classical music. And you know, that was fine with me. I had no trouble giving up those things, because I believed in what I was doing."

It was a slow realization. He knew that if he went on the mission for his mother's sake, that was not right. It had to be for himself. What made up his mind was a visit in White Bear from an Elder of the church who had been a missionary and a Marine. "It was kind of cool," Scott said. "I realized that I did believe in my faith. I thought about why I'm here, and it helped me understand just a little more of who I was."

That does not stop him from quibbling with some Elders over the issue of Mountain Dew. Banning Mountain Dew would have been a make-or-break prohibition for Scott. There is a standing commandment that Mormons cannot drink coffee or tea—"abstinence from hot drink, liquor, drugs and tobacco products," he said—but some church members interpret that to mean abstinence from caffeine. "When it says, 'Don't drink caffeinated Coke or Mountain Dew, *then* I'd have a hard time," he said.

About that mission, what exactly did a nineteen-year-old young American who spoke German (not a popular language in Russia) do to save souls? "First you're a foreigner," he said, "and then you have to tell them, in bad Russian, 'You're a heathen.' That doesn't work very well. It belittles people.

"Russian people are the most hospitable, caring people in the world. They're a little standoffish on the street—imagine after seventy-five years of communism some guy in a suit comes up to them and says, 'We've got to talk.' It's not easy.

"When we were proselytizing, we would run into drunk people, and this one guy said, 'You're KGB agents trying to capture those who are trying to change.'

"We said, 'Can't you tell we're Americans, because of our terrible Russian?' And he said, 'No that's a KGB trick.'"

Scott said it helped that he was an extrovert, with good social skills, and that he does not embarrass easily. "At first, all I could say was my name and 'I'm from America.' My partner was there a month longer, and he would finish the conversation for me."

Russia was a hazard post. "I was mugged right after I arrived, and had guns pulled on me. It helped to be forceful and self-reliant. I had a little more confidence and was able to work out the situation for the best. As my mom said, 'Most people have a guardian angel. You've got a squadron.'"

During his two-year posting in St. Petersburg, he was allowed to call home only two times a year: on Christmas and Mother's Day. Any other communication had to be through letters. "At the end, when it's time to go home, your parents can come out and do a little tour with you, but during the mission it's discouraged. No family, boyfriends or girlfriends."

The only exception to the phone rule is when there is a family emergency. While Scott was in St. Petersburg, his father died, after a long illness. Scott's mother was allowed to call then to check up on him.

"I felt that during those two years I became a better person and got more understanding of who I was. I had a stronger belief and a stronger testimony. And I know I touched other people's lives, and became a part of their lives, too.

"It is kind of awe-inspiring to know you touched someone. One gentleman had a severe drinking problem. It was ruining his life and his family's life. He'd be in a drunken rage and haul off and hit them. We said, 'Don't you want to be a better person, a better father?' '*Da, da.*' And we'd say, 'So how can you do that if you're drinking?'

"With conversations like this, we turned someone's life around. A lot of these people are struggling. In Russia, it's basically survival time, because there are corrupt politicians and the mafia controlling everything. So they don't get what they need. But if you help them get control of their lives, then that's important. I had something that the politicians and the mafia couldn't take away.

"It's just like the Peace Corps, but we were helping people spiritually, giving them a sense of hope. And that's what everyone wants. Contrary to what Jesse Ventura says, religion helps give people something to hold on to. It's not a crutch."

Now that Scott is back from his mission, he is no longer Elder Bennion. As Brother Bennion, he has the right to baptize and bless, and as a college student he is allowed to have a weakness for sixty-dollar flings in Vegas. He expects to graduate from the University of Utah in 2002 with a double major in Russian and political science. "And now I'm allowed to go out with girls and watch TV and movies," he assured me.

He's in the National Guard, in military intelligence, and will be certified as a Russian interrogator in May of 2000. Eventually Scott wants to enter either the CIA or the State Department. Hey, he's already got the black suit.

CITY YEAR

A program called City Year is almost unknown outside of the cities it serves. City Year takes volunteers as young as seventeen to work in Boston; Chicago; Cleveland, Ohio; Columbia, South Carolina; Detroit; Philadelphia; Providence, Rhode Island; San Antonio, Texas; San Jose, California, and Seattle, Washington.

The program was founded in Boston in 1988 by two roommates from Harvard Law School, Alan Khazei and Michael

Brown, and is the model for President Clinton's Americorps program, of which it is now part.

"It's a wonderful program," said Connie Nicholson, an educational consultant in Osterville, Massachusetts. "More students are becoming concerned about things like homelessness. The homeless used to be not even a part of our vocabulary."

John Sarvey is the executive director of the City Year program in San Jose, California, right in the heart of some of the most expensive real estate in the country. As a result, the San Jose City Year pays the most—$900 a month—and still finds that its volunteers have to stretch to afford housing. Moreover, 35 percent of the San Jose volunteers are from out of state, the highest percent in the entire program; that makes it even harder.

"Housing is definitely a challenge," Mr. Sarvey said. "We try to help them find the least expensive apartments in Silicon Valley, though that's an oxymoron. Usually five or six corps members take a two-bedroom apartment."

So what is there for ninety City Year volunteers to do in Silicon Valley? Plenty, since the boom economy does not extend to everyone in the San Jose area. "We work with children to help them do better in school and improve their reading and grow up as confident citizens," Mr. Sarvey said. The volunteers who come to City Year, he said, "are heroes going on their journeys. What heroes do is slay monsters and dragons, and all too many of our children have monsters and dragons in their lives."

As with all of the City Year program, there are strict rules. Uniforms (T-shirts, pants and boots are supplied by the Timberland Corporation and sport copious City Year logos) must be worn, with the shirt tucked in. There is to·be no visible facial piercing. Two of the City Year sites do drug testing.

"All of our programs emphasize that we are drug-free, because we're role models to children," Mr. Sarvey said.

Mia Ruiz-Escoto, a budding artist, came to City Year as a local kid who had struggled academically in high school. "The advisors did talk to me about college," she told me. "They did have high expectations. But I had a hard time with school. I was always wanting to paint or stay in the art room."

She said her father was in education. "My mother wasn't rich at all, but we weren't lower class, either." So she tried "the usual junior college," as she put it.

"Junior college is basically . . . it's very well-meaning," she said. "The whole concept of it makes sense: save money, take classes before moving to a four-year college. But I think it's almost like the land of the lost. People are not willing to commit to any direction. They're just there. They take a few classes and they drop a few."

She decided community college was not for her. "I needed a break," she said. She heard about City Year through a mentor and filled out an application. "It was really hard," she said. "It asks you a lot about yourself, and you have to reflect on what City Year would do for you. Also, they ask who the important people are in your life. And what qualities you admire."

Her interview went well, and she was accepted. Yet Mia wasn't quite sure what she was supposed to be doing. She expected to paint a mural. Instead she was assigned to Ryan elementary school to work with a school program for kindergarten through fifth grade.

Her ideas for the kids were so innovative, the school district hired her on completion of her City Year internship. And the program also led her back to school.

"I had been telling the kids to follow their dreams," she said, "and then I realized I wasn't doing what I wanted." A staff member at the school found out she was an artist, "and he pulled me aside and chastised me for not being in art school," she said. "'Do it for yourself,' he said. So now I'm going part-time to the San Francisco Art Institute.

"As of now, I'm just doing everything I enjoy," she said. "I'm working in the community, doing art and going to school."

And, she says, she got to meet the President of the United States. He was in town, his organizers heard about the City Year program (the model, remember, for Americorps) and invited the volunteers to the Fairmont Hotel to meet him.

"Then they took pictures," she said. "It was an incredible day. Who would have thought? My teammate, Zawdie McClendon, was living in a shelter and having every hardship you can imagine. And after we met the President, Zawdie was crying and said, 'I can't believe it. I came from the ghetto and I met the President.'"

MAYBE SOMETIMES THE RICH BENEFIT, TOO

Hamilton Simons-Jones had a City Year experience as far away from that of Mia and Zawdie as possible, both geographically and economically. Hamilton, whose parents run a small twice-a-week newspaper in Columbia County, New York, was the kind of bright kid who goes to Andover, the prestigious prep school in New Hampshire.

"If I hadn't gone to City Year," he told me from his room at Tulane University, in New Orleans, "at this point I would be very burnt out, like most of the other students—like my friends, getting drunk and not caring about much."

At Andover, Hamilton had problems almost from the very beginning. He says he was always the "shy kid who looked down at the path."

"Doubt killed me," he said. "I really think that the difference between someone and their potential is doubt. It's your own personal doubt about what you can do."

At the beginning of sophomore year, Hamilton was told he was not ever going to graduate from Andover. "I got in a little bit of trouble there," he said. "It was kind of 'goes to show you guys' when I graduated."

He had a great relationship with his parents, but saw himself in high school as a boy in a bubble. Even he cannot explain why. He just knows that something in him failed to connect.

After high school graduation at age seventeen, he said, "I had no idea of what I wanted to do, just not more of this, basically." The headmaster's daughter at Andover had done City Year and come back to do a presentation. That's all it took for young Hamilton.

"I thought, 'This sounds pretty cool.' I thought, 'I'm going to take a year, be on my own, party for a year.'" Best of all, he said, he could tell his parents he was doing a formal, credible program. "Because they wouldn't have said, 'Oh, just take a year off.'"

His roommate decided to do City Year as well, and the two of them applied to the Boston program. He put on his City Year uniform and prepared to have a good time. He pictured himself counseling gang members, something exciting and street.

And then he swallowed the City Year lesson. "Basically," Hamilton's favorite word, "City Year puts you in the culture of fairness and idealism. A real culture for you and the other three hundred people.

"At first, I'm sure I was a little cynical," he said. All corps members had to wear Timberland khaki pants with their shirts tucked in. "We were walking billboards, effectively, which was pretty good publicity."

Then he found himself introduced to the team members he would be working with for the next year. While Andover claimed to be diverse and multicultural, he felt the prep school diversity was pretty shallow.

"All the kids of the same race are sitting together," he said. "At Andover, everybody was from the upper class."

On his team at City Year were kids who needed to get their GEDs. One of the leaders had spent time in jail. Two of the kids on the team grew up in the area they would be working in, the South End. And teams were required to work closely together— no sitting at separate tables.

The South End, he said, was a pretty diverse area as well. "One of the teachers I worked with spoke Creole, Vietnamese, Spanish," he said. "The kids were mostly African-American, but there were a couple of Vietnamese."

Instead of working with teenage gang members, Hamilton found himself assigned to a day-care center, to the Moonbeam class—two-year-olds. Mr. Cynical Guy, who thought he was going to party and hang with the homeboys, found himself making cheese snacks and presiding over a group of infants whose biggest drama would involve potty training. "It's emotionally trying, working with two-year-olds and the ups and downs of their lives," he said seriously. His favorite part of the day: nap time, when they would lie down with the kids and rub their backs to put them to sleep. "It was great to have a nap time each day," he said.

The day began with fifteen to thirty minutes of physical training, jumping jacks to get the heart started, that sort of thing. He had to be at the day-care center at 8:15 in the morning, no excuses. If you were late, you would get written up. As Hamilton puts it, "'This is what it's going to be like in the real world' kind of deal."

At the end of the day, the corps members were free: to make their own dinner, relax, do laundry, all of the domestic details that children take for granted at home. "So I had to learn how to cook," he said, "with a simple how-to-cook book. I did simple, simple mom things, like mashed potatoes, baked potatoes. I could do a steak, but no frills. With cooking, like most things, you've just got to try it."

The program was almost militaristic, but kids also had enormous freedom, which presented problems to those who were not mature enough to handle it. One member on Hamilton's team was bounced out of the program. "He wasn't ready to make the step of not partying," Hamilton said. "I realized right at the beginning that I couldn't party, because I wanted to be on point for my kids in the morning."

His roommate from Andover quit the City Year program in October, complaining that all he was doing was making photocopies. "He wimped out," Hamilton said. "It's all about getting over those hurdles. In City Year, one of the things is, it's bigger than you are. The point is, we were always representing City Year. I understood it."

For Hamilton, City Year was about expanding horizons, working as a team, being flexible. Just like the military, City Year works because it turns ten individuals into a unit. Kids who wouldn't get up before noon if their parents' jobs depended on it will jump up at the crack of dawn to keep their teams from getting into trouble. Like Chris Smith, who joined the Marines to be part of a greater good, kids in a program like City Year, the Peace Corps, a foreign church mission, become their best selves because they represent not just themselves but an ideal, a country, an entire philosophy. When they connect with something bigger than themselves, their grasp approaches their reach.

It turned out that the day-care center didn't fill all of Hamilton's time. So at 1:30 in the afternoon, when his shift at the center was over, he moved to working on the Boston City Year newsletter. "With my newspaper background," he said, "I got into it."

One thing he learned was that he had to help others learn to do it. He became Mr. Delegate-It. He already knew how to write and edit copy. What he needed to do was help other kids in the program gain marketable skills. There were bad parts of the year's experience, he said, but "everything bad you learn from, too." (See John Dewey!)

One of the things that killed him was the long hours. He was required to work only forty-two hours a week, but he often found himself putting in seventy. "I'd get home at ten at night and I'd be *so* burnt out," he said.

"City Year for me, I gave everything I had, this altruistic side," he said. "City Year taught me how to see myself, and also how to present myself to others. I never would have been able to talk to you like this three years ago or write a résumé or get a job. Now I don't even smoke pot anymore, because it would make me lose my confidence."

In high school, Hamilton never participated in any extracurricular activities. Now in his third year at Tulane, he says he dives into all kinds of things. "Planning committees and boards, and I'm not a meeting kind of person," he said.

"I don't know where I was before," Hamilton confessed. "All through high school I never had any severe challenges. With City Year I figured out who I am; I figured out I could take on the world. When I graduated, my take was: The only thing between me and my goals was a little bit of hard work."

At Tulane in New Orleans, Hamilton found a pretty apathetic student body, even though he said there was terrible housing and real poverty just six blocks from campus. Today Hamilton is head of the Juvenile Assistance Program, which has four hundred Tulane students volunteering to work with kids between eight and seventeen, to help them with their study skills. He also runs the student Community Action Council, Tulane University (Cactus), which raised $50,000 for Habitat for Humanity to build a house. The shy kid who looked down at the paths of Andover has become a leader, building passion in others for community service along with housing for the poor.

"And now I'm a straight-A student," he said. "I decided I wanted to keep as many doors open as long as possible. And I realized that getting bad grades would close doors. So I realized it was just doing the work."

He is studying political science and the classics, "because I love studying the ancient Romans and Greeks," he said. "The poli-sci side of things, my parents kind of talked me into."

When he graduates from Tulane in 2001, he may well join the Peace Corps. He says he doesn't have a career path ahead of him, but Hamilton has become the kind of kid you would never worry about. You can tell he's going to go somewhere, because he's already been somewhere.

"People realize themselves, whether it's City Year or the Marines, or the New Party or Cactus," he said. "Most of the time you're not going to do it on your own. You need people to push you, to expand your comfort zone."

GOOD WORKS CLOSE TO HOME

In search of ways to expand horizons, the first step is finding a program. Sometimes the desire is there but the timing is bad. Many of the national programs start in September and have application deadlines in the spring. Your child might drop out of college in September and be at loose ends. One thing is clear: If a kid wants to take a year off, it's not enough to sit in the basement watching cable.

If your child is ready to get to work, there are any number of programs that can use his help. Robert Gilpin's book, *Time Out: Taking a Break from School to Travel, Work and Study,* now out of print, was filled with ideas about what to do. *Taking Time Off,* by Colin Hall and Ron Lieber, published in 1996, has dozens of stories about kids and what they did during a year off, including volunteer programs both here and abroad.

More immediately, parents and kids can go to the web. A site called www.servenet.org asks for a zip code. I typed in mine in New York City and back came fifty-nine options for volunteer work, from sleeping in a homeless shelter and cleaning up afterward, to being an adoption counselor at the ASPCA to learning to counsel pregnant women.

But some kids, my own son among them, don't respond to do-gooder programs like City Year or missionary work. My son never even completely signed on to giving Christmas presents to kids in the projects, which we did every year during Operation Santa Claus in New York. While he is a great kid, and has a big heart, volunteering for an organized charity was just not his thing.

If your son is like my son, and not going to join the Army, or go to Dynamy or Exeter or become a missionary, there is one last alternative to going out into the world and getting a job. And that is going to a counselor or advisor who has experience with thousands of these kids.

While lots of high school guidance counselors know how to get your kid into the state university, or can help Jared apply to an Ivy League school, few of them know the alternatives available, from programs that wrap the education pill inside a trip to Greece to those that send kids out West to string barbed wire. If nothing I've talked about so far seems right for Jillian, read on.

Chapter Fourteen

GET THEE TO A COUNSELOR

Why must every generation
think their folks are square?
And no matter where their heads are,
they know that Mom's ain't there?
—JOHN SEBASTIAN,
"THE YOUNGER GENERATION"

Picture this: It is April and you are meeting the other soccer moms out in the parking lot, surrounded by the Chevy Suburbans. All the other parents are chattering about their children's acceptance letters from Brown, UCLA, Stanford, the University of Michigan–Ann Arbor, the University of Wisconsin–Madison, Ole Miss, Texas A & M, McGill. The list goes on and on, with each parent nodding and saying, in turn, "Oh, that's a good school."

You would like to jump in, but your kid has been turned down by all ten of the schools he applied to. Or your daughter failed to get any of her applications in on time. Or your son has been wait-listed at his safety school. Your beloved child may even have announced that he is going to drop out of high school before graduation. What do you do?

You can turn to your minister, your priest, your rabbi—but they may not know any practical solutions. You can talk to school counselors, but if your child is in public school, they probably are not going to have much time or patience to spare. You can talk to a psychiatrist, but except for a prescription for Prozac (for *you*, Mom, not for young Jason), none of the solutions will be cheap. A psychiatrist may well suggest some combination of private therapy for Jason, group therapy for him and family therapy for all of you, perhaps with a therapeutic boarding school for Jason thrown in.

OK, so you're going to brave it out, walk into that circle and tell them that Jason is going to work at the local pizza shop for a while. Yeah, try that on the soccer moms.

Here's another solution: Throw yourself on the mercy of a counselor who has an entire client list made up of parents like you. If you feel alone among the soccer moms, you will feel like one of the crowd when you talk to Neil Bull (and his children, Holly, Sam and Neil), Bob Gilpin, David Denman, Gail Reardon or Jake Horne.

These folk are the avatars of time off, the sultans of the gap year. Once you talk to them, you will feel like a member of a select society, parents whose kids are so unconventional and creative they have slipped the bonds of earthly concerns and sailed off bravely into the world of brilliant iconoclasts.

NEIL BULL, THE GODFATHER OF GAP

My only problem with Neil Bull is that he makes a misfit kid sound like a genius and a year off sound like a sure thing. Neil is a charismatic figure who started the notion of a structured year off in 1980. His notion has become so popular, he says he now regularly gets queries from burnt-out lawyers who want to go off to Baku like their kids. (He takes on the lawyers, too, brave man.)

Cornelius H. Bull is the godfather of the gap year, and every person I spoke to deferred to him. He came to the idea of taking time off after a long career as an educator, both in the United States and abroad. Neil has a B.A. from Princeton (1950). He also has an M.A. from the University of Virginia (1960). He taught at the Lawrenceville School in Lawrenceville, New Jersey; was headmaster at a college in Istanbul, Turkey; at the Verde Valley School in Sedona, Arizona, and at St. Mary's Hall in San Antonio, Texas, before starting the Center for Interim Programs.

Now he has offices in Cambridge, Massachusetts, where I met

with him at his spacious co-op just a block from Harvard Square. His daughter, Holly, runs the Interim program in Princeton, New Jersey. "There's a litany of alternative approaches, because college has become so expensive and so many kids are having trouble," Neil told me when we sat down together. "They have no idea why they are going to school and the finances are so hard. They also see school as so boring. They feel they're not going anywhere."

Neil sees a sophisticated group of students, many of whom want to spend their year outside the United States. One gets the impression talking to him that these kids are secure in their decision to take a break even before they come to him. "Common wisdom is that an eighteen-year-old should be on a short chain," he said, sneering at the idea. "And the shibboleth that if they step out, they'll never go back? That's nonsense."

Neil sees a lot of prep school kids who come from Andover, Choate and Deerfield. These kids have the breeding, the background, the contacts, the education and the sense of entitlement to become successes. What they don't have is the ability to sit in a classroom one minute longer.

"A lot of them," he added, "lack self-confidence." And Neil knows just what to do about that.

From his years of living and teaching abroad, and his contacts in academia, the cultural world and the government, Neil has amassed a file of four thousand options for kids. The options can last anywhere from a few months to a year and include things like working with a musher in the Yukon, helping fix a sixteenth-century Syrian monastery, working on a horse-breeding farm in New York State, taking an internship at the British Parliament and heading off to an ashram in Bali. Some of the suggestions sound so esoteric they are nearly laughable: How about working with a Venezuelan ornithological ecotour organization? But, someone will want to do it.

When he talks about a kid named Nick who spent his interim time building a house in Wyoming, helping make a documentary about James Baldwin and working in a dive shop in Indonesia, you want to sign your own kid up and go along for the ride. Then he caps that by saying that this same kid also spent time on the island of Elba, where David P. Calleo (director of European Studies at the Paul H. Nitze School of Advanced Studies at Johns

Hopkins University) needed a cook, gardener and computer expert to do chores for what was essentially a summer-long summit conference for everyone from distinguished politicians and scholars to Ph.D. students seeking advice.

"Every dinner was a four-hour seminar in world affairs," Neil said, "and the kids who went there were expected to sit at the table and speak up."

Every year, Neil's company sees about two hundred kids, at a cost of $1,500 apiece, 60 percent of them from public schools. "I've never turned anyone down," he brags, "and I've never advertised." He also says he will offer scholarships and let kids pay off the fee over a period of time.

And while his contacts are elite, he says his programs are not. He sends kids off to work at an arboretum in Turkey, or an orphanage in India. What is important to him is that the programs don't cost the teenager anything other than plane fare. ("Any kid can make round-trip airfare to anywhere in the world working at a pizza parlor for the summer," he told me.) And he looks for programs that provide room and board, as well as the kind of challenges and real-life experiences teens need.

Ask Neil about his success stories and he is off and running. "I had a kid from Texas and he went to Bangladesh to work in an orphanage," he said. "And this kid said, 'I think the guy who is running the place is stealing money.'" Neil passed that information on to an official in Bangladesh who immediately asked if the student could take over until they could find a replacement for the administrator.

The student was eighteen, and the orphanage had kids in it who were as old as seventeen. What to do? The teenager put on a necktie as a symbol of authority and went to work running the orphanage. "And it worked," Neil said.

Another story: "I had a young lady from New York and we sent her off to England to work in a battered-women's shelter. Her mom went over to see her and said, 'Neil, she's running the place, and last year she couldn't clean her room.'"

Whereas in this country we don't trust eighteen-year-olds, he says, kids blossom when they go out into the real world, where they can actually accomplish something. He goes on, an endless fountain of tales about the kid in Baku who learned

Russian and joined a rock band, the kid who got into Oberlin by writing about the six weeks he spent working with the poor in Kentucky.

What Neil most enjoys is getting skeptical parents into his office to talk about their kid, the screwup. "I love to talk to parents," he told me. "I look them in the eye and say, 'You've got to listen.' I'm very cold-blooded with the parents. They have to leave if they're not quiet. Leave or be quiet," he said with the kind of authority only a past schoolmaster can muster.

His one concession to parents: "If they don't want their kid to go to Africa," he said, because of political trouble or disease, he will talk the kid out of an African internship.

"Beyond that, it's between me and the kid," he said. "Get out of their way most of the time, and they'll be fine. But you have to have that kind of faith. If they can write their own ticket, why shouldn't it work?" (A sobering note: Others in the field will tell you that some kids don't rise to the occasion, become frustrated and come back home. This kind of option works only if a kid also is resourceful and resilient, but kids are often more resourceful and resilient than their parents think.)

Then Neil went into a favorite gripe, one that in his book is right up there with the idiocy of ranking our kids by their SAT scores: Fathers, particularly the successful controlling fathers who want their kids to buckle down, get with the program and get back in the traces at school.

"Fathers say: 'They'll never go back to school.' Well it just doesn't happen. Fathers are hopeless," Neil said. "They are not a very enlightened biped."

One father who brought his son in to see Neil had a lot of agendas for his son. "And I said, 'This is your son's year off, not yours.' When I said, 'I'm going to send the kid some material, the kid said, 'You'd better send it to my father.' And I said, 'Your son has to buy this and take control of it. It has to be his experience. Otherwise it's not going to work.'"

Neil has seen them all, around three thousand bright loafers, restless youths, confused, unfocused, lost kids; he's seen kids who were burned out after years of trying to please their parent, kids who knew they needed a breather before settling in for another four or six or eight years of schoolwork. "This is the year they get out of prison," he said, the gleam of the maverick in his eyes.

"I don't think any eighteen-year-old belongs in college," he said. "I am dead serious.

"It used to be that college was about the life of the mind," he says dismissively. "Now it's just a job market."

After a consultation with Neil, you'll have the soccer moms at school agog as you describe Jason's decision to spend the next year turtle-tagging in Costa Rica, followed by a stint working with an Irish documentary filmmaker, and in the spring, studying painting at school in Provence. That's Provence in *France*, you know.

Let them brag about getting their kid into Georgetown after that.

ANOTHER GENERATION OF BULLS

Neil has three children, and they have all followed him into the business. His daughter, Holly, runs Interim's office in Princeton, New Jersey. Needless to say, Holly was brought up with the idea of taking time off. She did a stint in Hawaii, exploring the idea of becoming a marine biologist when she was seventeen before realizing that scientific research was not for her. Instead she went to Harvard and got a degree in education.

"We see the parents' dilemma," she said. "They want their kids to enjoy the benefits of a college education, but their child has no ability or no enthusiasm, or has a learning disability—those are the ones who really need a break.

"College is a rite of passage," she said, "but there can be others. Mostly it's getting away from home. As soon as the kid gets on the plane, we see a difference."

Holly says that Interim has changed over the years from a program that sends kids to expensive programs like NOLS, which charge essentially the same thing as college. Now they are working with kids who *need* the room and board.

And those room-and-board placements can become endangered if too many kids take them on and things don't pan out. One recent Interim kid had trouble living and working on an organic farm in Ireland. "We've lost some good room-and-board placements because the kids are not responsible," she said.

While some kids request an assignment with a friend or friends, she encourages them to spend at least part of the year alone. "They'll get a lot more out of that than out of going to

Nepal in a group of Americans. The cushioning protects them from learning.

"Our job," she says, "is to make sure we don't hurl them into extreme situations they can't handle. A lot of times when I sit down and talk to the students I see how tentative they are. Some are excited and game. Others are really nervous. If a kid has not done a lot of traveling in Asia, I say start in Australia. Or start in Europe. See how you do. Or go with others."

The important thing is finding the child's niche. "Some kids can go to a high-powered school, and they're turned on by it. If they're just sloughing through, that hurts. State schools, basically they're there to party.

"Parents say, 'My son has a wonderful social life.' So of course he'll focus on that. Who wants to slave over a test if you're bound to fail?"

Kids with learning disabilities do better with internships that are hands-on, even something like an internship at CNN, the Cable News Network, where there is constant stimulation. "It's nuts, but they love it," she said.

Mostly, she wants to give young people a chance to feel successful at something. "From six to twenty-one, that's a lot of years of feeling that you're coming up short. When you break that cycle and let them do nonacademic things, they come into their own.

"We put them in a school they don't want to be in and are surprised when they're like a mule digging in their feet. Either they dig in their feet, or they become passive, they just go through the motions. We give them alternatives."

Obviously this acorn did not fall far from the tree. Nor did her two brothers, Sam and Neil, who in the fall of 1999 opened a new sister company in Sebastopol, California, LeapNow (Lifelong Education Alternatives and Programs). LeapNow is offering programs similar to Interim's, but with a special focus on things that groups of kids can do together, specifically for those kids who are not ready to go out on their own.

The two brothers will take clients from west of the Mississippi, leaving those east of the Mississippi to Neil Sr. and Holly. (LeapNow can be reached at www.leapnow.com.)

The Bull brothers hope to broaden the appeal of the business their father founded and attract a new range of clients. They are hoping to double or triple their business.

They have also spent time developing a global network of mother and father hens, to watch out for the interns who are in foreign countries by themselves. "To have someone meet your seventeen-year-old daughter in India when she gets off the plane is very important," Neil Jr. said, "especially if you're sending her out for the first time."

LeapNow will charge $1,500 for consultations and programs over a two-year period, and $800 to plan a one-semester (or four-month) break.

Sam Bull is the executive director of LeapNow and used to run Interim's office in Boulder, Colorado. "I graduated from Princeton and I had no clue what I wanted to do," he said. "All I knew was that I was confused." And so he took the years from twenty-two to thirty to travel, work and explore. He was lucky in that one of his jobs was to write the descriptions for Interim's internships. "When I saw one that interested me, I did it," he said. "That was perfect training for what I'm doing now.

"I see young men, in particular, need to wander and be unstructured, where they can be a lone bull, get to a crossroads and say, 'Do I want to turn left or right here?' I spent weeks in Katmandu, weeks of just wandering and looking at things, just storing them inside for later." Everyone needs a bit of that, he says.

HERE'S ANOTHER WAY OF DOING IT

Milton Academy in Milton, Massachusetts, is one of those schools that make you want to sit under a tree and read poetry. Bright and shining kids scampered across the greens, seeming without a care in the warm May sunshine. It was near the end of the school year, and they had every reason to be happy. They were in the school that *U.S. News & World Report* rated the number-one prep school in the country.

Robert Gilpin teaches history at Milton Academy, which has 660 kids in the upper school. About thirty seniors a year are urged by Milton's counseling office (which has nothing to do with Mr. Gilpin's counseling service) to take a year off before going to college.

The Gilpin residence is hard by the Milton campus, deeply shaded by centuries-old trees and charmingly edged with lilacs. When I arrived, a worried mother and her son, definitely a galumphing Bobby, were coming down the steps after a consultation.

The Gilpin home seems designed to impress and to calm. Bob led me into the living room, decorated with antiques and dozens of family photographs. If your school's guidance counselor seems too timid, and Neil Bull seems too grandiose for your child, then Bob Gilpin may feel just right. He is the author, with Caroline Fitzgibbons, of *Time Out: Taking a Break from School to Travel, Work and Study,* a 1992 compendium of suggestions that many people think is the most comprehensive one around. Unfortunately, it is out of date and out of print.

"The kids I deal with are mostly sixteen to twenty-seven," Bob told me. "I started in 1988. It's not rocket science." He says he was sitting around at lunch with Milton's college counselor and everyone was talking about how Neil Bull was the only guy in town for kids who were not ready for college. "I thought, 'Hmmm. I have kids in the dorm who need a year off.' So I decided to take a sabbatical and write a book. In the process, people asked for advice. That's lived on. The book did not."

He says he is busiest in February, just before college acceptances go out. Demand reaches another peak in August as kids who have been accepted at college decide they simply can't go.

Teaching at a prep school, he is in a unique position to see both sides of the guidance counselor question; while counselors may know that a kid is not ready for college, it is extremely difficult for them to suggest it to the kid's parents. "I think prep school guidance officers feel pressure to produce statistics and do not look for the betterment of the child," Bob said. "Those people in private would endorse completely the notion of the year out for kids, but they can't advocate that publicly."

Parents, you see, have a very hard time resisting the urge to send Jared off to that college he just got into, a situation that can lead to his dropping out or, worse, flunking out. And just try to get Jared back into another college when he's got a miserable college transcript. "What most people don't know is, if you have a bad year in college it is the most difficult baggage to get rid of," Bob said. "It's very hard to move from college to college if you're carrying a 2.3 or a 2.5. Kids who don't identify their discontent with college will find themselves in a perilous situation."

And their parents will find themselves going broke—for

nothing. "College is the most expensive buffet in the world," Bob said, "$30,000 a year—and you'd better be sure you're hungry. I don't think every child is ready to take that plunge.

"As far as college is concerned," he said, "if you have the courage to opt out of the lemmings' rush to the sea, you're a special person. Kids are tired. They take time off because they're bored. They're burned out. They do it because they haven't done well and want to do better. Those who are upper-middle class, entitled and mobile take a year off to better their college choices."

Society joins forces to point kids straight at college, he said.

"Fred Hargadon, the dean of admissions at Princeton, said there was no reason in the world that we picked the age of seventeen or eighteen to go to college. In fact, twenty-one might be a lot better."

And it is not essential that you go off to Crete to have a learning experience. "You can spend a year bagging groceries in the Shop 'n' Save, and you can learn a lot," he said.

But that's not what counselors like Bob would suggest. For kids who have had a checkered career in academia, Bob often recommends something like the Audubon Expedition Institute. "What AEI does is what experiential education was meant to be in the first place," Bob said, "to take students to a site and live there, learning how it functions, experiencing it. And you get college credit. You can graduate from college through this program, which is entirely experiential."

Bob Gilpin charges $200 for an initial consultation, $500 for two visits. That, my friends, is a couple of pairs of high-end sneakers, and will be much more likely to take your son where he wants to go. Bob also has a $1,200 rate, which will cover any consultations up to a year. He has just the kind of patrician balance that makes parents feel comfortable with their choices. His website, www.timeoutassociates.com, offers access to his database for a set fee, for those who can't get to him in Milton.

MORE OF A COUNSELOR

Gail Reardon runs her business in Newton, Massachusetts, within ten miles of Bob Gilpin and ten miles of Neil Bull. In fact, she got into the business through Neil and once worked for Bob.

Her career path is instructive. She started out, in the sixties, working as a counselor for teenagers with problems with drugs or alcohol in Maine. Then she and her husband moved to Puerto Rico, where she taught at a college campus and worked with adolescents as a high school guidance counselor. Another move brought her to Massachusetts, where she began working with pregnant teens. A complete career change put her in a large bank, designing managerial programs. Then she changed careers again and began working as a fund-raiser for educational institutions.

"I'd done all these different things," she said. "I said, 'I don't want to get dressed in a suit and be in management.'" She briefly considered going into the Peace Corps. What she wanted was to get outside her own life. The only person she knew to turn to was Cornelius Bull, who helps adults as well as kids.

She went to ask him for help in finding a new direction in her life, and he in turn offered her a job. She has now had her own company for five years.

She works with a number of private schools in New York City, counseling kids who want to take a year, or a semester, away from academia, but she also works with public school students. "I have always wanted to reach students who aren't in private schools and boarding schools, students who haven't had those kinds of opportunities," she said.

What she wants to do, she said, is expose kids to exciting and unusual experiences. She says she can put a kid coming out of high school, with no research experience, in Vietnam studying the effects of Agent Orange. (An experience of this kind might not lead to a job in biotechnology, but it will make for killer dinner-table conversation in Darien twenty years later—"Now listen, when I was in Danang, children ate their vegetables.")

One of her students is going to the head of the Amazon; another is in Thailand. "NOLS and Outward Bound are fine if that's what a student is looking for, but it doesn't just have to be learning survival skills," she said. "You can study art, or reptiles. Experiences really run the gamut."

Gail says she has sometimes rejected clients who are just being Brendas. "I saw two girls who came to me and were immature and they wanted the grand tour of Europe, backpacking. I said, 'Go to Hosteling International.'"

She will also not work with teenagers who are unrealistic

about what they want. "I'll say, 'I can't get you on Broadway, or an internship with Fine Line Cinema.' I don't promise what I can't deliver."

Every year there is a hot spot, she says, a place that kids suddenly decide is the place they *have* to go to. It used to be Australia and New Zealand. Then it was South America and Latin America, she said. Then it was Europe. And now it is Asia, where she is particularly enthusiastic about Islandtime, a program in Hawaii, Thailand and Fiji run by David Adams. Islandtime allows an intern to stay in one place for nine months or a year while working with two or three different programs, studying ecology first, say, and then working for a local health clinic. The price tag is $1,695 a month.

Gail offers a free consultation, and charges $150 an hour or $1,000 for a complete program. When parents come to her with their children for a consultation, she says, a lot of issues get put on the table. "There's separation and what they wish they had done," she said. "Sorting out those issues is what we do.

"I tell them, my purpose is not to convince you about what you should do. I tell them it isn't for everyone. But everyone should have some knowledge that it's a real option. That takes some of the defensiveness out of the situation."

Nonetheless, she said, there was still a stigma about taking time off. "People think that the right kids from the right school and the right family go to the right colleges, especially here in New England," she said. "Because the only path that seems open is the one in front of them. It's only when you get through that experience that you see that, in fact, there were choices. Even the most reluctant parents of kids who have taken time off by the end of the year are so grateful."

INTERPOINTS

I asked Jake Horne, who runs a structured year called Interpoints out of Washington Depot, Connecticut, why so many "year off" advisors were located in New England, in a ring around Boston. "You could only do it if you were in Boston," he said, "because there are so many schools and so many freethinking people there. It's a high-volume place where one could start and pick up clients." His location in northwest Connecticut is, he says, surrounded by prep schools. Perhaps that is one reason why, when people think of Jake Horne, they think expensive.

Parents who define "the best" as "the most expensive," here's your guy. Jake Horne charges $2,750 to design a structured year for a student and four years of follow-up advice. And he is exclusive, too, taking about 35 students a year. All of his students, he says, are on the fast track academically and looking for fresh and stimulating experiences. (Translation: Take confused and wary kids elsewhere.)

"For the next four years, if they want to do something, or just need a reference point, I'm there," he said. He will also work with older clients, kids who have dropped out of college, on an hourly basis.

But his main clientele is made up of seniors in the nearby prep schools. "It became really clear to me that there were scads of kids leaving prep schools and going to college, and partying, transferring, blowing out," he said. "The culture doesn't give these kids an awful lot of grounding to reflect on what they want, or rites of passage or metaphors for passage to being adults. Outward Bound and NOLS and the Army have been the only resources for making these transitions, but that's changed."

His clients also come from public high schools in Greenwich or New Canaan or Farmington, Connecticut. "These kids have had pretty successful high school careers," he said, "but their brains are pooped. They've worked pretty hard. They need to take the time to recover. That's why most of my kids want to do that. It's not because they haven't gotten into Princeton."

Perhaps in Chicago, he says, there is a different pace and pressure. (No comment.) "But in the East there's this straight track: high school, college, graduate school and then a banker," he said. "Even kids who know they want to step off that track have a hard time doing it."

Luckily, he says, the parents of his clients "tend to be pretty cool people." "They themselves either took time before college or at least did junior year abroad. Or they are people who are eclectic. A fair number of my clients' parents are CEO's of corporations, but they have a different way of looking at the world."

While he finds that he has plenty of customers willing to pay for his time—"People who have their children at prep schools are used to paying for services"—he says that kids with gumption can create their own year off. "You don't need my service or Bulls' or anyone's," he said. "But we tend to offer some comfort for these kids to let them know they are close to the mark."

Basically, he offers comfort in two areas. Parents ask: If my kid does this, will he become a bum? And if my kid does this, will he be killed?

"Much of my business is related to addressing those issues," he said. While he notes that parents are "always neurotic," he also notes that he is the father of three daughters and that he would never put a kid in a situation that might be unsafe.

"Parents are concerned about whether kids have the judgment and can manage problems when they arrive," he said. "If they're in college, they're in a dorm, they're in classes. We buy into the illusion that they're safe. But if he's in New Zealand, is he going to be bungee jumping on the other side of the world? A lot of it has to do with parents relinquishing control, and the kid making the shift from kid to young adult making decisions. It takes practice."

Jake is not one to take on kids with an active problem with drugs or alcohol. "I am very clear with these kids," he said. "They have to have common sense, self-interest and motivation. If a kid has baggage . . . One kid is eighteen and she's an alcoholic. She needed to address that first, and I said that to her." Nor will he take kids who have serious ADD disabilities. "Kids with ADD have difficulty managing, and they don't fit my criteria," he said. "The kids who have ADD who work with me have the temperament, the criteria, they have control, common sense."

He says all this despite the fact that he worked at the Forman School, for kids with learning disabilities, for ten years. "I did the pre-prep, prep school, then Harvard route," he said, but he left Harvard in his junior year. It was 1971, he says. He hitchhiked around the country for six years. Then the woman who was to become his wife said, "Pull yourself together."

"The confusion dissipated and I went back to Harvard," he said. "I was passionate about it then, and finished in three years."

Now he is in the business of providing challenges. "That's organic to human nature," he said. "My kids are desperate to have that kind of experience. That's why NOLS is so successful. You come away clean and healthy and having done something remarkable."

He tells his clients that they may have to pay for their first internships. "What I tell them is that they're eighteen, they don't have a résumé, they have more to learn than to offer. They will start the front end of the year paying for the experience, whether it's art restoration or an archaeological dig. They pay for mentoring and training and structure."

That's in addition to his fee, of course, and airfare.

"By the time my kids are halfway through their year they are in a much more independent kind of environment," he said. "They learn how to figure things out. These kids have to be stretched, and when you do, they rise to the occasion."

His kids come back from their year with a different vocabulary, he said, having lived in different countries. And he makes clear that all of his kids *want* to go outside the country. Then, by the time they've been away for six or eight months, they will be ready to "reconnect" with the United States, he said, "perhaps through photographing wild animals in Yellowstone and living on a ranch."

But he says he cannot work with kids who don't have good judgment and common sense. "In the past, I've had one or two kids who couldn't make decisions," he said. "It was a nightmare."

He finds that he sees more young women than young men. "I think gals are braver," he said. "Guys get into schools because of their athletics. They're worried that if they take any time off they're not going to play varsity."

Parents are also inclined to urge their sons to make "responsible decisions," he said. Building guitars in England might not come under that rubric.

"Girls take good risks," he said. "They've been thinking about this stuff longer. Guys—well, I was really dumb until I was twenty-eight."

The bottom line for Jake: "Teenagers don't need to be sitting in the classroom. They need to be seeing and touching and smelling. That's why everyone loves labs." His program makes a lab of the entire world.

AND NOW FOR A PHILOSOPHICAL TAKE

Until the Bull boys moved to California in 1999, David Denman had the state, the whole West Coast, to himself. He has established his business in Sausalito, conveniently located in the heart of Silicon Valley.

But Dave is not some young pup. He's got the manner of a wise old man who has seen and tried everything when it comes to finding places for offbeat kids.

And he's also been around long enough to have memories like this. "I took time out of graduate school at Princeton Theological Seminary and went to Mississippi as a 'good Northerner,'" he said. "And I taught in the mid-fifties in a small college for blacks. It was the most seminal experience in my own life. It has given me a slant on what Gunnar Myrdal called the American Dilemma that I would never have had otherwise. In any discussion about race, I bring a different perspective because of that experience in Mississippi."

Dave works to find boarding schools for high school students as well as "arranging to place children in schools for naughty boys and girls," he said, referring to high-priced therapeutic schools.

But half of his time is spent on finding alternative solutions to kids just out of high school or taking a break from college. "College counselors are blithely shoving young people toward colleges without any thoughts about what it might lead to and for whom there may not be jobs," he said.

"How are kids supposed to know what they want to be if they've only been in school?" he asks. "They need to experience life in order to decide, to make an informed decision."

Dave charges $1,750 for what he does, whether it's boarding school placement, finding a place in a school in San Francisco or Marin County or whether it's time-out work.

On the last he works primarily with programs that offer room and board. "You can't take an eighteen-year-old, responsibly, and plop him somewhere in a strange place with no support," he says. And after the kid has gone out and tested himself in the real world, Dave says, "there's a college in the country for everybody."

One of the reasons I liked talking to Dave so much was that his been-there-done-that philosophy was developed close to home and is based in a lot of love. He has four children, three of whom were high achievers and one of whom was not.

"He took time out and extended it in Aspen, Colorado, working on the ski patrol and in numerous restaurants." This son ran for mayor of Aspen at age twenty-four. "He didn't get elected," Dave said, "but he told me, 'Dad, I never could have learned this in political science class.'"

Eventually he ended up with a culinary diploma. "In his early thirties now, he is the executive chef at the best restaurant in Telluride, Colorado. And he still gets to ski from eight in the morning to eleven. He's got two condos and a log cabin on ten acres—which is more than his older siblings have.

"The coda to my son's story," Dave said, "is that he married a wonderful young woman who graduated from Yale. And she brings him class." She flies him to Houston for the opera; he takes her camping and climbing.

ON THE OTHER HAND

I didn't see any of the aforementioned counselors, either before my son went to college or after he dropped out after two years. Partly, I was annoyed enough at him after the DWI report card, and had spent enough money, so that I felt it was his turn to do some work. And also he had a serious girlfriend. That put the kibosh on any program that would involve his going to North Carolina to learn crafts, or taking off to work on a ranch in western Australia.

Moreover, as Jake Horne said, any kid can come up with his own list of things to do. Using the combined wisdom of the counselors I spoke to, a kid's structured year should involve these things: The kid should be the one who makes the choices; he should earn all or part of the money needed for the year; the child should do more than one thing during the year; and whatever trips or internships are picked, the teen should be excited about the possibilities.

What is important is that the kid get out of the house and out from under his parents' rules.

Chapter Fifteen

GET A JOB

*Choose a job you love, and you will never
have to work a day in your life.*
—CONFUCIUS

If you ask a child in the United States what he wants to be when
he grows up, chances are he'll tell you "rich." Admirable, but not
practical. The problem arises when kids realize that what stands
between them and great wealth is hard work.

In 1993, when President Clinton gave his first State of the
Union speech, he talked about the value of work. After promising to establish apprenticeships, he said, "There is dignity in all
work, and there must be dignity for all workers."

I watched that speech with my best friend, Gini, in a bar at
the Edison Hotel, across from Lincoln Center. We were two
women who had come out of the Midwest—she, the daughter
of a factory worker in Cicero, Illinois; I, the daughter of a blacksmith in North Branch, Minnesota. Tears leaped to my eyes when
I heard the President laud the idea of work. Not wealth, work.

My father supported a wife and three children by working as

a blacksmith, a welder, a mechanic, a tool-and-die man, an inventor. During World War II he had been a shipbuilder in the state of Washington. At some point he had also worked as a steamfitter for the Great Northern Railroad.

He was the kind of man who did all that and then played mandolin and banjo and guitar in a local polka band at night. When he owned a service station, between pumping gas and fixing cars, he sat in his filthy office and did "Increase Your Word Power" in the *Reader's Digest*. When he was a young man, he had written notebooks full of poetry, mostly doggerel. Later, working in his own Mobil station, he always had a paperback book cracked open, whether it was a generic title by Frank G. Slaughter or *The Gingerbread Man*.

My mother was single until the age of thirty-eight, and she always worked too, first on the family farm in South Dakota, then in a cookie factory in Sioux Falls, and later at 3M in the Twin Cities in Minnesota. Eventually, she started a little grocery store in our small town, a convenience store that was eventually put out of business by a 7-Eleven.

After school I used to help her, measuring lutefisk into cardboard cartons, cutting wheels of longhorn cheese, stocking shelves, making ice cream cones, ringing up purchases on an old National Standard cash register and stacking groceries into tall paper bags set on a stool. I was the first person in my family to go to college, and when I went off to the University of Minnesota, my parents were not anticipating that I would become well-rounded or enlightened. My parents' one wish was that I would pursue something practical, like teaching, so that I could earn a living.

I come from hardworking people, and when I sat in that bar that night, it had been a long time since I had heard someone in government who sang the praises of people who just plain worked. And it was clear to me the President was not talking about people like me who work with their brains. He was talking about people who work with their hands.

"In the United States we don't value work as they do in Europe and many Asian countries," said Paul F. Cole, secretary-treasurer of the New York State AFL-CIO, as we sat in his office in Albany. "Work is devalued here. People look down their noses at people who work with their hands. And guidance counselors say, 'You are not successful unless you go to a four-year program in college.'"

Paul looks like the former Army Reserve captain that he is. But he was also a high school social studies teacher in Youngstown, New York, for twenty-two years. So he knew what he was talking about when he said, "If you ask a parent, a kid, or a teacher, or a guidance counselor about a job in manufacturing, they immediately go to 'Well, it's dirty machines.' They have a 1940s view of what a factory looks like."

Instead, he said, modern manufacturing is high tech and requires educated workers who do not park their brains at the factory door. It is the job of schools to make that and the rest of the working world known to students, he says.

What about Leon Botstein's notion, I asked, that high school should end at sixteen because kids are bored? "The diagnosis is right, the prescription is wrong," Paul said. "The prescription isn't to end school at sixteen. The prescription is to make sure those eleventh or twelfth grades are a valuable learning experience where kids begin to connect the world of school with the world of work."

Part of the problem, he said, is that American employers don't have any confidence in eighteen- and nineteen-year-olds. "In Europe they do," he said. "I've been to a number of factories and programs all over northern Europe. You see kids, young men and women, who are seventeen, eighteen, nineteen and very responsible. They perform quite effectively, quite competently, in the workplace. American employers just don't see that."

"You can go all over Europe and see young people in the workplace doing important work," he said. "The difference is they work to learn, our kids work to earn. Kids over here work at McDonald's or Foot Locker at the local mall, and they do it to get money to pay for the car or pay for the gas or get the latest Nike sneakers. There is no connection between what they do at work and what they learn in school."

And that's where Paul runs smack dab into "standards-based education." While the standards-based people want students to hunker down and drill, drill, drill on the questions that turn up on Regents, national and international achievement tests, Paul and people who think like him want kids out in the workplace, getting their hands into something and finding out what the working world is all about. Since there is not enough time in the day for kids to do that and to drill, students may have to choose.

At what age do they opt out of the "study-for-the-exam" track, and opt into the "school-to-work" track. In terms of college prep, you're either on the bus or you're not on the bus.

The people who advocate a bond between school and work say a student can do both; people who belong to the standards-based camp say they cannot, that their test scores will suffer.

A very short background paper: Education in this country has always been a political football. (Note the National Defense Education Act of 1958, which was supposed to make us keep up with the Ruskies in the space race.) Kenneth Hoyt, who is now at Kansas State University, was director of the federal Office of Career Education from 1974 to 1982. In the seventies, under him, career education (or vocational education) was on fairly firm footing. Then came the eighties, and Ronald Reagan's Back to Basics program.

Basics, apparently, did not include basics about career education. In the 1990s career education began to flourish again. President Clinton ran for election advocating the system of apprenticeships. In 1991, the Secretary's Commission on Achieving Necessary Skills (SCANS) report was organized, combining business and vocational educators. But during SCANS, the words "vocational education," with their whiff of shop class and low-functioning factory workers, were replaced by terms that had a lot of "pro"s and "tech"s in them.

These new terms were supposed to deal with the emerging need for technology workers, from people who repaired air conditioners to people who worked in computer-automated factories to lab technicians, health care workers and specialists in reading X rays and mammograms. An offshoot, School to Work, was launched in 1994. That was the year that Goals 2000, a national plan to do things like cut down on dropouts and encourage national standards, was started.

The other figure here is General Colin Powell, who in 1997 organized America's Promise: The Alliance for Youth, which has, as one of its tenets, the acquisition of "a marketable skill through effective education." General Powell's program advocates "job shadowing," having a kid follow someone around to find out what a job really involves. (Think of it as a one-day apprenticeship.)

All this was going on, way beneath my middle-class radar, while I focused on my son's PSAT scores, his entrance exams to special schools, his ability to learn a foreign language and his entrance into a boarding school. One reason it was beneath my radar was that these programs presumed a somewhat limited career in the "trades" or the "techs," while a college career seemed to promise a limitless future. It had worked for me; surely it would work for my son.

Now I was sitting with Paul F. Cole, and getting a refresher course on an entire branch of education that had eluded me and my son, a kind of education I had in fact avoided. Paul spent 1990–1992 working on the SCANS report and is, among other things, the vice chair of the National Skills Standard Board. He is also on the National School-to-Work Advisory Council. For members of the religious right, Paul Cole is ground zero, demon incarnate. Why? Let me quote some of the overheated prose in *Goals 2000,* a 1996 tract: "What we have gotten with Goals 2000 is a national—soon to be international—school system, as dreamed of and patiently planned for by socialists, one-worlders, and their fellow-traveler Utopians." (Just to make it clear, the terms "one-worlders" and "Utopians" are pejorative, even more than "socialists," perhaps.)

One whole chapter of the book is devoted to the National Skills Standards Board—in the words of *Goals 2000,* a "blueprint for our economic enslavement." What is giving the radical right such fantods? This pretty much sums it up (the book helpfully prints all of its big ideas in bold type): **"Who owns our children? Are they yours? Does the state (government) own them? Or are you willing to share custody of your children with the state?"**

Aha. The National Skills Standards Board will, when it finishes its work, define just what is required for each and every job in this country. The NSSB will then issue nationwide certificates that will declare that Jeremy has the skills to work as a secretary/receptionist in any state, or that Jennifer knows enough computer skills to work a lathe in an automobile plant from Maine to Tennessee.

And to get those skills, kids will need "some kind" of training, a phrase that turned up over and over from the graduates of White Bear Lake High School. They weren't sure if kids need to go to college, but "some kind" of training is needed.

To get a job in this country, people need training, and increasingly they get that training in community colleges, which jump in response to the needs of the surrounding community. If the county needs health-care workers, the local community college will add courses in nursing and being a health-care aide. If the town needs car mechanics for Fords or Chevys, Ford or GM is going to donate some cars to the community college and courses in "Repairing the Ford Escort" are going to be added.

What's interesting is that 30 percent of the people taking those courses, at either community colleges or trade schools, already *have* a bachelor's degree. In other words, they have gotten a college education, and now they need training to get a job.

A YOUNG MAN MEETS THE WORK WORLD

After two years of college, two years in which my son may have withdrawn from more classes than he passed, he agreed that he was going to take some time off, to live in an apartment in Rochester, New York, work and get himself pulled together. Nothing in the two years of very expensive college that he had had gave him any marketable skills, so he had to start at the bottom. He began by painting fences for his college, to pay off some of the damage to the apartment he and his roommate had rented.

Then he found work as a roofer for $7.50 an hour. Now, roofing is hot, dirty and hard work, toiling up on top of a building in July. It is no party, but he looked on the bright side: He was getting a bitchin' tan.

One fellow who turned up to do some painting for the same contractor was an ex-convict who had spent time in Attica.

Was I upset? Momentarily. But life offers some harsh lessons. One lesson my son learned was that you transport and sell cocaine, you go to Attica for four years. And the fellow made it clear that Attica was less of a party than painting, or roofing.

My son's next job was driving a pickup truck for the contractor he had been working for, who had lost his license. That meant my son had to get up at 6 A.M. to pick up his boss at 6:30 and drive him around in a rattling, old, rusty truck with ladders on the top. Not the cool image my son had cultivated while driving around in his little Mazda RX7 sports car.

His next job was delivering packages for UPS during Christmas rush. He got $6.50 an hour. During the entire Christmas season, jumping out of the truck and running bulky packages up icy sidewalks, he got precisely $1 in tips. "But I worked in some nice neighborhoods and I got to drive the truck," he said.

After that he spent three months selling vitamins at the mall, where someone backed into his car and bashed in his front fender.

Then he moved up to making $8.50 an hour ($300 a week take-home) working for a company that treats people's lawns. He had to take regular blood tests to make sure that he was not poisoning himself while he rid the lawns of weeds and grubs. It was during this job that he began to hear commentary from the citizenry of Rochester.

Old Italian men would come outside in their undershirts and tell him, "You're a nice boy. Go to college. You don't belong in a job like this."

Mothers would stop on the sidewalk and point at him. "If you don't stay in school," they'd tell their ten-year-olds, "you're going to end up doing something like that."

"Mom, at least I'm doing some good in the world," he told me on the phone. "I'm an object lesson."

"Look," I told him. "At least you've now had the worst job you'll ever have. Years from now you'll be able to say, 'This is nothing compared to pumping chemicals onto people's lawns.'"

IT'S JOB EXPERIENCE, STUPID!

While some educators praise the pure pleasures of learning, it turns out that students themselves *want* training. And employers, needless to say, want trained and experienced workers.

"What would be interesting is to go to Stanford and study something real, something you could actually use," said Scott Wainner, the twenty-one-year-old website multimillionaire who dropped out of Texas A & M. (Note to Scott: Stanford is already there, offering practical computer-related courses to all comers.)

Norm Fraley, manager of distance learning at Kelly Scientific Resources in Detroit, said: "I think we need to bust that learning-training stereotype, and get it out there that training is teaching how to do something functional."

Several of the kids from White Bear Lake made it clear that they felt that college did not prepare them for the working world.

Matthew Kummer from White Bear Lake is working in the field he studied in college. He is an on-air reporter at a television station in Peoria, Illinois, after earning a bachelor's degree in broadcast journalism from the University of Wisconsin, Eau Claire. Nonetheless, he said, "that four-year degree isn't going to get you anywhere unless you've done internships." It was his experience that got his foot in the door, not his degree.

Holly Major from White Bear Lake got a bachelor's degree in psychology at the University of Kansas in Lawrence. In her job of placing people in positions at Sprint's world headquarters in Kansas City, she says she looks at the applicants' job experience rather than at their degrees.

"In fact, the people who graduate with a telecom degree and apply for positions at Sprint are, many times, not qualified enough for the basic entry-level position in telecommunications," she wrote. If the company really likes someone they hire, she said, they will send that person back to school to get the education they need.

Chris Wlaschin Thomas, also of White Bear, said she was "not much of a book person," and that after high school she didn't want to study anymore. She went to technical school to become a medical secretary. "There are people who graduated from college and they work for eight or nine bucks an hour, and I make twelve," she said.

Don Peterson had a double major in business/marketing and international relations at Bethel College. "I came out with a great liberal arts degree," he told me. "However, I wasn't specifically prepared enough for a particular job. I was particularly lucky because I had a work internship through my school that gave me some marketing training. Without that, I would've had no experience on my résumé." He urged students to focus on vocational or computer training, "rather than waste the $60,000 it costs to pay for four years of college.

"I felt like much of my college education was not specific enough to prepare me for the workforce," he said.

YOUR TAX DOLLARS AT WORK

While middle-class parents were focused on getting Jonah and Janelle into Ivy League colleges, some schools in this country have been busy "partnering" with businesses in order to teach kids marketable skills. White Bear Lake High School is one of them. Rolf Parsons is a member of the White Bear Lake school board, and the parent of a child who graduated from the school in 1993. "We make a great deal of effort in White Bear Lake to find an opportunity to cooperate with business," Rolf told me. "I'm well aware that we need to train people to do more than go to college." He said he believes the school "is not serving half of the school population."

Brenda Selby, who graduated from White Bear Lake High School in 1993, is now earning $18 an hour working as an installer for U.S. West, with full benefits. She had been working since she was fifteen, she said, and had taken advantage of some of White Bear Lake's job training. (Remember, she graduated in 1993, before School to Work came on the scene.)

Just out of high school, she found herself with a new baby, no skills and no husband.

"I went on assistance," she said. "I didn't want to do that. I knew I needed some kind of training."

She decided she wanted to be an electrician. Public assistance paid all of her expenses for a two-year course of study in electrical construction at the Dunwoody Institute, a technical school in Minneapolis.

"A program called Stride, which they don't have anymore, paid for everything," she said. "When I graduated, I didn't have any debts."

While she was waiting for a spot to open up in the electrician's union, she heard about a job at U.S. West. "I said, 'Jeez, with the kind of training I've got I can do that: climbing ladders and poles, installing jacks and lines, going down into manholes.' They tested several hundred, and I was one of the top eight who took the tests."

Brenda enjoys the gender-bending aspects of the job. "People say, 'It's so nice to see a woman get the job.' Old women say, 'The phone man is here. Whoops, it's the phone woman.'" But even more she enjoys being able to provide for her daughter.

Moreover, now that she is working for U.S. West, she can begin to think about further education. "I know one guy who's been taking classes for five years to be a lawyer, and U.S. West has paid for it all," she told me.

SOMETIMES KIDS JUST NEED TO WORK

What can someone achieve without college? In construction, 44 percent of the workers have only a high school diploma, and 21 percent have less than that, according to the U.S. Department of Labor. That's why my son started there. And while construction can provide a good living, my son longed for an indoor job, one with air conditioning.

He could take a couple of courses, work for a couple of years and then become a certified electronics technician (repairing equipment from video cameras to televisions and audio equipment to microwave ovens). According to the Bureau of Labor Statistics, the median wage for that in 1996 was $619 a week, around $35,000 a year. I could just point him to www.careers.org and let him figure it out himself.

I sort of liked the idea of his becoming an air traffic controller. There's a competitive federal civil service exam that tests things like "abstract reasoning and three-dimensional spatial visualization," according to the Bureau of Labor Statistics. (All those years of playing computer games, put to some *use*.) The feds, who train all air traffic controllers, require that the trainee be less than thirty-one for some positions (there is a mandatory retirement age of fifty-six—this is a job for those with young reflexes), and have three years of work experience or four years of college, or a combination of both. Air traffic controllers are trained at the Federal Aviation Administration academy in Oklahoma City for seven months, and start at $30,000 a year. In 1997, they averaged $46,000 a year. Plus, they can retire after twenty-five years of service—with all the benefits of a federal employee. Not bad.

He could make technical drawings (he was always good at CAD), with a little bit of training in drafting. In 1996, according to the Bureau of Labor Statistics, drafters started at around $20,000 a year and could earn up to $50,000.

There were all those technician jobs, from broadcast technician to nuclear medicine technologist (full-time median pay of $36,000 in 1997, according to the Bureau of Labor Statistics). Some technician jobs just require hands-on experience. Others require a couple of years of training and a certificate. With the college he already has he could probably pick up the required credits in a year.

He could become a basic emergency medical technician. All that requires is 110 hours of classroom work and ten hours in an emergency room. He's always liked watching *Cops*.

And of course there are all those computer jobs just waiting for him to get his Cisco Certification or his MCSE.

He could be an entrepreneur and start his own business, from yard work to home repairs to installing high-end stereos and entertainment centers.

If he wanted, he could become a trader on the stock market. (Richard Grasso, the head of the New York Stock Exchange, does not have a college degree.) He could write (no degree required). He could join an entertainment company in the mailroom and work his way up (David Geffen).

There is practically nothing except professions requiring a college degree (doctor, lawyer, architect and so on) that he could not do. And if he was interested in those fields he could, without a college degree, become a practical nurse, a paralegal (among the fastest-growing professions) or a drafter.

In other words, there is almost no job that might be closed to him, and that includes the governorship of the state of Minnesota. All that is required is the will, because there is clearly the way.

HOW ONE WOMAN DID IT

Valerie Woodsen, forty-eight, of New Jersey is now a successful marketing executive in broadcasting. She did it without any college education. "Had I been forced to go to college," she told me, "I would have flunked out, because the parochial schools so discouraged me from wanting to learn."

Valerie grew up in a family of three children that moved several times in and around New York City—Harlem, Queens and finally Mount Vernon in Westchester County. "I guess you could say we were poor," she told me. "My mother was a barmaid and manager, and my dad was a gambler. When he worked, he was a chauffeur. Growing up, I didn't have an expectation about Christmas. I wouldn't know one year from the next what it would be. There might have been a chance you wouldn't have anything for Christmas. The money wasn't there."

What she does remember is glamorous Aunt Rachel, who was a maid for Bess Myerson, the former Miss America. "We thought she had the coolest life," Valerie said. "She went to parties all the time, dressed in these beautiful cocktail dresses. I wanted a life like Aunt Rachel's."

Valerie earned mostly C's and D's in high school. She didn't know what she was going to do after graduation in 1969 until a counselor mentioned that the J. Walter Thompson advertising agency was looking for minorities for a two-year program. (Valerie is black.)

"I immediately went to work," she said. "At the time it was the greatest place to work, a great party atmosphere. Every afternoon at 3 P.M. everyone would be in the bar downstairs." Ah, the creative life in Manhattan.

When she left J. Walter Thompson, she briefly tried Bronx Community College, and even more briefly tried modeling. Then she went to work for a chemical company marketing executive and really began to learn the business. "He encouraged me to grow," she says simply.

Her career took the usual twists and turns that make for an amusing story later but can feel like severe buffeting at the time. She tried the West Coast, mostly to get away from her family. And while she was there, working for CBS as a sales assistant, someone heard her voice on the telephone, realized she was black and hired her to read the news and be an overnight disk jockey on a black radio station. She did the early-morning news report, then took twenty minutes to record the sound bites for her overnight show; she was finished with work before 9 every morning. "And I was making a fortune—$25,000 a year to do this, in 1974."

When the station was bought by another company, she went back to the advertising agency side, always moving up, "because I liked working," she said. "I could throw myself into work and never worry about the hours."

Pretty soon she was a manager. "No one *ever* asked about college," she said. "In those days it wasn't important. It didn't become an issue until the 1980s, and by then I had the experience. In today's environment, I could never do what I did."

Valerie now has an eight-year-old daughter, and she *expects* her daughter to go to college. "I have these conversations and I tell her, 'You *have* to go to college, because it's the only way you can get interviewed [to work] in an office.' And that's to get an interview to be an assistant. A college degree is the requirement to be an assistant. That's *insane*."

On the other hand, Valerie sees an extraordinary sense of entitlement from the college graduates she hires. "These kids with college degrees, they're . . . hah, forget it," she said. "They have a total set of expectations: what they should be doing, when they should be promoted. I felt lucky to be promoted, and they expect it."

Whereas she was often asked to get coffee for meetings when she was young, she says she would never ask one of the new hires to get coffee. "They say, 'Get it yourself.' A totally different set of expectations."

After running her own company for seven years, Valerie recently went to work for the Infinity Broadcasting Company, a division of CBS. "I've become exceptionally good at the politics of corporate America," she says. She is running a division dealing with marketing and promotions and makes between $150,000 and $200,000 a year.

Despite her strong feelings about her daughter's going to college, the teachers at her daughter's progressive private school tell her she needs to ease up a little. "I was talking with her teacher last year and the teacher was saying, 'Don't encourage her to go to college. It might not be the right thing for her.' Her teacher and the school administrator were *both* doing this. Their thing was, they felt they weren't ready to go to college themselves, and they wish their parents hadn't forced them to go."

SUPPORTING EDUCATION, FROM A WORKER'S POINT OF VIEW

In his late seventies, Mattel Dawson is still working as a rigger at the Ford Motor Company's Rouge plant in Dearborn, Michigan, driving a high-low, a kind of forklift truck. Mat takes any overtime the company offers.

Donald N. Ritzenhein, assistant vice president of annual giving and development services for Wayne State University, said, "He works every day of the week—I mean, every day. He works twelve hours Saturday and twelve hours Sunday."

Mat makes $23.47 an hour and, because of the overtime, brings home almost $100,000 a year. Most of it he gives away to the United Negro College Fund, churches and education. Since

1994, he has given more than $1 million to charity. In 1999 alone he gave $200,000 to Wayne State University; over the years he has given the school more than $400,000.

Mat Dawson left school in Shreveport, Louisiana, in the seventh grade. He skips vacations, drives a 1985 Ford Escort and lives modestly. Even though he is divorced and has one daughter, he prefers to do good deeds with his lifetime earnings. His secret, he has said, is that he learned when he was young to work hard and to save a lot of his money.

But perhaps, I said to Mr. Ritzenhein, in addition to giving money to colleges and universities, Mat Dawson should allow students to "job-shadow" him for a day, and see what a real work ethic looks like. "It would be an interesting experience," he said. "From what I gather, he pulls his weight as a rigger. So far as I can see, he does his thing."

SOME LUCKY KIDS STARTED IN HIGH SCHOOL

Hillary Pennington is an executive with Jobs for the Future in Boston, and an advocate for Pro-Tech, part of the School to Work program. "Our particular interest is in creating learning strategies at the high school level and up that are more hands-on, applied and more intellectually rigorous."

When I talked to people about what was wrong with high school in this country, over and over they said there was not enough experiential learning. Kids sit in classrooms, bored with teachers blah-blah-blahing at the front of the room (what Paul Cole calls "chalk and talk"). Kids want to do something, and they want to do something real.

School administrators are coming around to experiential learning, Hillary told me, "but the dominant education policy is antithetical to experiential learning. New York State is a good example, so interested in academic achievement, a standard-based reform movement and ways to assess student learning. But assessment emphasizes fairly narrow academic content over their ability to apply knowledge to what they didn't see before."

Part of the reason educators remain wedded to the basics, she said, is that it is easy to give one test to everyone, and much harder to assess what it means for one kid to be "job-shadowing" a lab technician and another to be building a portfolio of computer-generated graphic art.

"Assessing complex skills is expensive," she said.

"So at the end of the decade we end up with two things at odds with each other." While the teachers believe that Pro-Tech turns kids on to learning, "they are worried about the test scores being reported in the newspapers. The measures we pay attention to, that the public cares about, are *so* hard to change.

"Students are saying, 'We don't want to take tests,'" Hillary said. "'They don't measure what we know.'"

There is another side to this. L. Sunny Hansen, a professor at the University of Minnesota, took a look at the School to Work program in the June 1999 issue of *Career Counseling* magazine. "Critics of STW," she wrote, "have accused it of tracking students, 'dumbing down' the curriculum, forcing premature decisions (e.g., career majors by grade 11), and of allowing schools to take over functions that belong to parents."

Professor Hansen pointed out that school counselors were expected to spend one third of their time on career development, leaving only the other two-thirds of their time for college counseling and personal and social development. Professor Hansen sees School to Work as promoting the needs of business over the needs of students. "One of the limitations of STW is that it focuses on students as workers and ignores other parts of their development," she wrote. "STW is workforce development, providing skills so that the U.S. can keep the international competitive edge with Germany and Japan. Students deserve to be treated as whole people. . . ."

She concluded that School to Work "is the latest bandwagon, driven by business and industry, implemented largely by vocational education, [and costing] billions of dollars."

Her complaints are a little hard to fathom, since the program is not compulsory; it is simply offering the alternative to kids who want it.

On the other hand, perhaps the School to Work program should be available later in life. Instead of trying to grab kids off the high school assembly line, maybe it's better to wait until they have tried college, or their first jobs, and discovered that they want something better. Then again, isn't her argument caving in to another lobby that may be just as powerful as "business and industry," which is to say the postsecondary college and university programs? Isn't School to Work simply providing another way for kids who aren't going to college?

Hillary Pennington said she has seen President Clinton's youth apprenticeship fall apart over such divisiveness. "I was on the transition team and worked with Richard Reilly, but for political reasons they didn't want [School to Work] targeted at the middle half," she told me. "They were worried it left out the top, the kid who goes to Yale, and the bottom, the kids who needed it most, and who were tracked out of any opportunity at all. Seven years of floundering. We put people into the position of thinking that they had to make an either-or choice about college. But the most powerful models blend the two. The best models recognize that not everyone needs a four-year college degree, but some postsecondary increments—and will get them anywhere that's practical."

Through running Pro-Tech in Boston, Hillary has found that kids who began working on a serious career path in high school (not in a video store at the mall, but in hospitals, offices, institutions) tended to go on to some kind of postsecondary education and to stick with it.

The Pro-Tech mission, she says, is to not leave our children's work lives to chance "under the guise of freedom."

"We want to track them to somewhere," she says. "Right now we track them to nowhere."

Putting everyone on the college track does not work. "The cost of college education and the number of boomeranging kids who come home anyway will put some pressure on," she said. "Corporate America will create some incentives. At some point there will be a need to look at the standards-based reform movements: Is that an adequate measure of our children?"

SO WHERE DOES AN EIGHTEEN-YEAR-OLD START?

A kid can still start at the bottom, like Valerie, and work up. Or a teenager can parlay some knowledge of computers into a job in an office. But almost everyone will need some form of training or certification.

Those in the career-training field like to make this distinction: The old vocational training led to a limited set of skills; the new "career" training will teach students how to learn, thus equipping them for the three or four job changes they will make through their lifetime. But what constitutes job training?

As my son learned, most low-level jobs do their training on videotape. That's how UPS did it, from customer relations to handling hazardous materials, and so did the lawn-care company. "But I got paid to sit and watch the video and take a quiz," my son told me.

One alternative is a paid apprenticeship, although the payment is sometimes a burden on the student. "That's how people used to do it," Jimi Petulla, the head of Career Connections, told me. Career Connections, based in Reno, Nevada, asks a $4,000 to $6,000 fee to arrange for an apprenticeship in radio, television, film and recording. Jimi promises to match a kid up with someone working in the field, within driving distance of the kid's house. By putting in fifteen to twenty hours a week over a period of eight to ten months, the apprentice learns all of the aspects of the job, he says, and gets the experience needed to actually become employed in the field.

"I started working on the radio at fifteen in my hometown in Pennsylvania," Jimi told me. "I came from a very poor family. There were ten of us, and college was not an option."

There were schools of broadcasting, he said, but they would take anyone who walked in the door. "They called it a screening process, but it was a joke," he said. "They wanted people who made less money, because you got a Pell grant right away," he said, referring to government loans. "They weren't selling a career, they were getting Pell grants."

Most of the people he knows in the recording business got into it just walking in off the street, he said. Which makes him critical of the college programs that take four years to teach someone how to produce a CD.

What he does is split the fee with the audio engineer or station manager or film producer who will train the apprentice. "I literally pay them to train the student. What I do is what they did back before there were schools. In the twelfth century, people would have thought it was crazy to put twenty students in a room with one master. It was the worst thing they could have done.

"The best way to learn anything is one person sitting down

and teaching one other person. Your family would pay for you to work with a master. It's a throwback to the Renaissance apprenticeship method. It works, and it's fast. A person either can do it or not.

"People assume that school works," he said. "It's not true, man. The people who end up getting work are the ones who do the apprenticeships."

People love to teach someone who's motivated, he said. But he's wary of anyone who thinks they are going to be recording Van Halen in six months. He looks for "people who say, 'I don't mind paying my dues and starting at the bottom.'"

By now, Jimi was talking fast. "A diploma is a scarlet letter in this business," he said. "It's a kick-me sign. People want to hire someone who's done it, not someone who's studied it."

Kids pay $25,000 and more to study film editing or audio engineering, he says. "The reality is you come out and you still have to go out and find a job. Ninety percent of those students get nothing. A small group will get an internship and work for free for a year. So I say, skip the school and let's find out if you can do this or not."

His program is not accredited, and he does not give diplomas, he said. "I don't want to. People think being accredited makes you legit. Getting people jobs makes you legit."

But kids don't have to pay Jimi for an apprenticeship. States like Colorado and Pennsylvania and Georgia and Missouri have begun offering apprenticeship programs for kids as young as sixteen. Pennsylvania is pushing apprenticeships in technology, Georgia in trades like electrician and plumber, Missouri in the skilled trades, Colorado in contracting and manufacturing. Apprentices who are accepted into the programs are paid modest salaries. As licensed journeymen, they can earn up to $30 an hour.

COLLEGE DEGREES FOR . . . SOME

The president of Boston University was criticized for suggesting that some of his students would be better off quitting school and becoming plumbers and electricians. It was seen as closing the door on kids who were struggling in school.

I say he was right. At some point, someone has to stand up and say, "Not everyone deserves a college degree," and that will only happen when companies admit that not everyone *needs* a college degree.

If money were considered the only way to judge success, those kids would be a lot better off becoming talented plumbers instead of second-rate liberal arts majors. As for their intellectual stimulation: Libraries are free, and so is PBS.

Or, to put it another way, a schoolteacher in Missouri earns an average of $35,000 a year. A heating and plumbing contractor or an electrician makes between $40,000 and $50,000. You can get to a schoolteacher with just one phone call; just try reaching a plumber or an electrician.

ON BECOMING A TRUCK DRIVER

The last thing I expected when I began writing this book was that I would be sitting in a flimsy office on a large lot in West Babylon, New York, being moved by a man who feels he changes lives by admitting people to a truck driver training program.

But that was before I met David Borsack. I had talked to Dave a number of times on the phone. He was convinced there was a news story in the "scandal" of truck drivers who could not speak English. The Department of Transportation requires that interstate truck drivers be fluent in English so they can read traffic signs. Many truck driver training schools, he said, allow drivers to scam their way through the written test (he claimed they were provided with the answers); the schools then train the drivers for their commercial driver's license (CDL) and send them out, unable to speak English.

A little background here: For immigrants, one of the easiest and most lucrative jobs available is driving a truck. The Bureau of Labor Statistics notes that there will be greater need for truck drivers in the years to come (especially if everyone keeps ordering books, clothing, antiques and furniture on the Internet). It is possible for someone to earn $30,000 to $35,000 a year driving a truck long haul. Owner-operators, who have their own rigs and are in business for themselves, can make $100,000 a year. Michael Starnes, an American, started by driving a delivery truck; in the 1970s he used $10,000 in savings to form a trucking company in Memphis, Tennessee. Today his company, M.S. Carriers, has thousands of trucks and grosses $400 million a year.

For years, Russian immigrants, even those who were doctors or lawyers back home, came to America and got their CDLs. Dave pointed to a picture of two of his graduates on the wall: Russians who came in, trained as a pair and have been working together—one sleeping, one driving—ever since. It has been their ticket to success.

"Immigrants are new to the country, desperate and in need of a skill," Dave said. Now the immigrants tend to be from the Ivory Coast of Africa—"tremendous work ethic," Dave said, "amazing dedication." But Americans also learn to drive trucks. And for a kid with a need to get out and go and no other discernible skills, driving a truck sounds ideal. And it's not just for guys: Companies like UPS are eager to hire women drivers, as well as minorities.

"Women think it's man's work—strength and size—but it's not," Dave said. The Commercial Driver Training School has about 8 percent women, often in the coach (that's bus to civilians) program, a shorter course.

So I went out to West Babylon to see Dave and the truck driver training school. The minute I saw him come toward me, I knew there was something wrong. He looked like a man who was being worn by his suit. Scleroderma, he told me later.

Dave, thirty-nine, is an interesting guy, the son of a truck driver who never graduated from high school. His father was never proud of what he did for a living, but he put two children through college on a truck driver's wages. Dave attended Long Island University and got a degree in journalism. He taught in the New York City school system for a year, "but I wasn't able to make a difference," he told me earnestly.

Then he spent two years teaching at a private school in Manhattan, the Allen-Stevenson school. He liked teaching and he liked coaching kids in sports, he said, but he felt he still wasn't able to reach the students.

He tried working for a brokerage company for a couple of years but wasn't happy with that either. Then he discovered he had scleroderma, a chronic disease that causes thickening of the skin and other problems. He had a wife and young child. And he needed to do something that would not be so stressful but that would allow him to work with people.

Thus Dave became the admissions director of a truck driver training school. And he found his mission in life. He can take poor kids, "people who are unemployed or underemployed and busting their butts to make $5.50 an hour," he says. And after four months in truck driver training school they can be making $12 an hour to start and get up to $18 or $19 an hour. "Twenty dollars an hour, that's the goal," he says.

The school is expensive, however: $4,455 for the four-month course in the big trucks, $1,295 for the shorter course in driving a coach. What really bugs Dave is that his students can't get student loans. After a scandal about default rates on student loans in the late eighties, he said, the government decided to crack down on proprietary trade schools. The primary transgressors were cosmetology schools and schools that taught "business skills" to poor people, taking their student loan money and leaving them with no skills. But the government decided to fall back on an old standard by which to judge education: seat time.

Henceforth, kids could get student loans for only courses that lasted at least nine hundred hours, he said. And he couldn't stretch truck driver training out to nine hundred hours, "not even if we included courses on smoking cigarettes and drinking coffee, which is something truck drivers do a lot of."

I liked Dave enormously, especially his ire over not being able to get student loans for kids to study something that would give them employment. "We're not ever going to have trained robots drive a truck," he said. "You've got to get a person to do it. And we have 85 percent placement rate in the first ninety days after they finish the course."

Outside, as we spoke, students were climbing up in the rigs and practicing tight maneuvers. "Most people are scared the first time they get up there," he said. "I think there's a great deal of pride to drive that big truck like a pro." Most of the people who become truck drivers, he said, like it "because of the freedom of not sitting with a boss all day."

"People use it as a way of getting away," he said.

We talked for a bit about middle-class values. Dave left teaching behind to admit immigrants and the unemployed to a school that could pave the way for their dreams. "Don't write about me," he said. "Write about what people can get out of this."

THERE IS ALWAYS TEMP WORK

In writing this book, I discovered that almost every aspect of what I was looking at stemmed either from the period right after World War II, when this country had a surplus of returning soldiers and the peacetime economy began to expand, or the 1960s, when the country had a surplus of educational reformers who wanted students to break out of the classroom.

Temping started in this country in 1946 with Kelly Services, which trained the clerical and secretarial workers who would step in when a company faced an emergency. (Kelly Scientific Resources is a business unit of Kelly Services.) Manpower and other temp agencies followed.

According to the Bureau of Labor Statistics, in 1997 more than 14 million Americans worked as temps. Kelly has even started a program to provide "temp" teachers—that is, people who can step in as substitute teachers, even if they don't have credentials in education.

Norm Fraley, Manager for Distance Learning for Kelly Scientific Resources, points out that lots of programs from community colleges to technical schools are spitting out people with very specific skills, skills that would get them immediate employment either as a temp or as a full-time employee. The key, he said, is some kind of certificate or skills test to show that you know how to do something.

The problem these days, he says, is not that there are not enough jobs, but that people have no idea what jobs are available, and what skills are needed to get those jobs. (Norm, meet Paul Cole and the National Skills Standards Board.)

Norm gets nearly evangelical when he talks about the mystique of helping a person find out what kind of job they would love so much, they would do it for free. "You do that, you are doing a favor for every employer, to find the people who would do the job for free, people who would say, 'This is what I'm here for.' Now you have a recipe for the perfect employee, because they're not employees anymore."

So I asked Norm, "Okay, what should my son do? He doesn't know what he wants to do, except it's not roofing or working for minimum wage or taking what he refers to as a 'butt-crack job.' He's bright, charming, knows something about computers, can rewire anything and wants to be proud of whatever it is he does."

"Let your son know that in life anything that's worth having has to be paid for in full up front. Maybe he's not ready for that wisdom," Norm said. "But he should go for the thing he loves, even if it's a lot of work."

And then he repeated what someone once outlined as the four steps of learning. "The lowest is unconscious incompetent, that's your eighteen-year-olds, who don't even know that they don't know. The next step," he said, "is the conscious incompetent, then the conscious competent, who knows what he's doing. And the last step is the unconscious competent, who does it without even thinking."

He concluded: "Often the biggest leap is from unconscious incompetent to the conscious incompetent." That's most kids when they encounter their first real job, something that challenges them more than ringing up purchases at a vitamin store. And that leap can be a profound one.

"The human mind," he said, "once expanded, never returns to its original size."

Chapter Sixteen

ON THE ROAD OF LIFE, THERE ARE PASSENGERS AND THERE ARE DRIVERS (PARENTS, HAND OVER THE KEYS)

There is nothing noble in being superior to another person. The true nobility is in being superior to your previous self.
—A HINDU PROVERB

Let's talk about letting go, because that's what this has all been about, letting go of preconceptions about what our kids can do, about what is acceptable for them to do. Sometimes letting go of the notion that they will get into the Ivy League, at other times letting go of the notion that they will go to college at all—and still loving them for who they are.

One of the hardest things for me to give up was the notion that my son would graduate from college. But when I reached that point, my life, and *his* life, became immeasurably better. I didn't really set him free (or myself) until I accepted, deep down, that that just might be the case.

You remember Elizabeth, the middle-class mom who was concerned because her son, the one who was moldering in the basement, joined the Army? Her son was in basic training when we talked the last time.

"It took me about a week to get used to his not being here," she said. "I raised him for nineteen years, and all of a sudden I'm not responsible. Somebody else is. My brain is having trouble shifting back and forth between 'He's gone!' and 'No, stay ready! Be alert!'"

With her son out of the house and in the hands of the U.S. Army, she has found, for the first time in a decade, that she is free to focus on work and her husband and on herself.

"I feel a certain freedom," she said. "Wow, I can do this job and I don't have to worry about him, or about rushing home. I don't live with this daily dread of what might have happened. It's strange. This is all still very new. Before he left, part of me thought I would always be responsible for him. I was beginning to think he was never going to grow up."

And then he did.

This mother never told her colleagues when her son was kicked out of boarding school or when he dropped out of high school. "Knowing the people I know, they're all big achievers and their kids are gifted," she said. "It made it hard to talk about it."

But when he went into the Army, she suddenly found she had something she wanted to say. "I let everybody know what he had done and that I felt proud of him. I actually felt a surge of patriotism. I watched this tape, *Freedom Isn't Free,* and I thought, 'That's right, my son is doing something for his fellow countrymen.' That sounds hokey, doesn't it?"

In the weeks before he left for basic training, she said, "I saw glimmers of a young man coming out. He had done something that didn't involve *me,* and that was good."

She has given up the idea that her son will go to college, at least for now. "He may be in some trade when he gets out," she said. "I've had to look at people in that line of work very differently. I think maybe I was kind of a snob. And this has helped me open my eyes.

"In my snobby middle-class way I thought he would follow the path I took. I was always waiting for him to turn into *me.* You know, I was lucky enough to go to college, but other people have other talents and other ways, and that's okay, too. It's made me more open-minded."

ACCEPTING THE OTHER

We think of America as a country that does not divide people by class, but consider this: We are charmed when the workmen in *A Year in Provence* wrestle with a stone slab table and then sit down to discuss politics over a glass of pastis. In Paris, you can't buy a loaf of bread at your local bakery without hearing from the woman behind the counter about her children, or her husband's problems with his liver.

But when is the last time you invited the mail carrier in for a cup of tea and a discussion of the latest bond issue? Perhaps in a small town, but in cities, the people who are not white collar are so often not visible to those who are.

When I began working on this book, I began talking to people who had otherwise been invisible to me: the waitresses and waiters, bartenders, the electrician and plumber, the manicurist, the post office workers, toll collectors, the woman who did my mammogram, the guys at the twenty-four-hour-a-day Kinko's, the people at work who do something obscure called "pagination."

Instead of "Nice day" and "Thanks," I began asking them: "How did you get into this line of work? What training did you have? Do you like it? How much do you get paid?" Instead of being offended, they were happy to talk about themselves.

I found out that the old waiter at a fancy steak house made $80,000 a year and that the young Frenchman at another restaurant, who had worked in New York City for only two months, was making $28,000 a year, by his calculation. He was working three nights and Sundays, and was living in Greenpoint, Brooklyn, a district he had to draw for me on the paper tablecloth.

I found out that the toll collectors on the bridge over the Hudson were making $11 to $12 an hour. And that the woman who did my mammogram was a technician who had done her associate's degree and then become certified. She made $35,000 a year.

I also found out that paginators at the newspaper (people who worked with computers to code in blocks for headlines, photographs and text so that they appeared in the right place on the page) had twenty hours of training and could make $50,000 to $60,000 a year. Who knew?

I started talking to all of these people because I could see my son doing these sorts of things (well, maybe not the mammogram). I had not talked to them before. As Elizabeth said, "I think I was a snob."

These were people with mortgages and children and boats and vacation plans. These were people who struggled like me to make a paycheck last. And if we began talking about our children, we had more in common than I had imagined.

WHY CHILDREN LEAVE

In Robert M. Sapolsky's wonderful essay on primates, "The Young and the Reckless," published in *The Trouble with Testosterone,* he writes: "It is a remarkable thing to observe: every day, in the world of primates, someone young and frightened picks up, leaves Mommy and everyone knows it, and heads off into the unknown."

At another point, writing about his own experience of going to college, he said, "Growing up, and growing away. Off to college, off to war, off to work in the city, off to settle in a new world—home is never the same again, and sometimes home is never even seen again."

Many of the parents I talked to had had to say good-bye to their children, not knowing when they would see them again: when Sarah Parsons went off to the Peace Corps in Turkmenistan, when Danny Siegle went off to work on an Alaskan fishing boat, when all of our children packed their bags and said good-bye, and really meant it.

Jacquelyn Mitchard is the bestselling author of two novels, *Deep End of the Ocean* and *The Most Wanted,* and a nationally syndicated columnist through Tribune Media Corporation. She lives in Madison, Wisconsin, where she is the mother of six, which means she has had a lot of experience in raising children and saying good-bye. She notes a growing conservatism in herself and her friends, mostly based on trying to hold on to things (including our children) as we get older.

"Those of us who grew up in the sixties," she told me, "our basic middle classness has reasserted itself. You start thinking less in terms of risking and more in terms of protecting."

And this happens, needless to say, just as your children are entering their "risking" years.

Jackie has seen her children go off in all different directions, including some who may not enter college. "It would be unreasonable to expect all of them to march to the same drummer," she said. "The impetus for my generation, my brother and I to go to college, is entirely different from the one for our grown and growing children. We were the first to go to college. That was an entirely different set of dreams. Our immigrant parents thought that college was a ticket to ride. Now I am forced to believe when I see it in my sons and my older daughter that there is more than one route to a successful and remunerative life.

"I fought this for a long time. I thought that you had to have the right college credentials. Now I'm seeing that it's not true. It's scary and it's exciting at the same time."

I had called her because of a column she wrote about her then fifteen-year-old son, whom she called an "indifferent student."

"My son, who is sixteen now, he is so smart it's staggering," she said, and you could hear the pride in her voice. "He's a science wiz who can put anything together, motors, anything. It's like math and science concepts were in his bottle as a baby. Yet he doesn't set great store in hauling home the A's. He does just enough to get by.

"I hope he goes to college. But he makes the case that he could just design websites for a living. It's a whole new world, isn't it?"

She, like many baby boom parents, has a kind of admiration for her kids' restlessness. After all, the baby boom, despite its talk about going with the flow, has turned out to be remarkably middle class and hardworking.

"One of the things I regret is that I marched right through college," she said. "I got out when I was twenty. I lock-stepped right into the mold and started making a living. And I have not gotten up from the desk since. If I regret anything, it's that I didn't do those things that other people did. I didn't travel and live in Montana and work on a horse ranch."

She need only look at her second husband to see the possibilities for her kids. (Her first husband died young, leaving her with a batch of children to raise.)

"My husband is in his thirties, an artist and a woodworker," she said. "And I'm twelve years older. He went to college on the ten-year plan while working full-time and only gradually accumulated enough credits to graduate.

"And you know what? No one ever says, 'Chris, how long did it take you?' He had a happy life where he explored all kinds of things. If our kids do that, it would be superb."

LOVING AND LETTING GO

I know that I did not begin to have a good relationship with my son until I was no longer telling him what to do. And I felt I had a right to tell him what to do as long as I was paying his bills.

That makes it very hard to have a pleasant Thanksgiving dinner. Along with the "How's the weather up there?" and "How's the car working?" comes the inevitable "Are you going to pass that physics course or not?"

It is not pleasant when a credit card company is calling to tell you that your son has run up $1,000 on his card at the local car parts store, and has not made his monthly payments. Or when it is clear that he is partying a lot and studying only a little.

Letting go means really letting go. It means accepting your child as a separately functioning human being. It means insisting that he move out of the house and begin supporting himself. The real world will provide lessons that he will ignore when they come from you, the nagging mom, the bossy father.

And handing him the car keys to his life means accepting that there are going to be accidents along the way. You can count on it. Sometimes they will be fender benders, sometimes major crashes. Letting go means that the power is going to be turned off in your child's apartment at least once, and the phone may or not be turned on this week. Your child may well come up short on rent, and it is not a crime to help out—once in a great while. But what works best of all is letting them learn for themselves.

For some kids, experience is not only the best teacher, it is the only teacher. And chances are that most of them, if they've been raised in comfortable homes and don't get involved with drugs, will not end up on the street.

My son recently drove to a concert in Baltimore with his best friend, Mike (4.0 average, computer major, still in school). The two of them had enough money for gas and concert tickets. They did not have enough money to stay in a Motel Six. So they slept in their car in an underground garage, which in August reached sultry temperatures. "We woke up and the car was like a sauna," my son said. "We could barely breathe. It was four in the morning and we were both sweating like mad. We just had to get out of there and start driving home, to get some air."

Sleeping in an underground parking garage? It's going to happen.

And you know what? That will be an experience my son remembers for the rest of his life. That, and the number of times he has run out of gas and had to push his car home.

When he comes home, he immediately sets to work making my world work better. He cleans out the rain gutters on the house in the country, puts up the storm windows, winterizes the attic, sets the clock on the car radio. He puts his hands on my computer system and suddenly the printer, the flatbed scanner, my Internet service provider, my software, all work the way they were supposed to.

He also has informed me that he can fix my roof in a weekend for about $300 in materials. So you see, I have grown my own private roofer. There are compensations.

He also educates me in the ways of machinery. I think my car is "being uncooperative" when it doesn't start on a cold morning, and that my computer gets "tired" after a long day.

"Mom," he'll say, "it's a *machine.*"

He has a committed and settled relationship with his girlfriend, a lovely young woman who is still in school (studying business, of course). Recently he asked me for a subscription to the newspaper in Rochester, New York, for Christmas. (What? My son is reading a newspaper?) "Yeah," he said, "I pick it up every morning, fifty cents, and clip things out for friends, things they might not know about." He also asked if there was a way he could get the weekly science section of the *New York Times.* "Mike and I like that section. Especially the stories about the expanding universe," he told me.

So you see, he does have an IQ above that of an eggplant.

He talks these days about wanting to go back to school and study something. He's thinking about studying computer networking, maybe at a community college, maybe Cisco. He wants to work at something clean, something he can do indoors. These days, he says, he doesn't even mind putting on a button-down shirt.

"I don't want to be a bum," he tells me.

"Don't worry," I say. "You won't be."

There is not a conversation we have these days that does not end with the words "I love you."

Of course, there are some children who are going to be like comets. They are in such a hurry to get out and take on the world, they will leave us in the dust.

Some of those children will end up like Scott Wainner, a website millionaire at age twenty-one who still calls his mother for advice. Some, if we're lucky, will turn out like Scott Bennion, the Mormon missionary and soldier, or Hamilton Simons-Jones, the Tulane political activist, or Staci Linklater, the entrepreneur hair colorist in Vegas.

They are all on their journey, and may God bless them and keep them safe.

Talking about a troop of baboons he was observing, Robert M. Sapolsky wrote, "All this only reaffirms that transferring is awful for adolescents—whether they're average geeks opting for the route of slow acceptance or rare animals like Hobbes who try to take the troop by storm. Either way, it's an ordeal, and the young animals pay a heavy price. The marvel is that they keep on doing it."

Humans, he notes, are the most widely distributed mammal on earth, because of this deep-rooted instinct to get out and move on.

"To hell with logic and sensible behavior, to hell with tradition and respecting your elders, to hell with this drab little town and to hell with that knot of fear in your stomach. Curiosity, excitement, adventure—the hunger for novelty is something fundamentally daft, rash and enriching that we share with our whole taxonomic order."

Would we humans have it any other way?

Coda

The call came, as most of those calls do, without warning. I picked up the phone and there was my son, calling from Rochester, New York, sounding grave.

"Mom, I've got something to tell you," he said.

A mother's mind reels at moments like that. Even in the smallest pause, we steady ourselves for what will come. His girlfriend is pregnant. They are getting married. No, something worse. He wrecked his car (again). Someone is hurt. Someone is ill. Someone is in jail. This can't be good news.

But no. This is what he said. "Would it spoil the thesis of your book if I went back to college?

"I've been thinking about it, and I think I'm ready," he said. "It would feel good to be a student again. I want to study"—well, you can fill in the rest from here. He wants to study computers, of course, and who doesn't?

I told him, no, it wouldn't spoil the thesis of my book if he went back to college, part-time while he worked. I told him that the thesis of my book is that people shouldn't go to college before they are ready. What I didn't tell him was that I, of course, had come to the conclusion that college might actually be unnecessary. I didn't tell him that because if your child feels that college is necessary, for him to get a job, or be proud of himself, or keep up with his friends, then you still want him to go. You want him to go for himself.

I say that despite believing that mass attendance at college may someday be seen as a quaint twentieth-century notion, something that was popular there for about fifty years, from the end of World War II until the end of the century. Can you imagine, people will say in 2020, that nearly two-thirds of high school students went to *college*?

Because we are always out of step with our children, it made perfect sense that, just as I was ready to abandon the idea of anyone really needing college, I would find that my son did.

Not too long after that, a friend sent me a copy of the speech that the columnist Anna Quindlen gave at Villanova University in Pennsylvania in the spring of 1999. She was addressing the graduating seniors, but it's good advice for anyone, even someone who is thinking of skipping college . . . for now.

"You walk out of here this afternoon with only one thing that no one else has," she said. "There will be hundreds of people out there with your same degree; there will be thousands of people doing what you want to do for a living. But you will be the only person alive who has sole custody of your life. Your particular life. Your entire life. Not just your life at a desk, or your life . . . at the computer. Not just the life of your mind, but the life of your heart. Not just your bank account, but your soul.

"People don't talk about the soul very much anymore. It's so much easier to write a résumé than to craft a spirit. But a résumé is a cold comfort on a winter night, or when you're sad, or broke, or lonely, or when you've gotten back the test results and they're not so good. . . . You cannot be really first-rate at your work if your work is all you are. So here's what I wanted to tell you today: Get a life. A real life, not a manic pursuit of the next promotion, the bigger paycheck, the larger house."

Or I might add, the manic pursuit of an expensive degree, before you know who you are. Students: Before you get the rest of your education, get a life.

Index